ERRATA

Due to the number and complexity of illustrations, some errors have occurred. The following corrections should, therefore, be made:

p. 39, line 8: Substitute, "We now return to the study of the situation where"

p. 39, Fig. 3-24: Label the points where vertical segments beginning at V_1' and V_2' intersect the baseline G and G_2 respectively. Lable the man's head E.

p. 39, Fig. 3-25: Label the focal point P.

p. 40, Fig. 3-29: Change any label A to A'; change any other label A to A''.

p. 41, Fig. 3-34. Add label B as in Fig. 3-33.

p. 48, Fig. 4-18: Label I_V should be H_V.

p. 57, Figs. 5-7 and 5-8: change V of V_SV vertical to V'.

p. 67, Fig. 5-34: Transpose labels V' and V.

p. 77, Fig. 6-13: Draw a vertical diameter through the circle.

p. 115, This drawing is Fig. 8-11.

p. 131, Fig. 10-3a, from left to right: Label first arrow reflection point I; label second arrow tangency point II, label second arrow end point IV, and label third arrow end point III.

p. 132, Fig. 10-8: Label third arrow from the left A.

p. 132, Fig. 10-9: Replace label a with α and label b with β.

p. 138, line 14: Substitute "point B'. What are the shaded side of the cone."

p. 139, Fig. 10-29: Change label S on ground shadow to S''.

p. 160, Ex. 28, line 6: Substitute, "onal AD. You can see that AB is a half-diagonal of the new square, so if you."

p. 160, Ex. 28: Transpose labels C and D.

p. 163, Ex. 38: Transpose labels V_1 and V_2.

p. 165, Ex. 46: Move label V_2 to the point further right.

p. 166, Ex. 53, line 2: Substitute "FC the V_1 vanishing point" for "FC and V_1 vanishing point."

p. 168, Ex. 59: Change labels D' to C'.

p. 169, Ex. 66: In lower figure, from left to right, working top to bottom, mark first vertical C and F; second vertical B and A, third vertical D and E.

p. 172, Ex. 74: Change labels A and D of longest vertical to A' and D' respectively.

p. 172, Ex. 77: Change A, B, and C in the structure on the right to A' and B' and C'.

p. 181, Ex. 115: Transpose labels V_2 and V_1.

p. 181, Ex. 117, line 2: delete reference to Fig. 2-105.

p. 185, Ex. 144, line 3: Delete reference to Fig. 2-114.

UNDERSTANDING

Radu Vero

PERSPECTIVE

CALVIN T. RYAN LIBRARY
KEARNEY STATE COLLEGE
KEARNEY, NEBRASKA

VNR **VAN NOSTRAND REINHOLD COMPANY**
NEW YORK • CINCINNATI • TORONTO • LONDON • MELBOURNE

Photograph on page 6 by Sanda Blassian Vero

Copyright © 1980 by Litton Educational Publishing, Inc.
Library of Congress Catalog Card Number 79-337
ISBN 0-442-29089-6 (cloth)
ISBN 0-442-29088-8 (paper)

All rights reserved. No part of this work covered by the copyright
hereon may be reproduced or used in any form or by any means—
graphic, electronic, or mechanical, including photocopying, record-
ing, taping, or information storage and retrieval systems—without
written permission of the publisher.

Printed in the United States of America

Published by Van Nostrand Reinhold Company
A division of Litton Educational Publishing, Inc.
135 West 50th Street, New York, NY 10020, U.S.A.

Van Nostrand Reinhold Limited
1410 Birchmount Road
Scarborough, Ontario M1P 2E7, Canada

Van Nostrand Reinhold Australia Pty. Ltd.
17 Queen Street
Mitcham, Victoria 3132, Australia

Van Nostrand Reinhold Company Limited
Molly Millars Lane
Wokingham, Berkshire, England

16 15 14 13 12 11 10 9 8 7 6 5 4 3 2 1

Library of Congress Cataloging in Publication Data

Vero, Radu.
    Understanding perspective.

    Bibliography: p.
    Includes index.
    1. Perspective—Technique.   I. Title.
NC750.V45   742   79-337
ISBN 0-442-29089-6
ISBN 0-442-29088-8 pbk.

CONTENTS

INTRODUCTION

There are many good manuals on perspective drawing. Most of them treat the same basic problems according to the same basic principles, but each with a different method and with more or less comprehensible drawings. However, no matter how accurate, precise, and understandable is the written demonstration of the problems and no matter how clear, elegant, and faultless are the drawings, most students get lost in the intricate jungle of construction lines and fail to grasp the simplicity of perspective drawing. Even in colleges, a surprisingly large number of students lose contact with their lecturer's explanations and, in most cases, lose their interest in perspective drawing as well.

The main reason for this failure is not any inability on the part of the student; rather, it is due to neglect of the training that should precede the study of perspective drawing. To clarify this point, we will compare perspective drawing to boxing. The rules of boxing can easily be learned and used in a fight. However, this is not enough for the fighter to win or even to stay on his feet against his challenger for any length of time; the boxer must also go through a serious and varied training of his natural abilities. He has to develop his nervous system for quick reflexes, he has to improve his lungs for a resistant breathing, and he has to train his muscles and learn to balance his weight. Nerves, lungs, muscles, and balance exist in every individual, but their improvement is possible only with training, and achievement is impossible without it. Unfortunately, the particular type of training necessary for understanding perspective drawing has been entirely ignored. This is probably because mental training is a more subtle notion than physical training and because lecturers and writers of reference books about perspective drawing have neglected the fact that preperspective training requires special attention. What we sometimes wrongly regard as talent is in fact a gradual, discrete and continual self-training of interested children at play with their own imaginations. This way of playing is common to the great majority of children, and while some of them abandon it for other interests, those who persist through the later years of adolescence are potential creative artists.

However, as this manual deals exclusively with perspective drawing, we will try to analyze the process of "thinking in perspective." Like boxing, perspective drawing has rules and principles that can be easily learned. All these rules belong to euclidean and projective geometry. We assume that our students have clear notions in these fields. But the neglected necessary training deals with the mental process we call "vision in space." This is the ability to project images on a mental screen prior to any attempt at transferring them to paper. For the untrained student, the mental images are blurred and lacking in precision, whether they are the details of a person's face, a color resulting from the combination of two or more different tones, the shape of a building, or even a simple straight line. The general mistake of untrained students is to try to work directly on paper without a precise visualization of the image, thus losing the three-dimensional values of the construction lines. The trained student will project a definite image on paper, and his construction lines will make sense in space.

The second and more important ability to be trained is the manipulation of mental images. Whether he is visualizing points, lines, solids, or colors, the student will need to modify, move, compose, replace, translate, rotate, intersect, and build them in accordance with a precise sense of space in order to achieve a desired result. Without this ability it is impossible to imagine lines running toward the horizon, planes changing position, solids being raised one on top of the other, and, more generally, perspectives of the same complex spatial structures seen from various points of view. The student will need the ability to play with shapes in time, to imagine them in motion, and to visualize perspective four-dimensionally. Only when this mental training has been completed does the student gain the full ability to visualize. And only after visualizing the problem can he start to transfer a mental image onto paper, using the technique acquired in the study of perspective rules and principles.

Our experience with students, architects, and renderers has convinced us that learning perspective drawing is not a matter of talent. It is only a matter of revitalizing the neglected and sometimes forgotten ability to see in space mentally. We endeavor here to develop this ability and bring it to maturity, and therefore we have designed this book as a collection of progressively more challenging mental exercises. Although we will devote further study to the rules and principles of perspective, our aim is to train your perspective vision more than to offer a complete course in this discipline. Once you have fully acquired this mental capability, you can complete your studies with any of the very good books already on the market.

So, starting with the premise that all masterpieces are born in a mental vision, we offer the following method of improving imaginative power:

1. Never start a new exercise before having a clear picture and a complete understanding of the previous one. Even if some exercises seem to be ridiculously simple, do them anyway.

2. Imagine the exercise in motion. We will help you.

3. Do not use your pencil before obtaining a very clear mental image of what you want to sketch.

4. Try to see your image on the paper before actually drawing anything, so that when you start to use your pencil, it will trace out the image you have projected mentally on the blank paper. You will not always succeed at the beginning, but you will improve with practice.

5. Don't lose patience, no matter how long an exercise may bother you. Most important, do not look at the solutions before finishing the whole chapter. After studying each chapter completely, return to each exercise, recall your solution, and check it with the answers.

6. Do not be satisfied to solve just the exercises in this book. Intentionally, we provide only one specific type of perspective problem. Invent your own exercises and perspective situations. Thus you will work on your imagination too.

7. If the geometry we use is beyond your knowledge, do not take our statement for granted, but find it in reference books and familiarize yourself with it. If you neglect such things, it will be more difficult later to understand other, more complex statements.

8. If you have a rather good knowledge of theoretical perspective but encounter difficulties in the actual construction of a rendering, first read Chapter 8, Theory of Perspective, and only then return to the first chapter. If you have little or no knowledge of the material, begin at the beginning.

1. MENTAL EXERCISES

This chapter contains 100 exercises. You should work them mentally without using a pencil and paper. Except for the starred exercises, which have short answers at the end of the chapter, there are no other answers or explanatory drawings, so you have to make the first efforts alone.

*1. How many points are necessary to determine a straight line?

2. Imagine a point. You can do this by thinking of the point as a star in the sky or as a dot on paper. However, such a point is actually a three-dimensional body. Try to imagine a dimensionless point and, while seeing it in your mind, to define it as a unique and purely abstract place in space.

3. Imagine your point in motion. Move it one inch to the right and then one inch to the left on your mental screen. Then do the same thing vertically. Alternate the vertical and horizontal translations, increasing the speed, until you can see a cross.

4. Use the same point as before, but change the angles and the length of the translations. Choose at random one of the directions and send the point straight to infinity, trying to imagine what happens there. (Nobody has succeeded so far in actually imagining infinity!)

5. You have imagined the previous exercises on a frontal mental screen. Now send your point straight ahead of you. Imagine yourself shooting a bullet toward a target in front of you, but reduce the speed and abstract so that it becomes a point, while you can follow its motion.

6. You have seen the point running to the target. Now imagine only the place of impact as the final place of your point and bring the point back and forth again several times on the same straight line. This is easy. But now go beyond the final target toward infinity. Your point will go on indefinitely, although it remains in your field of mental vision. If the point runs straight on a trajectory that is perpendicular to the line uniting your two eyes, you will have the impression that the point doesn't move. However, if the point should have dimensions, you will realize that it moves because its size will decrease until it vanishes. The *vanishing point* is a basic notion in perspective, and you will encounter it frequently later in this book.

7. Try now to give the trajectory a slight angle, such as 5° to the perpendicular you used in Exercise 5. This time your point will move, and you will see the movement until the point vanishes toward infinity.

8. Return now to the point that runs back and forth on a definite distance in Exercise 6. If this distance is straight, your point defines a line. You can enrich this definition by imagining the line as the distance between two motionless points or as an infinity of immaterial points stretched between the initial and final points of the line (segment).

9. If the previous line continues to move toward infinity, you will obtain the same image you had when the point was running toward infinity. This is correct because a line, being defined by the motion of a point, will behave in the same manner as it moves toward a vanishing point, with the difference that the moving point vanishes entirely, while a line will stretch toward infinity without disappearing.

*10. How many lines can pass through a point?

11. If you consider the moon sufficiently distant from yourself for this exercise, mentally trace a connecting line between the moon and the tip of your finger. As we all know, the moon moves slowly toward the horizon, and you can consider your finger motionless. Therefore the connecting line will also change angle, and you can imagine this change to the limit when the moon goes beyond horizon. However, you know that the moon continues its rotation, so you can also continue imagining the connecting line going through the earth, beneath the line of the horizon.

*12. Give the correct definition of two parallel lines.

*13. Are the sunbeams coming to the earth parallel?

14. Now imagine yourself having a gun in each of your hands, so that you can shoot two bullets simultaneously. We know that not even the best marksman could shoot two simultaneous bullets in perfectly parallel directions, but we will accept such a deed as theoretically possible. So the two bullets will hit the target at a distance equal to the distance between your two hands. Correct? Even if you move the target ten, one hundred, one thousand miles or no matter how far away from you, the bullets will hit it at the same distance as the distance between your hands. This is the theory. However, to your eyes, this distance diminishes in direct proportion to the distance between your eyes and the target, until at the vanishing point the two bullets *seem* to vanish into each other. This is one of the most important statements for understanding perspective: Perspective drawing is *not* the representation of real shapes but a distorted image of real things, objects, and bodies as seen by the observer.

*15. What solid is a sheet of writing paper?

16. Stop imagining for a while and observe a few common objects around you. A simple sheet of paper resting on your desk will present to your eyes pairs of nonparallel edges. You know that these pairs are parallel, but your eyes perceive them as going toward a joining point. Watch carefully and remember through repeated observation that that joining is *always* somewhere beyond the distance between your eyes and the remote borders of the desk plane; if you don't know why, you will find the answer in Chapter 3. Also watch a plate or other circular surface lying on a desk; you will almost always see the circle not as a circle but as an ellipse. There is only one case in which parallels remain parallels and circles are not distorted: when the surfaces are precisely frontal to your eyes. This is also something to remember, an essential observation in perspective drawing.

*17. Can you find the centers of a square and of a rectangle without measuring?

*18. How can you find the center of a circle?

19. Let us return to your mental screen and try to play with the geometry of a circle. As you probably know, one of the definitions of the circle is the totality of points at a given distance from a point called the center. Now mark this center mentally on your screen and consider it fixed where it is. If you attach one end of an imaginary thread to this center and to the other end a stone, you get the image of the circle by rotation. Or if you attach one end of a stick to the center and rotate it, you obtain the area of a circle. This is very simple and you already knew it, but you have always worked it on a piece of paper or seen it diagrammed in a book. What is new is to imagine it only, exchanging the thread and the stick, rotating them faster and slower, and varying the length of the radius.

20. Imagine a square with 90° vertical and 0° horizontal edges on your frontal screen so that the intersection point of the diagonals falls exactly on the center of your mental screen. Now, if you mentally trace a horizontal line through this center, the square will be divided into two equal halves (upper and lower). And if you consider this horizontal middle line an axis, you can slowly rotate your screen so that the square will rotate too, becoming more and more distorted. Can you describe this distortion to yourself? Let us analyze what happens. While the axis remains unchanged, the lower edge of the square comes forward toward your eyes, while the upper edge gets more remote. They both remain parallel to the axis, but the lower edge becomes larger (being closer to you) and the upper edge becomes smaller. Once the rotation has started, so that these two edges become unequal in length, the vertical edges will not remain parallel. Rather, according to the increasing difference in the size of the horizontal edges, the angle between the two vertical ones will increase (i.e., if the angle between two parallel lines is considered 0°, for a rotation of 90°, the angle will become 180°). Taking into consideration the initial conditions of symmetry, we see that the distortion of a rotated square at any angle will be an isosceles trapezoid.

21. Repeat Exercise 20, replacing the square with a rectangle with the longer dimension either horizontal or vertical. You will obtain similar observations. You will thus realize that perspective distortion, in certain conditions that are to be studied, makes confusion between a perspective square and a perspective rectangle very possible.

22. We hope that you successfully imagined Exercises 20 and 21. However, if you failed, take a square piece of paper, a book, or any rectangular surface and, by placing your hands at the middle of its right and left edges, turn it slowly while observing that the statements made in the preceding exercises are correct. Again, don't use pencil; just try to understand. Then mentally repeat the two exercises.

23. Imagine again the square described in Exercise 20, but instead of tracing a horizontal line through the center, trace a vertical one. Now the rotation will be done around this central vertical axis, as would happen to a door hinged at its middle. You will observe that this time the vertical edges remain parallel while changing length and the horizontal ones change angle.

24. A very important remark: In both the exercises about the square and the exercises with rectangles, we have a pair of parallel edges and a pair of nonparallel ones. The nonparallel ones, which in the preceding cases are equal in length in any particular position, would meet in one point if mentally extended. For each angle of rotation, there will be another intersecting point. And as the number of positions determined by the rotation is theoretically limitless, we will have a limitless number of intersection points. One of the characteristics of these points is that they are collinear; that is, they move on a single, straight, infinite line, which is vertical or horizontal according to the position of the rotation axis. We are not yet in a position to demonstrate this statement, but it can be established. The lines containing the points of intersection are called *vanishing lines*. Except for the horizon line, which is the only vanishing line to be actually experienced in nature, all vanishing lines are theoretical tools for perspective drawing, but most students, accustomed to the horizon line, are unaware of the fact that there is an infinity of vanishing lines to be utilized. Do not forget that the horizon line is *your* horizon line! You will understand this better in Chapter 3.

25. When we spoke about the square or rectangle, we did not give any specific dimensions for the edges. This means that if you inscribe another square within the square of Exercise 20, preserving the parallelism of edges, or a rectangle within the rectangle of Exercise 21, the edges will undergo the same distortions. The question you have to answer on your mental screen is where the nonparallel edges of any such squares or rectangles will intersect. Just think about the following definition of parallel lines in geometry: Any group of parallel lines (forming an angle of $0°$ between them) unite at one point, at infinity.

26. While preserving the basic conditions given in Exercises 20 and 21, trace vertical or horizontal lines *not* through the center of the square or rectangle but at different distances from the center, so that they remain parallel to one pair of edges. Then repeat the rotations. Repeat this extremely important exercise until your mental screen records such rotations with no difficulty whatsoever. If your images are correct and your sense of geometry doesn't betray you, you will realize that the virtual points of intersection of the nonparallel lines are situated in the same plane in which your square or rectangle is situated, and so you will have a clear picture of the horizon line as the vanishing line of a plane.

*****27.** Is the horizon line of a calm sea a straight line?

*****28.** What geometric figure is formed between your eye and two boats floating on the sea's horizon line?

29. Imagine yourself standing on the seashore. If a rectangular raft floats on the plane of the sea so that two edges remain frontal to your eyes and the two others are perpendicular to them, then the two latter ones are not parallel; their extensions unite in one point. Can you "see" where this point is located?

30. Because of its floating, the raft changes position so that no pair of edges remains frontal to your eyes any more. What happens to the pairs of edges? Since no pair of edges remains frontal to your eyes, no pair remains parallel. In this case *both* pairs of edges become convergent, each pair intersecting in another point. As we said, the raft is theoretically situated in the plane of the sea, and the vanishing line of the sea is the horizon line. If a boat sails on the sea on a straight trajectory (*any* straight trajectory that is not parallel to your frontal screen), you will be able to see the boat until it vanishes on the horizon line. Through abstraction, we see that all straight lines situated on the sea plane will vanish on the horizon line, and through generalization we see that all straight lines situated in a plane vanish at the vanishing line of that particular plane. This seems to be a lot of theory, and it is usually explained with drawings, which make it easier to understand. But we remind you that those having a trained ability to visualize in space have no problems in imagining the statements explained above, and we want you to make this effort too in order to gain this ability.

*****31.** When a boat goes beyond the sea horizon line, what disappears first and why?

32. We return now to the square described in Exercise 20. It is frontal and undistorted and has two diagonals. Obviously, the diagonals divide the square into four triangles. Now, by slow mental rotation, study what happens to these triangles. There is no substantial conclusion about their distortion, but this is a very easy and profitable exercise, because later you will have to deal with many triangles and you must get used to their distortions.

33. Let us now imagine our square in a diamond position (edges at $45°$ to the horizontal and vertical) and rotate it, considering first the horizontal diagonal and then the vertical diagonal as the axis. This time (remember the raft) each pair of parallel edges will become symmetrically distorted, and they will intersect in two points at equal distances from the center of the square. Does your image agree with this statement?

34. If the square is rotated *almost* 90° around its diagonal, from the initial frontal position to the position in which the plane of the square becomes *almost* perpendicular to your eyes, the intersection points of the two pairs of edges come closer to the square. Can you say where these points of intersection are situated when the rotation is exactly 90°? You may find this exercise very difficult. If necessary, you can make an exception: Take a pencil and trace the different positions of the square rotated around its diagonal while extending the pairs of edges to their intersection points. As this is your first attempt to use pencil and paper, do not forget that (in case your rotation goes around the horizontal diagonal), the upper triangle has a smaller height because of its greater distance from your eyes, while the lower triangle has a larger one because it is coming closer to your eyes. If you forget this and make the square rotating as in a technical drawing, your pairs of sides will remain parallel no matter what the rotation angle. This is a very common and confusing error made by people trained in technical drafting when they try to sketch an object in freehand perspective, without the help of construction lines.

*35. What is the numerical relation between a regular hexagon and its circumscribing circle?

36. Considering again the square from Exercise 20, let us inscribe a circle of diameter equal to the edge of the square. Before rotating, observe that the circle intersects the two diagonals in four points and also is tangent to the square's edges in four points, exactly at the middle of each edge. You know from geometry that the four points of intersection with the diagonals are at equal distances from the center and can be considered the corner points of another inscribed square. This is helpful to remember because the rotation distortion of these two squares will give you eight points of the perspectively distorted circle. You know that any perspectively distorted circle is an ellipse, but we want you to follow this distortion "cinematically" in your mind, thus getting familiar with the relationship between the angle of rotation and the type of ellipse that results.

37. If you inscribe the same circle in the diamond-position square from Exercise 33 and rotate the diamond around its diagonal, as before, of course the diamond and the circle will be distorted. Can you say what is the difference between the circle's distortion in the previous exercise and the distortion in the diamond? Can you explain why?

38. Preserve your mental circle as it is, imagine its horizontal diameter (which previously coincided with the middle horizontal line of the square and was situated on the horizontal diagonal of the diamond), and rotate the circle around this diameter. This is like holding a record with the fingers of both your hands on a horizontal diameter and rotating it in front of your eyes. Whether you circumscribe a square as in Exercise 20 or in the diamond position *or in any position at all*, the distortion of the circle thus rotated will be the same, while the distortion of the differently positioned square will vary according to its angle. This gives you the answer to the previous exercise as well.

*39. Can you see a circle drawn on a sheet of paper as a straight line?

*40. How long will the line obtained in the previous exercise be?

41. Let us stop for a while at one particular position, namely, at a 45° rotation around the horizontal diameter of the circle inscribed in the initial square. As we said, the upper half of the square (and the circle) is smaller, being farther from your eyes, and the lower half is larger because it is coming toward you. The square becomes an isosceles trapezoid and the inscribed circle an ellipse. You know that an ellipse is defined by its major and minor axes (diameters), which before distortion are the two perpendicular diameters of the circle and coincide with the two middle lines of the square. In the case of our particular 45° rotation (think carefully!) the distorted circle *looks like* a frontal ellipse but doesn't preserve its frontal properties. The major diameter of this ellipse does *not* coincide any more with the middle line of the square but is somewhere below it. The actual rotating diameter of the circle becomes a line uniting the two points of tangency of the ellipse with the square. This is very easy to verify with pencil and paper, but again, you must train your ability to visualize and work it out mentally. Don't stop trying even if it's hard.

42. After all these difficult exercises, let us return to some easier ones, in which we will try to get used to a mental process that might be called *abstraction.* The first one is to imagine yourself standing on a straight road. The road crosses a plain. There is nothing else but you, the road, the earth, and the sky, and the road is so long that you cannot see its end. (Actually, most books on perspective drawing begin with this classical situation, but we look for something else.) However, you practiced before with the two parallel bullets, so you know that your road will "look like" a single point on the horizon line. Having now a more detailed vision in your head, we suppose that you can imagine sand, pebbles, grass, or earth on both sides of the road, which might be gray from asphalt or yellowish from dust, and the sky clear blue or cloudy. Of course, you can go further and imagine trees, traffic, people, airplanes, birds, and whatever might occur in the vicinity of the road in your mental landscape. But the problem we face now deals with the reverse process: to simplify, to reduce, *to abstract*, not to add. We ask you to reduce the image of the road to the minimum necessary. The result will be three lines: the two edges of the road and the horizon line. We have abstracted what is essential, an operation that enables us to enjoy some advantages:

(a) These three lines enable us to imagine *any* road, *any* land, *any* sky, *any* colors or additional accidents or materials, without changing the basic pattern.

(b) We obtain practice in the fundamentally necessary operation of switching mentally from object to abstraction *and back*. Most books on perspective drawing describe, state, and demonstrate only the abstracting step in perspective, neglecting the switching process.

(c) We can decide about the position of our perspective road (in relation to your eyes) by changing only the essential, abstracted lines. When the positioning is satisfactory, we can return to the actual, detailed structure of our proposed landscape or any other rendering.

Let us see how it works:

43. Imagine the previous road crossed by another. Abstract. We say that the essential is five lines. Do you agree?

44. Observe that the five essential lines are not necessarily a crossroad but any pairs of parallel lines crossing each other on their way toward the horizon. These pairs of parallel lines cross each other. When we want to indicate that this abstract shows a crossroad, we must "clean" the intersection, thus obtaining the four corners of the two intersecting roads.

45. Suppose that the two pairs of parallels represent not a crossroad, but two long strips of clear, transparent plastic. Do you think that the intersection has to be cleaned as in the previous exercise?

46. A pair of cylinders of equal diameters intersect in the same image as the two pairs of parallel lines. They will be represented also by the same abstractions. But, of course, the actual intersection is totally different, and we won't ask you to visualize such a complicated intersection if you don't have previous knowledge about it. What we want to emphasize is that the abstraction of any perspective structure can be the result of many objects and can be translated into many images. What differentiates one final pattern of lines from another is the logical structure.

47. In our previous exercises, the logical structure, the key to the definition and identity, is the way the intersection is treated. A four-corner intersection represents the crossroad (Fig. 1-1a), a continuous intersection represents the two transparent plastics overlapping (Fig. 1-1b), and two perpendicular ellipses represent the intersection of two cylinders (Fig. 1-1c). What represents the intersection of two vertical walls?

48. Figures 1-1d, e, and f look absurd. However, they can illustrate strange and unique cases of perspective. Figure 1-1d might be two intersecting walls that are cut in a slant at their ends. Figure 1-1e is the intersection of two pipes that have been flattened at the point of intersection. Figure 1-1f is a normal road intersection on which, at the front edges, two solid spheres have been laid. These descriptions have certainly been oversimplified. For instance, in Figure 1-1e, the flattening of the pipes must progress gradually, not only at the intersection point.* Then the two lines determining the shape in perspective have the distance of one diameter (D) between them. Flattening the pipe into a vertical line gives us the size of $\pi D/2$, half the length of the circle, which is larger than the diameter ($2r < 3.14r$). This means that in perspective the intersection will be larger in vertical measurement, and thus our drawing is not correct. And yet, if we replace the two cylinders with two frustums of cones (Fig. 1-2), calculated so that D_2 will be twice D_1 divided by π ($D_2 = 2D_1/\pi$), the flattened line will look like the perspective view of the diameter "under certain conditions."

1-1   *1-2*

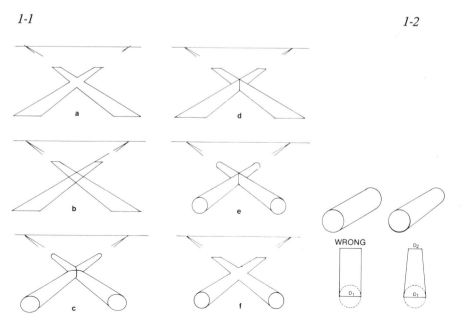

*You don't have to learn this.   15

49. Similar speculations and alternate solutions can be found for the other odd-looking figures. Try to see them.

50. Figure 1-3a is absurd. In order to produce a logical drawing, you must either preserve the idea of the three cylinders (Fig. 1-3b) or preserve the straight prismatic idea (Fig. 1-3c). Can you find another one?

1-3

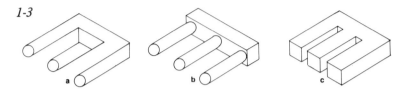

*51. What geometric figure is formed between your eye and the edge of a building?

52. Let us return to abstraction. Actually, abstraction will be exercised here much more in connection with descriptive geometry than with perspective, because without a clear understanding of different intersections, perspective drawing remains a difficult mystery.

Imagine a match box. Abstract it. You obtain a parallelepiped. This abstraction can appear on your mental screen either as a solid or clear glass or as a number of straight lines (12) outlining your abstraction. At this point you must concentrate your mental efforts on *seeing* the twelve lines in space, to realize that some lines cross the others in *your* image but do not cross them in space. In the same way that you have already learned to change the position of a straight line on your mental screen, try to arrange this abstract matchbox in different positions. This is certainly a very difficult mental operation but also perhaps the most important one so far. To make it easier, use the following exercises:

53. Imagine first one, then two, then three surfaces of the matchbox in motion and carefully observe their distortions.

54. Imagine the matchbox as an opaque solid. Then you will see not more than three surfaces at a time, sometimes only two and in certain instances only one. But as you turn the matchbox in different positions, some of the three surfaces will disappear behind, while the hidden surfaces will become visible to your mental eye. If this description seems confusing, let us try another way. You know that many modern buildings look like a matchbox. Now, if you imagine yourself in a car riding around such a building, you will sometimes see only one wall of the building (when your car is in front of it) and sometimes two (when you drive closer to a corner). You will not see the roof or the base. Mentally drive your car around the building as many times as is necessary for you to see the continuous changes with no effort at all. Then imagine yourself flying around this same building in a helicopter. This time the distortions of the walls will be different. If your helicopter flies close to the ground around the building, you will experience changes similar to the ones you had when driving the car. But when the helicopter rises above the height of the building, the roof will start interplaying with your other walls. However, you will not see more than three surfaces (two walls and the roof) at a time. Once you master these views as well, reduce the building to the size of the matchbox and then abstract it to twelve lines. If Exercise 54 is no problem for you, you should skip Exercise 55.

55. If the above practice was difficult and you did not succeed in visualizing the intersecting lines, compromise: Take a matchbox or a cigarette box and repeat the operations described in Exercise 54 and see what happens, while remembering that "looking" is different from "seeing." You can *look* at a pair of eyes and say that they are beautiful, but you can *see* them and realize their shape, size, color, and proportion. Here, seeing is a process of visual understanding that involves not only an emotional reception of visual data but also a process of mental analysis, of logical understanding.

56. Extend your mental exercises by enlarging and reducing the size of the matchbox, by varying the distance between it and your mental screen, and by changing ratios between its dimensions.

57. Take the particular case when all edges of the parallelepiped are equal. You have a cube. In which particular position will your mental image show this cube as a hexagon? And what will the three surfaces look like?

58. Repeat Exercise 54 with a pyramid instead of a parallelepiped.

*59. How many square sheets of cardboard do you need to form a cube if the dimensions of one sheet are 100 × 100 × 1 millimeters?

*60. What solid is a dime?

*61. What solid is a thread?

62. Consider a salami. The abstraction of a salami is a cylinder. Suppose the two ends of the salami are cut perpendicularly to its axis. If the cylinder stands on a table (with the axis vertical), driving around it will give you no particular changes. There are no edges to appear or disappear while turning around. The only definition of the cylinder is its end, the circle. Your task is to understand the distortions of this circle corresponding to different positions you take and to imagine its continuity on the hidden side of your image.

*63. How many points are necessary to determine a plane?

64. Only when you are sure that the previous exercises are solved, try to repeat the operations by imagining *two* matchboxes standing, one beside the other. While turning around with your imaginary car, see how one box covers the other one gradually. An interesting instance is when one edge of the closer matchbox comes to touch one of the edges of the other box. Geometrically speaking, your eye and the two edges belong to the same plane. This also means that the straight line from your eye to any point situated on the first box's edge will also touch the edge of the other box in a certain point. However, it may happen, because of the relative positions of your eye and the boxes and the distance between the two of them, that a straight line between your eye and a point on the first edge will not touch the second edge but will pass above it. In this case you have to make a small but essential effort and imagine that the next edge can be visualized as a virtual, limitless vertical line. Once you have succeeded, you will see that the eye line will intersect this virtual portion of the edge somewhere, because any two parallel lines belonging to the same plane can be intersected by another line that is not parallel with them. Once you master this type of operation, you have made a great step in understanding perspective drawing procedures.

65. It should be clear that your eye, the first edge, and the second edge belong to the same plane. Even taking only the two edges, we can determine a plane. What happens when your eye and the first box's edge form a plane which, as a result of your moving around, fall *not* on an edge of the second box but somewhere around the middle of a wall? The intersection of your imaginary plane and the wall is an imaginary vertical line. Can you imagine this line?

66. We have been using a new concept, *intersection*. Now, in order to clarify it, we will return to a number of simpler exercises and see how it works. You will be asked to use your mental ability, adding an imaginary knife and different nonabstract solids. Your knife will be used to cut these solids in a perfectly straight way (geometrically speaking, the knife's blade will move in only one plane). Imagine first a piece of hard cheese in the shape of a parallelepiped. To cut a slice means to cut a portion of cheese by moving the knife parallel to one of the rectangular surfaces of the cheese. If the cut is correct, the slice will be another thin parallelepiped in which the cut surface is identical with the parallel surfaces of the piece of cheese. Only its thickness is different. Of course, you can cut as many slices as you want and, if you do not change the direction of your knife, you will obtain the same result. Let us now translate this experiment in an abstract geometric sentence: A plane intersecting a parallelepiped parallel to one of its surfaces will give an intersection surface identical to that surface.

67. Cut your cheese with a knife that is not parallel to one of the surfaces. The intersection obtained will be a larger rectangular surface. While one of the edges will remain equal to the corresponding edge of the cheese, the other will become longer. There is no difficulty in understanding this, and we believe that from practical experience and elementary knowledge of solid geometry you know it, but the main thing is to make this operation only mentally.

68. Cutting the cheese with a plane (your knife) that is parallel to *no* edge will yield a totally different section, which is difficult to visualize. While in all former intersections the angles remained 90°, this time each angle of the section surface will be different and all four edges will change size. However, try to visualize what happens.

69. Cut the cheese so that your knife will (a) make a 45° angle with the frontal vertical surface of the cheese and (b) cut this surface in two. The resulting slice will be a prism of triangular section. Can you describe this prism in more detail?

70. Cut a salami. First consider the salami a cylinder of circular section. Then cut it with your knife perpendicular to the salami's axis. The result will invariably be another circle. But if you slant your knife, the section will be not a circle but an elongated curve, an ellipse. The more you slant your knife, the more elongated the ellipse you obtain. Suppose your salami has an infinite length and your knife cuts it through the circular section's diameter all along this infinite length. What is this section going to look like? If you fail to give the correct answer immediately, try first to visualize the knife cutting through the diameter (longitudinal section) of a short salami.

*71. What solid is the moon?

*72. What solid is formed by your eye and the visible circle of the moon?

*73. If you consider one point of the visible circle of the moon from the previous question and the eye, you obtain a straight line. What is the angle between this line and the radius of the moon that intersects this line?

*74. What type of parallelepiped envelops a sphere better than any other?

75. We cannot go further before intersecting planes with a sphere. The geometric demonstration is rather complicated and has no place in this book, but keep in mind that no matter where we cut a sphere with a plane the section will be invariably a circle. The largest circle will be obtained by cutting the sphere through its center, the smallest when cutting close to its surface. Also, when we again start traveling around a sphere either with a car or with a helicopter, nothing will change: The sphere will remain the same from any point, and if we keep flying at the same distance, not even its size will change. Perhaps you cannot explain why this happens, but we will give you the demonstration later in Chapter 6.

76. Cut a sphere in half, dispose of one half, and make the other one stand so that the circular section is vertical (in practice this is impossible, but we can accept it in theory). Turn around it. The moment you face the section frontally you will see a circle. When you face the opposite side, you will again see a circle, the same. When you come to the profile position, where the section and your eye belong to the same plane, you will see half a circle. Right? In between these three positions there is an infinity of other positions. Describe them to yourself.

Now put this book aside for a few days and reinforce your newly acquired vision by practicing the following three exercises:

77. Try to remember, repeat, combine, and complicate as many of the first 76 exercises as you can, of course, all mentally.

78. While walking in town, compare your mental achievements with the observations you can obtain from changes of shape of buildings in relation to the position of your eyes. Also try to abstract the buildings and structures you see into their basic geometric solids.

79. Take an actual knife and make as many sections as you can, using fruits, vegetables, bread, salami, cheese, or whatever you can find that can be cut. Follow these steps:
(a) Decide the precise section you will cut.
(b) Imagine what this section will look like.
(c) After cutting, compare the section obtained with what you had in mind before.

80. So far we have intersected different solids with a plane. Now let us go on to the intersection between two solids. For this we will imagine some practical examples. Imagine a nail entering a piece of wood.

81. If the nail is driven perpendicularly to the surface of the wood and then extracted, the hole remaining will reproduce the shape of the nail, which is usually a cylinder. On the surface of the wood, the hole will be a circle. You know this because at this point we deal with the intersection between a cylinder (the nail) and a plane (the wood surface).

*82. Under what conditions is a cylinder intersecting a prism of square section tangent to all four lateral surfaces of the prism?

83. If the nail is driven *not* perpendicularly to the surface of the wood and then extracted, the entire hole inside the wood will again reproduce the shape of the cylinder. But the intersection of this hole with the surface will be an ellipse. Right?

84. Suppose the piece of wood is a cube and the nail driven in at a slant comes out of the cube through a surface adjacent to the first. In this case the hole will look like a cylinder that is cut at its edges by two ellipses, which might be equal or not. Two questions: In which case will the ellipses be identical? What will be the angle formed by the nail and the two surfaces?

85. Generalize the images you have acquired by changing the nail to a water pipe going through earth or thick walls or to a tunnel going through a mountain. The problem is basically the same, but some details make the visualization slightly more difficult.

86. Abstract to solid geometry and imagine as many intersections of cylinders with parallelepipeds as you can in order to accustom your mental vision to the respective intersecting surfaces. Try also the almost impossible, to imagine the nail as a prism of square, rectangular, and hexagonal section and see if you can define the intersections. Do not worry if you cannot.

87. Imagine nails (cylindrical) intersecting *corners* of parallelepipedic solids. Again, this is difficult, and you shouldn't insist too much.

88. Review Exercises 64 through 76. In these we dealt with a plane cutting different solids. If the cutting plane is vertical and the cut solid stands on horizontal ground, we can imagine easily that the vertical plane will also intersect with the horizontal ground, which is also assumed to be a plane in a straight line. Indeed, if we cut any solid standing on any flat, plane ground, we can see that the knife will leave a trace on this surface, a straight line which theoretically can be extended indefinitely. This intersection between the ground and the knife plane is of invaluable importance in perspective drawing, because with its help we can define a considerable number of perspective construction points. So far we ask you only to imagine such ground intersections and understand that these lines are the ground limits of any vertical section of a solid by a particular vertical plane. Later we will see that the intersection plane can be also slanted and will leave a similar straight trace on the ground.

89. In order to make it easier to see a slanting plane that leaves a straight trace on the ground, imagine a hinged lid over an opening in the ground and, while rotating this lid in different positions around the hinges, observe that the line of contact between the lid and the ground remains the same.

90. Imagine yourself standing on a street. Imagine another person near you starting to walk toward the other end of the block. The walking person, as you can expect, will seem *to you* to be diminishing. You can also infer that if this person reaches the horizon line, he will be so small that he will look like a point. If he travels in a straight line, his head will also travel in a straight line, above the line where his feet touch the ground. So if you know his basic traveling line and his height when he is close to you, you can determine at any point in perspective how much he will diminish in height.

91. If you abstract the former process and instead of a person imagine a vertical line (segment) traveling back and forth on a straight path between you and the horizon, you can get a precise sense of the variation of height of this line depending on distance. What will be the height of this vertical traveling line at a distance halfway between you and the horizon? (Actually, the

question is inaccurate, and we speak only about the *apparent* half distance. The real middle is somewhere else, but we will study this in a later chapter.)

92. Try the same exercise first with a frontal wall of rectangular shape and then with a train car, both moving toward the horizon, and then with a cylinder *rolling* toward the horizon and back. Repeat the exercise with a ball (sphere).

93. You have seen in the preceding exercises that the size of all the objects varies with the distance. What kind of movement doesn't alter the size? The answer is, any motion that keeps the object at the same distance from your eye. Consequently any circular movement with the center at your eye will show you an object unchanged in size. On the other hand, we said that sizes do not change as long as the motion is happening in the frontal plane, which does *not* have all of its points at equal distances from your eye, and this is a contradiction. We will clarify this contradiction later, in Chapter 9, but for the time being try to think about it and find some answers if you can.

94. Imagine two persons on a road, very far apart from each other and from you. You would like to determine which of the two is taller, and the only way to tell is to bring both of them together. But if you imagine two poles (vertical lines) fixed in the pavement and far apart from each other, you cannot bring them together. So you have to imagine some other method for comparing their heights. You know that two vertical poles (parallel lines in space) belong to the same plane. Their points of connection with the pavement not only belong to that plane but also determine the intersection between this plane and the earth, a line that can be extended mentally to the horizon line to give the vanishing point of this particular line. Also, the moving tops of the two poles (recall Exercise 91) will vanish at the same point. Now the problem is simple: If the poles are equal in height, one single vanishing line will touch both heads; if the poles are unequal, we will have two vanishing lines for the heads.

95. Add a third pole that does not belong to the previous plane. This complicates the matter because you will have to verify the heights using two vertical planes, one for each pair of poles.

96. Suppose the three poles are equal in height. Can you imagine a triangular roof mounted on these poles? Can you extend your vision to four equal poles mounted on the corners of a rectangular plane and cover them with a rectangular roof?

97. Can you fill the spaces between the poles with walls so that you get a rectangular room? Can you still imagine the unseen walls hidden by the front ones?

98. Can you mentally add another floor above the ground floor obtained in the previous exercise?

*99. What solid is a bagel? What solid is the trace left by the earth in its orbit around the sun?

*100. Imagine that two spheres are tangent and a plane is passing through the point of tangency. What should be the relation between this plane and the line joining the centers of the two spheres so that the plane will be tangent to both spheres?

Answers

1. Two.
10. An infinity of lines in the plane and in space.
12. Two lines that intersect at infinity are parallel.
13. No, but the angle between the beams is so small that for practical purposes they can be considered parallel.
15. A parallelepiped.
17. Yes: at the intersection of their diagonals.
18. Trace the circumscribing square and intersect the diagonals.
27. No, it is an arc of circle, but the circle is so large that we can consider it straight.
28. A triangle.
31. First the bottom disappears because the boat travels on a sphere.
35. The radius of the circle and the edge of the hexagon are equal.
39. Yes, when the eye and the sheet are in the same plane.
40. It will be equal to the diameter of the circle. You should be able to imagine a more accurate answer after reading Chapter 3.
51. A triangle.
59. One hundred.
60. A cylinder.
61. A cylinder.
63. Three.
71. A sphere.
72. A cone.
73. Ninety degrees. This means that the line is tangent to the moon in that point.
74. The cube.
82. When the diameter of the cylinder's section is equal with the square's edge.
99. Toruses (the first circular, the second elliptic).
100. The line is perpendicular to the plane.

2. PRACTICAL EXERCISES

This chapter contains 165 exercises. You should work them mentally first, then translate your images onto paper. Don't forget: Before drawing anything, try to obtain a precise mental image and endeavor to see it on the paper so that when you start using the pencil, the drawing will fall more or less on the image you have projected mentally. The more nearly identical the drawing is to your image, the closer you will be to achieving a good vision. Every exercise is answered at the end of the book, but don't jeopardize your efforts by taking the easy way and looking at the answers before you have solved the question. We also recommend that you not check the answers at all before the whole chapter has been studied. After finishing this chapter entirely, return to the first exercise, solve it again, and then check your result with the drawing and explanations at the end. Only when you feel that you must know the answer, immediately, should you allow yourself a glimpse at the solution, but then try to understand why it is so without reading the explanation. And do not use a ruler or compass. All your drawings must be freehand.

1. Mark three points so that the lines joining the middle one to the other two form a 90° angle.

2. Trace the letter V so that the two arms form an angle of approximately 45°.

3. Trace four points at random and then join them with as many lines as possible. How many possibilities are there, and how many connecting lines will you have in each case?

4. Trace the letter V upside down and draw a horizontal line through its top. What *perspective* image do you obtain?

5. In the preceding exercise we gave two-dimensional information in order to accustom you to the perspective, three-dimensional interpretation of a flat drawing. Now, while preserving the horizontal line from Exercise 4, change the angle formed by the two arms of the letter V and make several drawings. Can you interpret perspectively what happens?

6. Now imagine the letter W upside down (or a freehand M) and connect the two upper corners with a long horizontal line. You might be tempted to think that this problem is very similar to the one in Exercise 4, but it is not. From the perspective point of view you are dealing with a different concept. The problem would have been similar to the one in Exercise 4 if the requested drawing had been ⋏ .

7. Take some liberty with the former exercise by considering two V's upside down instead of a W. Start playing in your imagination with the two V's, changing the distance between the two points on the horizontal line. To make it easier, compare the situation with two bells hanging from a horizontal iron bar and imagine the two V's hanging just as the bells would. You can obtain innumerable images, depending on the directions in which the V's "hang," the distance between the points, the length of the lines, and the intersection of these lines. Try to exhaust this cinematic game mentally, and then trace some of the more interesting positions on paper and analyze them from the perspective point of view.

8. An interesting and very common particular case of the preceding exercise happens when the two V's hang from the same point on the horizontal line, still able to dangle independently. If your mental vision is good, you will realize that the dangling lines never intersect with each other except in the hanging point. Why? What is your perspective conclusion?

9. Repeat Exercise 8 while changing the angle between the arms of the two V's at random. You know that we try to visualize lines imagined in a plane frontal screen and then interpret them in depth, three-dimensionally. As we said before, by varying lines you can exercise your imagination for all possible changes occurring in perspective drawing. This particular exercise deals with the different possibilities for seeing different roads (or parallels) situated on the earth. Is this statement complete?

10. Consider now a limitless horizontal line and somewhere on your mental screen a 5-inch vertical line crossing it. (The value 5 has no real importance except to give you an approximate size.) If you interpret the resulting drawing in perspective, you can say that the horizontal line is the horizon line and the vertical is a tree or a pole. So far there is no precise information about the height and location of this pole on the earth, because we have not decided whether the vertical is cut by the horizontal at the middle or at some other point, because we can move it to the right or to the left on our mental screen, and because we have no indication whether this vertical line touches the ground at all. However, if we draw the upside-down V in a certain relation to the vertical, our problem starts making sense. Can you see what happens?

11. Let us try a slightly more difficult visual problem. Again take the upside-down V hanging from the horizon line and cross it with a horizontal line, of course parallel to the horizon line. The two points where this new line intersects the two arms of the V determine the length of the line. Now, on each point raise a vertical line (pole) having the same dimension as the horizontal one and join the tops of these lines with another horizontal line. You have obtained a vertical square on your mental screen, and because its upper and lower edges are parallel to the horizon line, the square is frontal. You can also say that this square is a frontal wall, a screen within your mental screen, a frontal square tile, or any frontal square object. Actually, you realize, it is only a surface without depth. But we have not given you any specific information about *where* on the upside-down V you should build this square, so now you can construct another square and another one and another one wherever you want on the V. If your second square is very close to the first one, your image will show you two squares, the closest larger than the second, and you can say that they are two square pieces of glass, two wire squares, two thin frames, or whatever. However, with a small effort of abstraction, you can imagine the two squares as *belonging to*

the same object. Indeed, if you imagine a transparent glass tile, you will see the front and rear frontal squares exactly as in the preceding description. The problem starts becoming really difficult (and this is one of the first difficult problems in perspective drawing) when the tile (or wall or any opaque body) is not transparent any more, so you can see only one or two edges of the smaller rear square and you actually must imagine its shape. However, in order to have the complete drawing of the tile, the two squares are not enough. You know from geometry that the tile is a parallelepiped, that is, a prism having a rectangle as its section. In our case the section is a square and the thickness of the tile is its height, so altogether this shape in space has twelve edges. What we have done so far is to determine the two squares, so we need besides their eight edges another four edges in order to have the tile completed. And here we are, back to the upside-down V! The two bottom edges of the tile are segments of the two arms of the V lying between the two squares. Which are the last two edges?

12. In the previous exercise we said that you can imagine as many squares as you want using the same way of building them on the upside-down V. So you can imagine an infinity of such squares, one after another, from the closest point to your eyes to the tip of the V. But instead of mentally building an infinity of squares, let's try actually thinking in perspective: Take one square and slide it on the V, back and forth (always remembering that it will grow or diminish as a function of the distance between the two arms of the V). In this way you will obtain both a complete infinity of squares and the image of an infinite parallelepiped. Most important, once you master this mental exercise, you will have acquired one of the most delicate and fruitful ways of thinking in perspective, because only when you can play mentally with points, lines, surfaces, volumes, and objects, as we said, can you draw in perspective. Only by moving points can you imagine straight or curved lines; only by moving lines can you actually "see" the planes, the intersection of planes, or the surfaces determined; only by moving planes or surfaces can you determine volumes. And in our exercise you move a surface in order to "see" the volume determined by it.

13. This exercise will give you two ways to imagine a cube in perspective. The first is to slide the square toward the horizon, moving it a distance equal to the edge of the square. Of course, this is an approximation, because you cannot determine exactly (at this stage of the course) the distorted length of an edge, but you can build a rather satisfactory image of the cube. The second method is to rotate the square 90° around its lower horizontal edge until it lies flat on the upside-down V. If you imagine this rotation in profile, the upper point of the vertical edge describes a quarter of a circle. When you return to your initial image (remember Exercise 26 of Chapter 1), this quarter of a circle will be seen as part of an ellipse. You might ask: Why should I learn about these two ways of building a cube, when I can visualize it anyway, right in front of my eyes? We do not doubt that you can see the cube and many other solids, but this doesn't mean that you can actually put them on paper correctly. Besides, some complex surfaces distorted by perspective can be handled only by having an excellent training in translation (sliding) and rotation, and we are preparing you for them.

14. The second method of building a cube was the rotation of the frontal square around its lower edge. If this square belongs to an endless plane, a vertical surface, can you say where the intersection of this plane with the earth is? What does it look like?

15. If we rotate the square 90°, it becomes part of the plane of the earth. We know that the vanishing line of this plane (the earth) is the horizon line. But if the rotation of the square is (let us say) only 80°, where is its vanishing line?

16. We will now deal with the basic square of the cube, the square lying on the ground and determined by two horizontal lines and two segments of the upside-down V. It is time to stop talking about the upside-down V, because by now our imaginations are used to the idea of representing two or more parallel lines running toward the same vanishing point on the horizon line. We can describe the two nonfrontal edges of the basic square as parallel lines intersecting in a point on the horizon line. The problem is to trace another square adjacent to the first one and situated either at its left or at its right. In this case we know that they will have one edge in common, and this edge is one of the vanishing, distorted lines going to the vanishing point. As the closer edge of the first square is parallel to the horizon line and thus frontal, it is not distorted and its length will be the same for the next square. Therefore, if we extend this edge and take its length once more either to the left or to the right, we will have the second edge of the new square. Can you now complete the square?

17. Using the same method, you can trace a full row of frontal squares.

18. Mentally trace one diagonal of the first square. This is a line belonging to the plane of the earth, so by extension it will vanish in some point situated on the horizon line. Now trace the diagonal of the same direction in the adjacent square. Where does this diagonal vanish on the horizon line and why?

19. Trace the diagonals of the same direction of all the squares you previously imagined. Where do they intersect with the horizon line?

20. Now trace the diagonals perpendicular to the first ones and repeat the reasoning. Do you reach any interesting conclusion?

21. You have traced in the first square the two diagonals, thus obtaining the central point of the square. How can you divide this square into four squares, each having one-fourth the area of the initial one? (This is very simple.)

22. If you solved the previous exercise, keep the image in your mind and think about how to build another pair of squares behind the two frontal squares. You will see that the image is very similar to the one obtained in Exercise 21, but you have to reverse the reasoning.

23. Draw a chessboard. The problem is to do it without using any measurement, just using the diagonals and edges. If it is difficult to imagine it right away in perspective, think about it first on a frontal, nondistorted mental screen to see what happens and then return to what we know in perspective.

24. Imagine a large square divided as before into four equal, smaller squares. You can easily trace a diagonal in each of these four squares so that these four diagonals form another square in a diamond position. This particular square, as you can see, has no frontal edges. If the initial square's edge is a, and thus the quarter square's edge is $a/2$, can you calculate the edge of the diamond square? This is a mathematical question, but it is good to solve it in order to be able later to deal with measurements in perspective.

25. You remember the initial cube. Now trace a vertical wall on one of the diagonals. Forgetting the perspective distortion, is this wall square or not? And if not, why?

26. Imagine again a square on the earth with two edges parallel to the horizon line H. Can you divide this square into nine equal squares?

27. Can you divide a perspective square into *any* number of equal squares you choose?

28. Take the same square we talked about in the last several exercises.

Trace one diagonal. Can you build a new square in perspective so that this diagonal becomes its edge?

29. Can you build more than one such square adjacent to it?

30. Can you divide one such square into 4, 9, 16, . . . equal squares?

31. So far we have dealt with squares. Return to the initial square with two edges parallel to the *H* line. Can you build a rectangle whose vanishing edges are equal to the square's edges, while the frontal edges are 1.5 times as long as the others?

32. Can you trace a rectangle in which the vanishing edges are *a* and the horizontal ones are *na*, where *n* is larger or smaller than *a*?

33. Can you build a rectangle in which the horizontal edges are *a* and the vanishing edges are 1.5*a*?

34. Trace on the ground a segment that is *not* parallel to the *H* line. Can you divide this segment into three equal segments? (Do not forget that these equal segments will not look equal because of perspective distortion.)

35. Consider the same segment from the previous exercise. Can you divide it in any number of segments whose lengths are determined but unequal to each other?

36. Imagine the *H* line and a horizontal segment on the earth. Between the *H* line and this segment trace another horizontal segment of arbitrary length. This segment might be equal to, larger than, or smaller than the first one. How can you determine which of the three possibilities is correct?

37. If you have a segment *AB* parallel to the *H* line and a given point *C* between the *H* line and *AB*, how can you determine a segment *CD* parallel and equal to *AB*?

38. Trace the *H* line and a segment *AB not* parallel to it. You already know that the vanishing point of *AB and all its parallels* is the point where the extension of *AB* intersects the *H* line. Given a point *C* on the ground, can you trace a segment parallel and equal to *AB* through *C*?

39. Can you find a simple method of tracing another segment equal and parallel to segments *AB* and *CD* from the previous exercise exactly halfway between *AB* and *CD*?

40. Imagine a square and its diagonals, in perspective. You can say that the square is composed of four equal triangles. If you draw only one diagonal, you obtain two adjacent triangles. Can you draw a triangle similar to one of these two so that each edge of the new triangle is twice as long as the first?

41. How would you draw a triangle similar to the one in Exercise 40 but only 1.5 times as large as the initial one?

42. Let us think in motion. Imagine our square as a sort of platform on wheels. Of course, we preserve the abstraction of this platform and do not actually see any wheels, but we imagine this platform moving on two rails that are situated exactly under the horizontal edges of the square. (Actually, in the abstraction, the rails are extensions of these edges.) Can you imagine this motion and how the square is distorted as it changes place on the rails?

43. Can you imagine the same square's distortions when *you* move on a line parallel to the *H* line while the square is stationary?

44. Imagine a square moving toward the horizon on its vanishing lines. Draw the square in several of the positions it passes through.

45. Imagine a square moving in a diagonal direction. Although the situation is slightly more complex, draw several stages in this new motion.

46. Imagine now that a square moves toward the horizon, not in a diagonal direction and not in the direction of a vanishing edge, but in any slanting direction determined arbitrarily by some relation between one point on the square and another point on the ground. Do you have, after all the previous exercises, any difficulty in drawing some instances of the square's motion?

47. Can you repeat all of Exercises 40 through 46, replacing the square with a rectangle? (This exercise has no answer because all laws explained for the square are valid for the rectangle as well.)

48. Imagine a perspective square in a diamond position. This means that pairs of edges go to two vanishing points, while one diagonal remains parallel to the *H* line and the other vanishes on the *H* line, intersecting it in an angle of 90°. (Remember this point of intersection as the eye-point.) Can you construct translations for this type of square like those in the previous exercises?

49. Imagine a square in any perspective position on the ground. Can you draw an inscribed circle? Most perspective problems have to be solved by finding some essential points of the figure you wish to draw. Therefore, before trying to draw the circle in perspective, recall from plane geometry some of the properties of a circle inscribed in a square. First find the four points of tangency between the circle and the square, and then find the four points of intersection of the circle with the square's diagonals.

50. Build a perspective circle circumscribing a square.

51. Can you draw a regular octagon in perspective? Remember that an octagon can be built in plane geometry with two equal squares having the same center but positioned at an angle of 45° with respect to each other.

52. Can you draw a regular hexagon in perspective? There are many ways of approaching this problem. With your present knowledge, the easiest way (although it may seem rather complicated) is to start by inscribing a hexagon in a circle and then inscribing the circle in a square; this will determine the necessary construction points of the perspective hexagon. For this particular exercise you will probably need to refer to the answer, but try to do the construction before looking at it.

53. Given a regular hexagon in perspective on the ground, can you construct adjacent hexagons in a honeycomb pattern around it?

54. Imagine a rectangular yard within which a tree is planted somewhere, at an arbitrary point. The problem is to obtain the exact location of this random point within the rectangle. (This is an extremely useful exercise, because in most cases finding a point in perspective depends on other points of

reference, and your inventiveness can always find a solution. We give you only one.)

55. Imagine a rectangular yard cut into two unequal areas by a slanting fence, which is not parallel to any edge or diagonal of the rectangle. If you have the plane drawing, how can you obtain the perspective image of this sectioned yard?

56. Imagine a river that is very irregular in shape. If you have a map of it, how can you find the best approximation of such a river in perspective? (Hint: Remember that an artist who wants to enlarge or reduce an irregular drawing uses a grid of squares.)

57. If you have a square in perspective on the ground with two frontal edges (parallel to the *H* line), can you build such a vertical square on any of its edges?

58. Can you build a frontal cube in perspective?

59. Motion again. Imagine that the basic square is a lid hinged on one of its vanishing edges. This lid can be rotated around the hinges to 180°, until it lies flat on the other side of the initial square. This lid can stop at any angle, having a theoretically infinite number of positions. Can you draw the lid in perspective in *any* position?

60. Can you build a lid on a ground square hinged on a *frontal* edge so that it makes an angle of 45° with the ground?

61. On the *diagonal* of the same square (having two edges parallel to the *H* line) build another perspective square with all edges equal to the diagonal.

62. In order to familiarize yourself with the method, construct another square on the other diagonal of the basic square. (Since this exercise uses the same method as Exercise 61, it has no answer.)

63. Suppose you have on the ground two adjacent frontal squares (with collinear frontal edges). Trace their diagonals, one in each square, so that the two diagonals make an angle of 90° (in perspective it doesn't appear so). Then build a vertical wall on each of the diagonals with a height equal to the edge of one square.

64. Let us forget about the basic squares for now. Trace the *H* line and two intersecting lines on the ground. The problem is to build on these lines two intersecting walls of arbitrary height. The height, which is the same for both walls, is given at some point on one of the lines (not their point of intersection).

65. Trace the *H* line and any irregular W shape on the ground. Can you draw, in perspective, four walls of equal height built on this W?

66. Given a vertical wall, can you divide it in half horizontally?

67. Can you draw in perspective a vertical chessboard?

68. In Exercise 67 you divided a vertical square into 64 smaller squares. Can you find a simpler and much quicker method to obtain these divisions, using only *one* diagonal?

69. Can you divide a vertical rectangle into an odd number of equal vertical strips? (For the solution of this problem, first look back at Exercise 34.)

70. Divide a vertical wall into any number of horizontal strips in any proportion.

71. Given a vertical square, draw an interior square (like a window) exactly at the center of the wall. Disregard the size.

72. Given the same vertical square wall, draw at its center another square whose sides are half as long as the sides of the first.

73. Motion again. If you have a vertical *frontal* square that moves to the right or left on a rail under its bottom edge and parallel to the *H* line, then no matter how far the square moves, it remains frontal and therefore undistorted. But try to imagine a vertical square that is *not* frontal, although it

moves on frontal rails as before. How will this square be distorted in different positions, and how can you determine at each instance its shape in perspective?

74. Imagine the vertical square as a door hinged on one of its vertical edges and able to rotate a full circle (360°) around this edge. Although you do not yet have the knowledge to give a precise solution to such a problem, try to give an approximate method for showing this door in perspective for different angles of rotation.

75. Given a square vertical wall that is not frontal, can you "move" it on rails that are neither parallel to the *H* line nor parallel to the wall's vanishing edges?

76. We saw in Exercise 9 how to divide a vertical wall into any number of equal or unequal horizontal strips. Now trace a V on the ground, draw two walls on it at any height you choose, and divide them *both* into equal horizontal strips. This exercise will be basic for the rendering of multistory buildings in perspective, when you deal with many floors.

77. As before, draw a V-shaped pair of walls and divide them into a number of floors. Then draw a similar V-shaped construction on the ground, slightly closer to the *H* line, thus indicating that the new pair of walls is further from your eyes, and find a way of giving these walls the same height and the same number of floors as the first. Do not forget that the second pair of walls is completely unrelated to the first, except for having the same height and number of floors. (This exercise requires an additional "trick"; think in terms of virtual, nonexistent walls uniting the first pair of walls with the second.)

78. Build a ground square with two frontal edges (again!). On this base build a cube. Then divide this cube into eight equal cubes.

79. Trace a basic rectangle, erect a parallelepiped on it, and divide it into eight equal parallelepipeds. (This exercise is a variation on the previous one and has no answer.)

80. Trace the same square and the cube on it and then divide the cube into only four equal parallelepipeds; that is, instead of dividing it into eight equal cubes, you will obtain solids whose dimensions are 1, $\frac{1}{2}$, and $\frac{1}{2}$ times the cube's edge. The problem is to *remove* one of the upper parallelepipeds so that the remaining solid will look like a stair of two steps.

81. Can you build a stair of eight steps of equal height and depth? This may seem to be difficult, but if you remember the vertical chessboard, you will have solved the toughest part of the problem.

82. So far we have used the expression "vertical wall" for a vertical rectangular or square surface without thickness. Start practicing the construction of vertical walls that have various thicknesses, remembering that the cubes you have already constructed are such very thick walls.

83. Can you cut a door in a thick wall?

84. Draw a vertical (three-dimensional) wall and divide it in half vertically.

85. A pyramid is a solid that has a polygonal base and a top point joined to the base with as many triangular surfaces as there are edges of the basic polygon. Pyramids can be *symmetrical* (when the top is vertically above the center of a regular basic polygon) or *irregular* (when the top is not above the center of the polygon). The Egyptian pyramids are symmetrical pyramids with square bases. Can you draw such a solid in perspective?

86. On a perspective square with two edges parallel to the H line, raise a symmetrical pyramid of height equal to the edge of the square.

87. On the same basic square as in Exercise 86, build a pyramid having its top directly above some point P that is on the ground but *outside* the square. Make the height of the pyramid equal to the edge of the square.

88. Given a basic hexagon, raise on it a pyramid whose height is six times the edge of the hexagon. You will obtain a solid very much like many church steeples.

89. Build a perspective cube with a square pyramid on top of it. The total height is to be $2a$ (a being the edge of the cube).

90. Create different exercises by taking squares, rectangles, and other prismatic solids, adding on their top the corresponding pyramid and varying its height. (There is no answer to this exercise.)

91. We saw in Exercises 59 and 60 how to establish the perspective of a lid rotating around hinges. Now let us see how we can build a slanting surface without the complication of motion. Given a square on the ground (no matter how its edges are placed in relation to the H line), can you build over it a slanting roof that has one of its edges on the ground and the opposite edge supported by two poles of equal height? Remember that *over* the other two edges of the square you will have two vertical right triangles.

92. In Exercise 91 you obtained a slanted roof. Can you add onto it another roof slanting symmetrically down from the top, reaching the ground at the same distance from the center as the first one?

93. Draw the simple slanted roof of Exercise 91 on a cubical house.

94. Imagine the previous structure having only the roof and the two lateral trapezoidal walls (each composed of a triangle on top of a square). Assuming that these two walls are quite thick, can you remove the roof and show them in perspective?

95. Having solved Exercise 94, build a horizontal floor joining the two walls at a height half the distance between the ground and the lower part of the roof.

96. In order to have better light for workers, many factories are covered with repeated slanting roofs called saw-tooth roofs. Draw such a structure, consisting of several repetitions of the unit obtained in Exercise 93.

97. Usually a roof has four slanting surfaces corresponding to the four walls they cover. When the walls form a square, the roof looks like a square pyramid, and we have already studied it. But when the building has an elongated rectangular shape, the four surfaces of the roof consist of two trapezoids intersecting on a horizontal crest and two lateral triangles reaching the crest at its two ends. The problem is to put in perspective such a four-surfaced roof where the building is an elongated rectangle and the crest is half the length of the elongated rectangle.

98. Trace a circle on the ground in perspective. In order to do this, first draw the circumscribing square. Build on it a cylinder that ends above the *H* line.

99. Build a vertical cone within the cylinder built previously.

100. Build a cylinder lying on the ground (that is, with its generatrix, not its circular section, on the ground).

101. Build a cone with its generatrix lying on the ground. (This problem is not as simple as for the cylinder, and with your present knowledge you can solve it only approximately.)

102. Build a vertical cone upside down.

103. If a cylinder lying with its generatrix on the ground rolls toward the *H* line, what trace will it leave on the ground? How will it look at different instants in its movement?

104. When a cone is rolled on a plane, what geometric surface is covered? How does it look in perspective?

105. A sphere never distorts in perspective. Can you explain why with the help of geometry?

106. On your perspective field, with the center superimposed on the eye-point, draw a circle (its center is on the line joining your eye to the eye-point on the *H* line). This circle will represent a sphere. You know that this is the circle of tangency of the visual cone starting from your eye and touching the sphere. Therefore this circle is not the largest one that could be obtained as a section of the sphere. To find the precise diameter of this sphere is a problem depending on the distance between you and the sphere, and you do not yet know how to handle measurable perspective. However, you can draw an approximate cube around this sphere, which touches each face of the cube at its center point. Now try something else. Draw the same cube far to the right or left according to the translation method you have learned and imagine how the sphere will be inscribed. To your surprise, the visible circle of the sphere will contradict the statement made in Exercise 105 and will look like an ellipse. Can you give an explanation?

107. Can you say what circle our eyes see when looking at the sun?

108. Let us now learn a few helpful tricks in perspective drawing. You know that, in any square on the ground, each pair of edges run to a vanishing point on the *H* line. But suppose you have only two edges of the square (forming a right angle) and only one vanishing point (the other is so far away that you cannot place it on your paper). First using your complete mental field, including the other vanishing point, imagine what happens. What "trick" or "tricks" can you use to complete the square?

109. The same problem in space. You have one rectangular wall crossing another rectangular wall, no matter the angle between these two walls. The first wall vanishes at a point V_1 on the *H* line, and the other vanishes at V_2, which is too distant to be reached on the paper, so the only indication you have about the second wall is its length on the ground. Use a trick to complete this second wall without the help of V_2.

110. Given the data from the previous exercise, complete a full parallelepiped.

111. Suppose you have just one wall, with the horizontal edges vanishing at a point *V* beyond your reach, as in the previous exercise. How can you divide this wall in half horizontally without having the vanishing point?

112. Divide the same wall into three horizontal strips. (This exercise has no answer.)

113. Given two unrelated walls of the same height in perspective, divide them into horizontal strips, not necessarily equal, but identical on both walls. Find the trick of transferring the divisions from the first wall without measuring the divisions on the second.

114. Take five unrelated and randomly distributed points on the ground, raise a vertical line from one of them, and then raise verticals on the other four, preserving the same height.

115. Take five irregularly distributed points on the ground, and through one of them trace a segment on the ground parallel to the *H* line. Find equal segments parallel to the *H* line through the other four points.

116. Given five unrelated squares or rectangles on the ground in perspective and their respective vanishing points, raise a definite vertical on one corner of a single square and then construct solids on all these surfaces having the same height. (As this exercise is a synthesis of methods used in the previous ones, there is no answer.)

117. Given a square or a rectangle on the ground, *dig* a cubic or parallelepipedic hole in the earth of depth (approximately) equal to any one of the surface's edges.

118. Given a rectangle on the ground of width a and length $2a$, inscribe another rectangle of width $a - n$ and length $2a - n$, no matter what n is, so that the remaining "frame" has four sides of equal width.

119. Given the former double rectangle in a plane, raise a first solid on the exterior rectangle and above it another solid raised on the interior rectangle. Height is unimportant.

120. Repeat the former exercise by adding yet another solid recessed the same distance from the one below. You will obtain a skyscraper shape made of three superimposed solids. (Although this exercise requires a lot of additional construction lines, there is no new method involved in it, so we give no answer.)

The purpose of the next 45 exercises is to familiarize you with the concepts of light, shadow, and color. We hope you have answers for most of these questions, and our answers should be used only for comparison with yours.

121. Do you know what light is?

122. In space, astronauts are surrounded by darkness and can clearly see the stars, the sun, and the earth. Can you explain the darkness?

123. Why is the earth's atmosphere luminous during daytime?

124. Why is the moon's sky black even in daytime (when the sun is above the moon's horizon)?

125. What does *black* mean?

126. What happens to light falling on a black surface?

127. What does *white* mean?

128. What is a white surface?

129. What is a red surface?

130. Why is the sky blue?

131. What sometimes gives the sky a yellow-reddish tone?

132. Why does a white surface, when lighted by a red light, look red?

133. What makes one white surface reflect better than another white surface, and why?

134. Why does the eye receive more or less reflected light from a surface when this surface changes its angle?

135. Why do we perceive distinctly the three visible faces of a uniformly colored cube in front of us?

136. Why then can we see the face of a cube that receives no photons from the source of light?

137. Why is the shadowed side of a half-moon not visible?

138. What is the geometric difference between sunlight and the light emitted by any other source on earth?

139. Suppose you are in a totally dark room. On one of the walls there are two very small holes situated on a vertical line, one above the other. If two light beams coming from the same source pass through the holes and fall on the floor, can you tell whether the source is the sun or some light source on earth?

140. Imagine a white screen, positioned so that the sunlight falls perpendicularly on its surface. Interpose a square, nontransparent panel between the sun and the screen and parallel to the screen. You obtain a square shadow on the screen. What is a shadow, and what does it look like in this particular situation?

141. Put your hand between the sun beams and a wall that receives the sunlight. Move your hand closer to or further from the wall. Does the shadow become larger or smaller in this process?

142. Use the screen described in Exercise 140 and the square panel, but instead of the sun use a light bulb. Describe the shadow, first stationary, at equal distances from the screen and light bulb, and then in motion.

143. In Exercise 139 we asked you to imagine yourself in a dark room and analyze the direction of light coming from a light source, penetrating through two small holes and falling on the floor. Whether you are in a dark room and a hole permits one beam to pass, or you are in full light and one material point floating in the air casts a point shadow on the ground, the geometry of the phenomenon remains the same, because we only reverse the process without changing the data. The vertical *distance* between the ground and the hole (or material point), the *distance* between the hole (or material point) and the cast light (or shadow) on the ground, and the *distance* between the same cast light (or shadow) and the basic point on the ground where the vertical line starts form a right triangle. Can you analyze this triangle and its relationship to the source of light? (This question is so fundamentally important to any shadow construction that we urge you to look at the answer immediately after trying to give an answer, check your own with ours, and learn the complete explanation.)

144. Given the light source, its projection on the ground, and a vertical stick on the ground, find its shadow.

145. In the former exercise, introduce a vertical square panel between the stick and its shadow. If one of the edges of the vertical panel touches the ground, can you see how the stick's shadow is projected on the panel?

146. Build the shadow cast by the panel in Exercise 145.

147. Try to build the shadow cast by two adjacent panels forming some angle at their edge of adjacency. (This exercise is an extension of the former one and has no answer.)

148. Repeat Exercise 146, this time putting the panel in correct perspective with respect to a horizon line and the vanishing point of the two horizontal edges of the panel. What can you say about the relationship between the shadow's upper edge and the upper edge of the panel?

149. What is the shadow region of a coin when the light source is the sun?

150. What is the shadow region of a coin when the light comes from a light bulb?

151. What is the shadow region of a square facing the sun?

152. What is the shadow region of a square facing a light bulb?

153. What is the shadow region of a thread crossing the sun beams?

154. What is the shadow region of a thread crossing light bulb beams?

155. What is the shadow region of a microscopically small material point facing the sun?

156. What is the shadow region of a microscopically small material point facing a light bulb?

157. What are the colors composing white in the solar spectrum?

158. Which of these colors are primary? What does primary mean?

159. What are the secondary colors?

160. If secondary colors result from the mixture of the primary ones, we infer that white is a mixture of red, blue, and yellow. If this assumption is valid for sunlight, why does mixing red, blue, and yellow paint result in a gray tone but never in white?

161. When we say *gray*, we generally think of a mixture of white and black. Why then are combinations of blue and orange or red and green also called grays?

162. A red cube standing on grass shows you two surfaces in full light and a third one in shadow. What, roughly, will be the color of the shadowed surface?

163. Why do remote mountains look blueish?

164. What gives a picture a strong impression of sunniness?

165. Why do caves and open windows facing the sun look black?

3. HORIZONTALITY

What the Horizon Actually Represents

You, like many other millions of people, have never traveled in space. However, science fiction movies have placed us in spaceships leaving or approaching some mysterious planet or the earth. We admired the growing planet from the window of the spaceship traveling toward it and landed together with the astronauts. But in all these sequences, one observation of paramount importance for our study was lost. So let us travel in imagination again from space toward the earth with full attention concentrated on the growing outline of our cosmic home. The earth is a sphere that can be seen clearly from millions of kilometers away. Seen from the sun (a distance of some 150,000,000 kilometers), the earth would look like a pinhead, and the closer our imaginary trip brought us, the larger it would look. We saw in the previous chapters that the cone with its apex at our eye and its base tangent to a sphere will be tangent to one of the sphere's circles, and only when the distance between the eye and the sphere is infinite (or, for practical purposes, large enough) will the circle of tangency coincide with the largest circle of the sphere. Now, the ancient Greek verb *horizein* means "to divide" or "to separate," and its present participle is *horizon*, "dividing" or "separating." As the circle we see while watching the approaching earth (or sun or moon) separates the planet from the sky, we can call it the *horizon circle*. This horizon circle becomes larger and larger as we come closer to the earth. But the horizon circle is also the tangent line between the earth's sphere and the cone emerging from our eye, and it becomes smaller as the distance diminishes, as shown in Fig. 3-1.

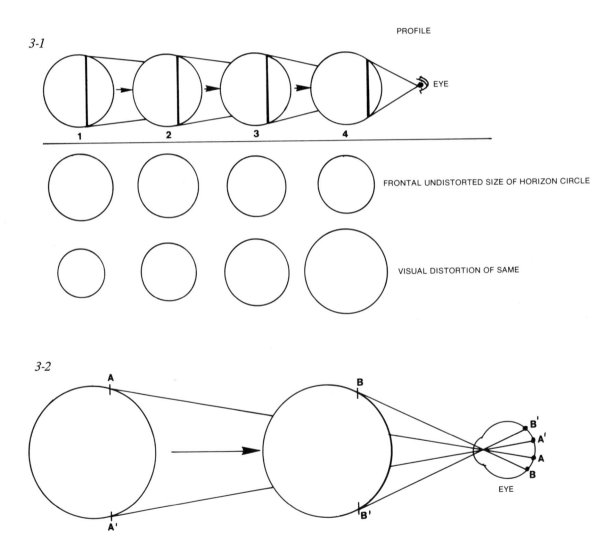

3-1

PROFILE

EYE

1 2 3 4

FRONTAL UNDISTORTED SIZE OF HORIZON CIRCLE

VISUAL DISTORTION OF SAME

3-2

A B

B'
A'
A
B

EYE

A' B'

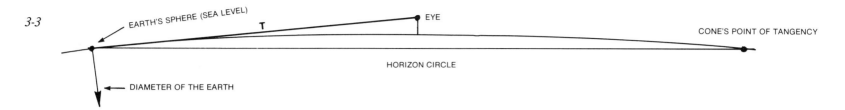

EARTH'S SPHERE (SEA LEVEL)

T

EYE

CONE'S POINT OF TANGENCY

HORIZON CIRCLE

DIAMETER OF THE EARTH

The question is: How is it possible that while the horizon circle becomes smaller, our image of it becomes larger? The answer is simple: Look again at Fig. 3-1 and see the angle of the tangent cone; it becomes larger and larger, and its projection on the retina becomes larger as well. Figure 3-2 is an exaggeration but shows clearly two instances of the motion of a ball approaching the eye and its projection on the retina.

Now let us find the "missing link" lost in the science fiction movies. We have seen that the horizon circle grows and grows until . . . what?

Suppose the spaceship is going to land on the sea. This is convenient for our study, because a calm sea has no valleys or mountains and theoretically is the earth's most spherical surface. So we are in the spaceship and see the horizon circle coming closer to us. The circle gradually becomes so large that we cannot see it in its entirety in one glimpse but must turn our head in order to encompass it completely.

Finally we reach the sea, and standing on the imaginary deck of our floating spaceship, we look around. We are in the middle of the sea, there is no shore in sight, and we can contemplate the horizon circle all around us. So, to understand better what happens, we will do some simple calculations (see Fig. 3-3).

First we calculate the distance between our eye and the horizon circle according to the power of a point to a circle, which says that the product of the distance from a point to a circle (H) with the sum of the same distance and the diameter of the circle (D) is equal to the square of the tangent to the circle from that point:

$$H(H + D) = T^2 \quad \text{or} \quad T = \sqrt{H(H + D)}$$

Knowing that D (the earth's diameter at the equator) is 12,750 kilometers and that the average height of the human eye (H) is 1.70 meters, we calculate

$$T = \sqrt{(12{,}750{,}000 + 1.70)\,1.70}$$

$$= 4655.642 \text{ meters}$$

Now we calculate the radius (R) of the horizon circle by similarity of triangles, as shown in Fig. 3-4:

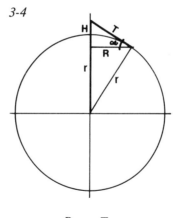

$$\frac{R}{r} = \frac{T}{r + H};$$

$$R = \frac{6375 \times 4655.642}{6375.0017} = 4655.6408 \text{ meters}$$

To calculate the cosine of angle α we use

$$\cos \alpha = \frac{R}{T} = \frac{4655.6408}{4655.6420} = 0.9999997$$

hence

$$\alpha = 0°10'$$

which is close enough to zero to consider R and T practically parallel. Also, for practical purposes, our eye can be thought of as situated at the center of the horizon circle, and we know that from the center a circle appears to be a straight line. Hence the horizon circle on the sea appears as a continuous straight line, which we call the horizon line. Repeating the calculations for the view from the height of a skyscraper (let us say 200 meters), we obtain

$$\alpha = 0°28'$$

which is again a very small angle. Again, T and R can be considered parallel.

Next we try to see the horizon from a jet plane at a height of 10 kilometers (10,000 meters). We obtain

$$\alpha = 3°12'$$

At this angle the horizon begins to fall under our eye line, but the horizon circle is still so large that the eye can hardly perceive its curvature. As long as the height remains small in relation to the earth's radius, the radius of the horizon's circle and the tangent from the eye can safely be considered parallel. This is why we have the impression that no matter where

33

we are standing (on a ladder, in an airplane, on the top of a skyscraper, or on the ground), the horizon line is *always* at the height of our eye (Fig. 3-5).

Try, if you have the opportunity, to ride in an outdoor elevator. The horizon line will move up and down together with you.

To think of the horizon line as being at the same height as your eye is an error but a permissible one. Perspective drawing would be impossible without this convention. Another permissible and fundamentally necessary error is to consider the earth flat, horizontal, instead of a sphere, because the surfaces in a perspective drawing are too small to permit the perception of any spheric curvature.

Look at Figure 3-6. In the perspective drawing *AC* is ignored and replaced with *AP*, the horizontal (virtual) plane of a flat earth. The horizon line is the end of the part of the earth that is visible to our eye, so according to our convention, the horizon line becomes identified with the intersection of our eye-level plane and the plane of the earth at an infinite distance. And because the earth disappears at the horizon line, we also call it the vanishing line of the earth.

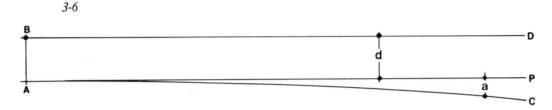

3-5

3-6

a = *exaggerated difference between the earth's curvature (C)*
    and (P) the virtual plane of the earth
d = *height of the eye*
BD is parallel to AP (and by acceptance to AC), so they intersect
    at infinity.

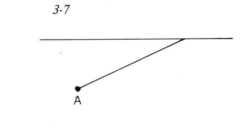

3-7

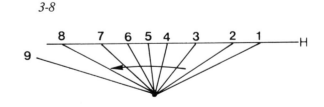

3-8

The Concept of Vanishing

In this chapter and in the previous ones we have used the term "vanishing line" in two different senses. In the exercises we regarded any segment as belonging to an infinite line that vanishes on the *H* line in a vanishing point uniquely associated with the group of parallels to which that particular segment belongs. In the previous paragraph we called a vanishing line the sum total of all vanishing points on the horizon line; that is, we identified the horizon line with the vanishing limit of the earth's plane. As we have accepted that the horizon line can be identified

with the infinite limit of the earth's theoretical plane, it follows that all lines traveling on this plane toward infinity will end, or vanish, on the horizon line. Indeed, if we take a point *A* (Fig. 3-7) and trace an infinite line through it toward the horizon, this line will end on the *H* line. So no matter what other line we draw through *A*, or no matter how we *rotate* the same line around this same point *A* (Fig. 3-8), its limit, its vanishing point, will be situated on the *H* line. For the infinite number of possible differently directed lines on the earth we will have an infinity of vanishing points on the *H* line, resembling an open fan.

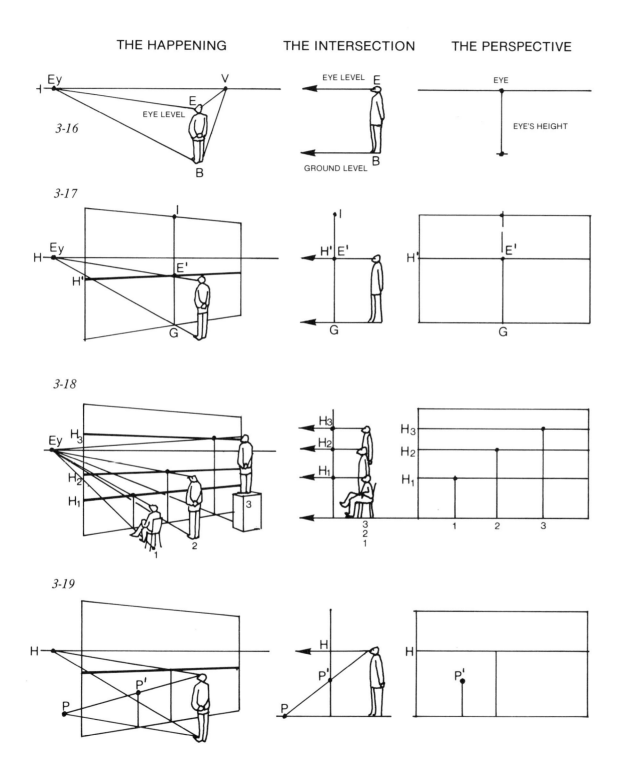

THE HAPPENING THE INTERSECTION THE PERSPECTIVE

3-16

3-17

3-18

3-19

horizon line on the projection plane as an indefinitely long, horizontal straight line.

Now, Fig. 3-18 shows three instances, in which the observer is sitting, standing, and at the top of a ladder. We repeat the H line construction for each one. The projected H lines on the projection plane vary according to the height of the observer, and you should realize that if the observer does not move to the right or to the left, the intersection IG remains the same, while E' moves up or down. So far we have considered the point on the horizon line so that we can establish the horizon line projection on the projection plane. But the working principle remains the same for *any* point situated on the ground (Fig. 3-19). Point P, the eye, and the ground line form another vertical plane, another intersection line between this plane and the projection plane, and hence the vertical that determines the intersection of PE with the projection plane in P'. If we trace a line PE on the ground (Fig. 3-20), this line will be easily constructed on the projection plane where P' and E' already exist. The characteristic of this line, which vanishes in E, is that it is parallel to the ground line EB ($E'G$ in projection).

Now, if we take two points M and P on the ground (Fig. 3-21), the method of finding their projection on the projection plane remains the same. Points P and M on the ground vanish in V on the real horizon, and V also has a projection on the projection plane in V'. For three points P, M, and S (Fig. 3-22), the problem remains the same, and the multitude of lines you see in the illustration is just the repetition of constructions for each point overlapping in a rather confusing pattern. But once we understand the mechanism of construction, we can detect that whatever happens on the gound is distortedly represented on the projection plane. Moreover, lines PM and MS intersect in M, because these lines have different vanishing points; that is, they are not parallel so they must intersect somewhere. We are now in a position to analyze how two nonparallel lines intersect, starting from their vanishing points.

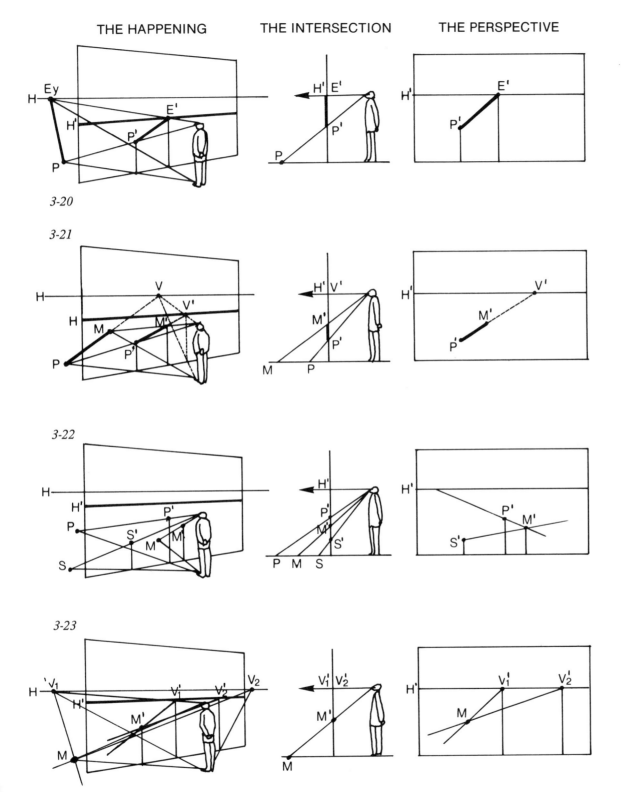

THE HAPPENING **THE INTERSECTION** **THE PERSPECTIVE**

3-20

3-21

3-22

3-23

So let us take two vanishing points V_1 and V_2 (Fig. 3-23) on the real horizon and find their projections on the projection plane's horizon in V'_1 and V'_2. Take at random two lines on the ground vanishing in V_1 and V_2 and intersecting in M. We can also find M', the projection of M. It is enough to trace V'_1M' and V'_2M' to obtain the correct perspective projection of the two intersecting lines. Now let us assume that two nonparallel lines intersect in a point M situated exactly under the feet of the observer (Fig. 3-24). The illustration shows that the two vertical planes represented by triangles EV_1M and EV_2M will give us simultaneously the projected vanishing points V'_1 and V'_2 and the ground points G_1 and G_2, which are the four points necessary to draw the two nonparallel lines. As both lines are vertical, V'_1G and V'_2G are parallel. This explains the baffling situation when two nonparallel lines intersect somewhere but appear parallel in perspective projection (see Fig. 3-13d again).

We can state now that two lines intersecting under the feet of the observer always appear parallel in projection.

The fifth case occurs when two nonparallel lines go in opposite directions from their vanishing points and intersect *behind* the observer. We would like you to practice in a similar drawing the construction of two such lines, taking point M_B as shown in Fig. 3-24.

Lines on the Earth

For a while we will forget about complicated constructions and familiarize ourselves with the perspective play of points, lines, curves, and surfaces on the horizontal plane of the earth as seen projected on the projection plane by the eye of the observer (who, from now on, is yourself). We will neglect precision in the construction of distances or measures, because our aim in these chapters is ease in handling the free perspective constructions, not the measurement

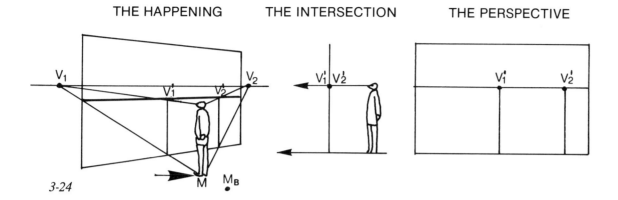

THE HAPPENING   THE INTERSECTION   THE PERSPECTIVE

3-24

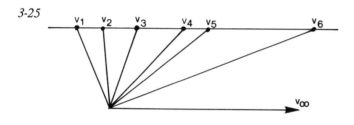

3-25

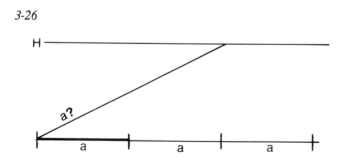

3-26

of precise relations among them (which will be studied later, in Chapter 7). It is much more important to exercise your eye and determine perspective relations for basic shapes than to start with a complex and rigid system of measuring, as we will often show in the following chapters.

We now return to the study of a point where two intersecting lines on the earth vanish at two different points on the H line. Before going further, let us return to the lines passing through one point on the ground and discover another helpful situation (Fig. 3-25). We have seen that any line passing through a point P must have a vanishing point V somewhere on the H line. With every rotation of the line, no matter how small, the vanishing point changes position. The smaller the angle between the line and the H line, the more remote V is. As our projection plane is limited in practice (either by our visual field in space or by the paper on which we are drawing), the location of the vanishing point becomes more difficult, until the line rotates so that it becomes parallel to the H line. By definition, this line is then perpendicular to the visual line (EyE), so it can be thought of as constantly preserving the same distance from our eye. If the distance doesn't change, any dimensions of this line or any dimensions on it remain the same, undistorted. This is an advantage, because many perspective problems need at least a reduced number of initial measurements, which can be taken on frontal units of length. In Fig. 3-26 we can double the length a on a frontal line, but without measuring perspective we cannot precisely represent the same dimension a in an angular position. And here is another word of advice:

It is of paramount importance that you exercise your eye in appreciating and defining any length a in depth distortion without the help of measuring perspective.

Throughout Chapter 2 we asked you to build a ground square in perspective especially in order to exercise your eye in such appreciation. But this appreciation must be checked against the points you subsequently construct in perspective because, as you will see, the whole composition will depend on your initial choice.

The infinity of lines that can be drawn on the ground can be straight or curved. We have seen that all parallels vanish at the same vanishing point; we have also seen that lines having two different vanishing points are not parallel. Any two nonparallel lines must intersect somewhere, even if the intersection point does not appear on the projection plane. But let us devote the following paragraphs to visible intersections.

The strange perspective drawing in Fig. 3-27 shows a line AE that vanishes in the eye-point and a frontal line AB intersecting it in A. It follows from our previous discussion that AE is perpendicular to the projection plane and its extension goes under the feet of the observer. Since AB is parallel to the H line, it is clear that the angle of intersection is 90°. Now look at Fig. 3-28, where E is the same and $A'B'$ is still horizontal. But this time EA' is slanted. What could be the real angle between EA' and $A'B'$? Or EA'' and $A''B''$? Remember that all lines having the same vanishing point are parallel so EA, EA', and EA'' are parallel, and all of them intersect with horizontals at an angle of 90°.

Now suppose that from two vanishing points V_1 and V_2 a great number of parallels intersect in an angle of 90° (Fig. 3-29). This angle remains the same wherever a pair of lines intersect, whether in point A, A', A'', B, C, or any other imaginable intersection point. Of course, the angles almost never appear as real, and their distortion can be precisely determined with the measurable perspective; but even after this determination, the perspective *might* look false, clumsy, and mechanical. The real decision must be made by your eye, and the first concern in starting a perspective drawing, after establishing the horizon line level, is to determine the pair of vanishing points for perpendicular bundles of parallels of the major elements in your composition (Fig. 3-30). If your composition has to be built around an important 90° corner, then by lightly sketching a few directions from it, you

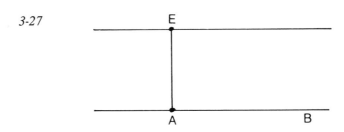

3-27

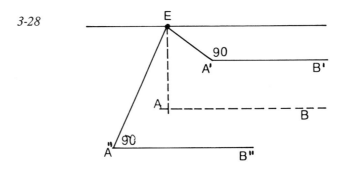

3-28

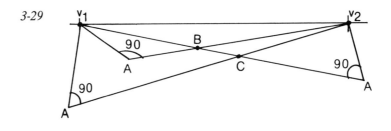

3-29

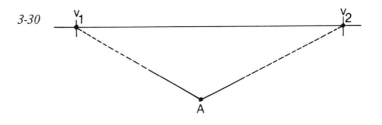

3-30

3-31

3-32

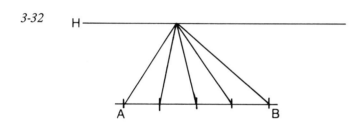

3-33

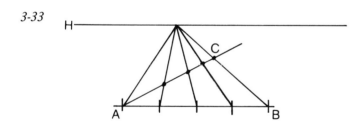

3-34

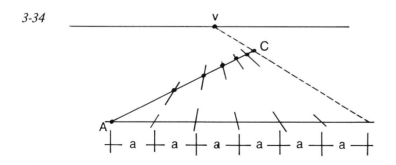

will obtain the desired vanishing points for all other lines parallel to these two perpendicular directions. This method probably seems very unorthodox, but in most cases the results will be much more in agreement with your mental vision of the composition than those obtained with any of the mechanical procedures that will be studied in Chapter 7.

Once you have decided about the vanishing points, the construction starts taking shape point by point with the help of a few geometric principles. The first problem is to divide a segment in perspective into a definite number of equal or unequal smaller segments. If the segment is frontal, there is no real problem. In frontal projection there is no distortion, and we can directly divide the segment AB (Fig. 3-31) into as many equal or unequal segments as we wish.

Notice that if we take this segment and join its ends to *any* vanishing point on the H line (Fig. 3-32), the resulting stripes going toward the horizon will be rectangular (and equal in this illustration). If we draw a slanting line AC from A (Fig. 3-33), this line will be also divided into several equal segments, since it is intersecting a number of equally distanced parallels. Thus, we have come to the reverse problem of dividing a slanting line AC (Fig. 3-34) into, say, six equal segments. To do this we take horizontal AB of any length, divide it into six, and find the vanishing point of BC. By joining V to each point of division on AB, we obtain the divisions of AC in perspective distortion.

Surfaces on the Earth

We will take a great step and try to realize how a perspective square should be drawn. Before knowing how to build a square with precise methods, approximate the length of its edges in perspective distortion, remembering that if a square is situated halfway between the two

41

vanishing points V_1 and V_2, as in Fig. 3-35 (i.e., with A on the central line perpendicular to the H line), segments AB and $A B'$, which are equal in reality, will continue to be equal in projection, and as A moves toward one of the vanishing points (Fig. 3-36), its edges will become proportionally shorter (AB' to V_1) or longer (AB to V_2). The square is completed by tracing the two parallels V_1B and V_2B', which intersect in the fourth point of the square, C (Fig. 3-37). If the square has two frontal edges (Fig. 3-38), then V_1 is identified with the eye-point (Ey) and V_2 moves away toward infinity. If AB is defined, AB' depends on your appreciation.

Let us see what we mean by "your appreciation."

As you can see in Fig. 3-39, all angles formed by pairs of intersecting lines that vanish in V_1 and V_2 are equal and the number of possibilities is infinite. When you have decided where V_1 and V_2 are located, trace a number of intersecting pairs of lines; this "net" will give you a choice of various rectangular surfaces. Your trained eye will be able to appreciate which of them most nearly represents a square, like $ABCD$ in our illustration. This approximation, of course, is not validated by any precise measurement, but since a perspective square can suffer such an enormous number of distortions (depending on your eye distance and height), your choice will be acceptable. However, only the first square demands the approximation of dimensions; all remaining construction details will be determined with the methods we know.

Returning to our three-step diagrams, we will understand the approximation of choice even better. In Figs. 3-40 and 3-41 we see the observer looking at a square, the first with two edges parallel to the H line, the second with two vanishing points within his visual field. The only thing that varies is the height of the eye, which determines the height of the horizon line on the projection plane and consequently the distortion of the square's image. Between the two situations shown in these diagrams there

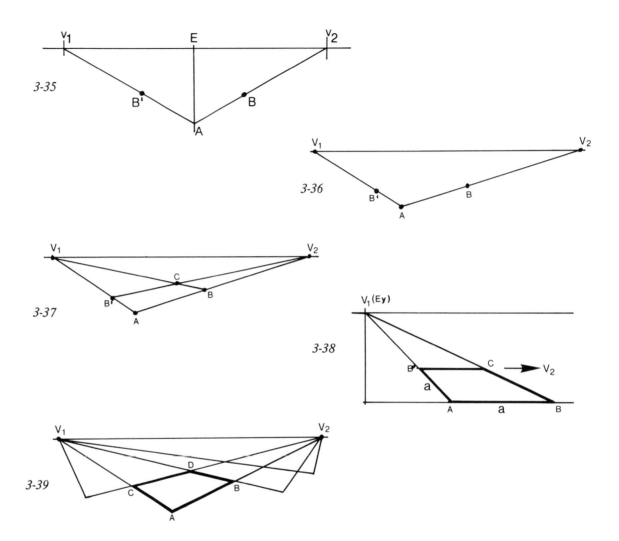

3-35

3-36

3-37

3-38

3-39

are a great number of different distortions corresponding to small changes in the observer's height. You will learn in Chapter 7 how the distance between the observer and the projection plane determines the distance between the two vanishing points, and we hope that even before learning this, continual practice will develop an empirical appreciation of the initial parameters

of your perspective renderings. We studied in Chapters 1 and 2 how to build the diagonals of a square, how to build additional squares beside the first one, how to determine the proportions of a rectangle starting from a square, how to play with diagonals in any type of rectangle, and how to construct triangles, hexagons, and other regular polygons.

THE HAPPENING   THE INTERSECTION   THE PERSPECTIVE

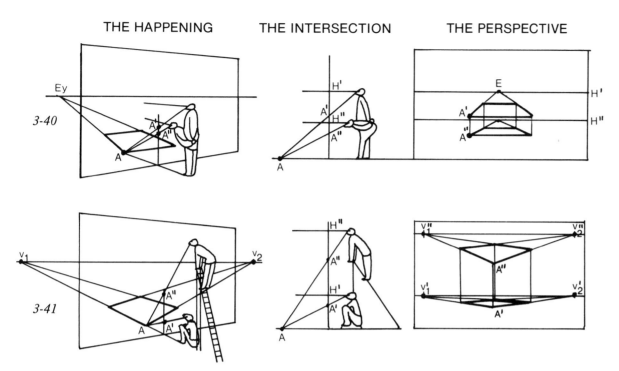

3-40

3-41

We can consider the asymptotes the diagonals of a rectangle, and since we know how to draw this rectangle in perspective, we can immediately find the two axes. The distance *AA'* projected in *aa'* gives us the division ratio, measurable with the known method (Fig. 3-44).

For irregular curves, where finding specific points is practically impossible, the solution is the square grid as shown in Exercise 56 of Chapter 2.

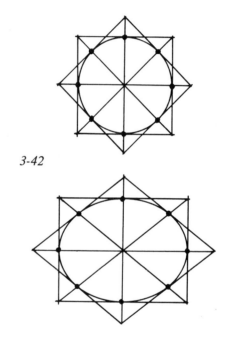

3-42

Only after knowing the construction of figures whose edges are straight lines (which, as we have seen, can all be related to a basic square) can we understand the construction of curves in perspective. Any regular curve, such as a circle or an ellipse, can be circumscribed about or inscribed in some square or rectangle. Figure 3-42 shows the necessary eight points of tangency and intersection of a circle and an ellipse, on which these curves can be drawn in perspective by first constructing the respective squares and rectangles. For irregular curves, parabolics, and hyperbolics, the easiest system is to find an appropriate number of straight lines and points that can envelop and determine the proposed curve. For instance, a hyperbola is determined by its two perpendicular axes, its two asymptotes and the distances *AO* and *OA'* (Fig. 3-43).

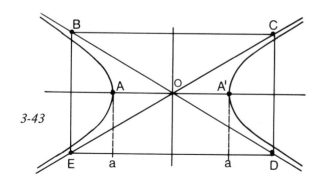

3-43

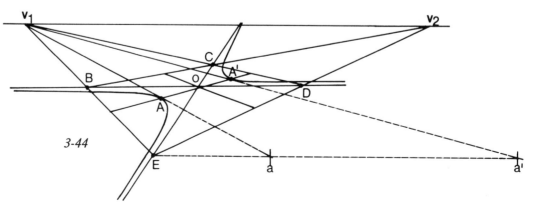

3-44

4. VERTICALITY

A vertical line can be defined as a line perpendicular to the earth's surface, as the trajectory of a material point from any position in space falling to the earth's surface under the influence of gravity, or as the shortest distance between any point in space and the center of the earth. The last definition is interesting because it shows that two vertical lines are *not* parallel as long as their intersection is not at infinity. However, as perspective must make some compromises and, indeed, the distance between two verticals falling within an earthly observer's visual field is so small compared to the radius of the earth, the angle between two verticals can safely be considered zero. Thus all verticals in perspective drawing are considered parallel. Moreover, we have already accepted that in perspective the earth's surface is flat, so necessarily, all lines perpendicular to this plane must be considered parallel.

Once we have accepted the principle of parallelism of verticals the task of constructing verticals in perspective becomes considerably easier than constructing lines on the earth's surface. Let us return to the three-step diagrams and analyze verticality.

The distance between the observer and the vertical, the height of the observer's eye, and the position (*p*) of the vertical in relation to the line *EyE* (Fig. 4-1) are sufficient to determine a vertical. In Chapter 7 we will develop the analysis of these relations.

In order to obtain the perspective rendering of what he sees, the observer introduces the vertical projection plane (Fig. 4-2). Now, the most practical choice for the distance from this

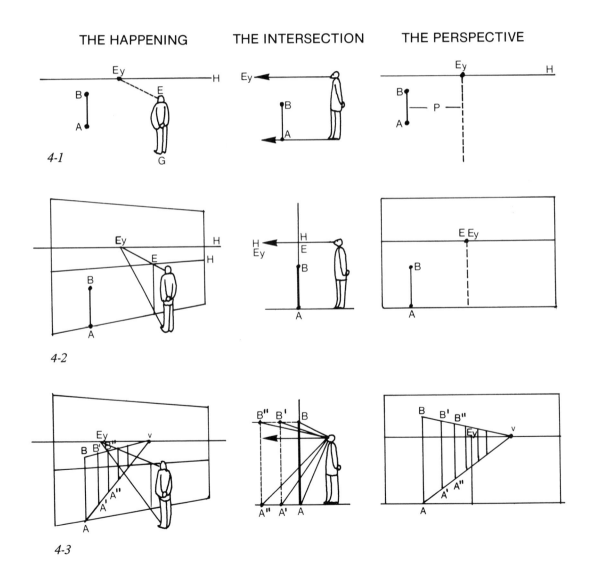

THE HAPPENING   THE INTERSECTION   THE PERSPECTIVE

4-1

4-2

4-3

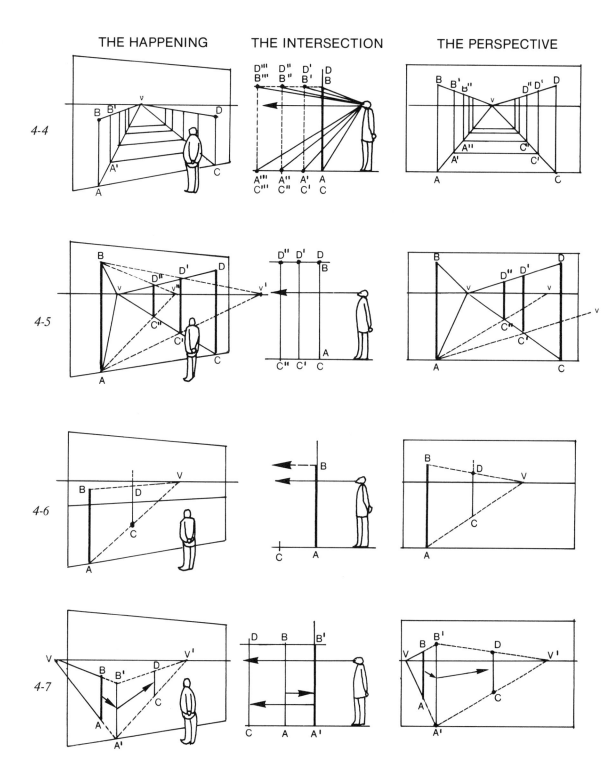

THE HAPPENING   THE INTERSECTION   THE PERSPECTIVE

4-4

4-5

4-6

4-7

plane to the observer (which may be chosen arbitrarily) is such that the vertical AB is in this plane. In this case (which is, however, not always possible) the true dimension of AB remains unchanged. This is therefore a method of simplifying the measuring procedure.

If we join A to *any* point V on the H line and then join B to the same V, all verticals traced between AV and BV at any point A' (Fig. 4-3) will have the same height as AB. We demonstrated this so many times in Chapters 1 and 2 that you should now be able to accept this statement readily.

Suppose we take two *equal* verticals AB and CD on the projection plane and trace their vanishing path toward a common vanishing point V (Fig. 4-4); then any line $A'C'$ on the ground parallel to the projection plane will give us verticals of equal height, equal distance, and equal distortion. Of course, even if $A'C'$ is not parallel to the projection plane (Fig. 4-5), the height of the two verticals at A' and C' is the same, but their apparent height is different. This enables us to raise a vertical of determined height when we know the height of a vertical AB situated in the projection plane and have the location C (Fig. 4-6) at which the vertical is to be raised. We extend AC to the H line and obtain V, then join V to B, and vertical CD will have the height of AB in perspective distortion. We can also think the other way around; suppose you have the vertical CD (see Fig. 4-6 again) and want to find its true value on the projection plane. Then join V to C, extend it to the base of the projection plane, obtaining A, raise a vertical at A, and join it to the extension of VD at B. So we can generalize as follows: If we have a vertical AB situated randomly on the ground (Fig. 4-7) and a point C situated so that AC goes much beyond the limits of our projection plane toward its vanishing point, then the equal vertical height at C can be raised through the intermediary of another point A' so situated on the projection plane that it can form a line $A'C$ that vanishes in an attainable vanishing point V''. Now we can generalize even further: The height of an arbitrarily situated vertical line can be obtained anywhere else on another vertical, even without the help of the projection plane, as shown in Figs. 4-8 and 4-9.

Suppose that, given vertical AB and point C, we are asked to raise a vertical CC' in C of the same height as AB. It can be seen that the vanishing point of line AC is too remote to use. But the choice of an arbitrary V will help us obtain $A'B'$ in *any convenient place* so that $A'C$ vanishes at an accessible point V'.

In Fig. 4-10 the same problem is solved with different choices of the location of A' (or A'', A''', etc.). All are good and give the same result. There is also another advantage in studying Fig. 4-10. This illustration, if kept in mind, will help you draw two or more vertical walls intersecting one another in a unique vertical line. Each wall, according to its angle of rotation, has a different vanishing point, but their common intersection, the place that determines their equal height, is the same for all.

Once we know how to construct verticals of the same height, the problem of verticals of unequal height becomes very simple. We will say that, given a vertical AB and a point C (Fig. 4-11), we must build at C a vertical n times higher than AB. So we extend AB multiplied by n and obtain AD. With this operation we have returned to the former problem of finding equal verticals. We already know how to find CD' equal to AD.

The next problem is to divide the distance between two verticals into two, three, or any number of parts, equal or unequal. We saw in the previous chapters two methods for the division of AC (Fig. 4-12); these are (1) the additional frontal line equally divided and (2) the checkerboard method.

The same illustration (Fig. 4-12) shows the simplest way of dividing the space into two. While looking at this illustration, imagine a double door, three electrical poles on a road, or three trees. You should, from now on, adopt this kind of exercise: For any abstract illustration find mentally a practical application and, when working with the pencil, start from *your*

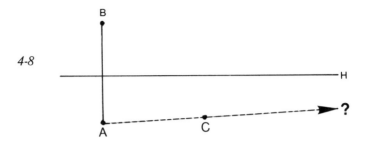

4-8

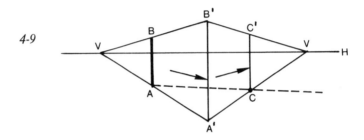

4-9

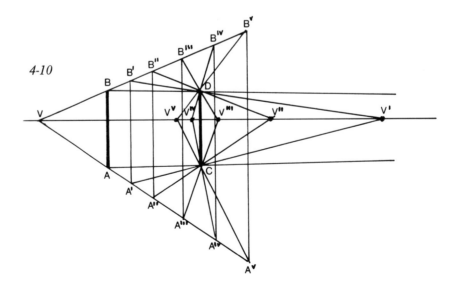

4-10

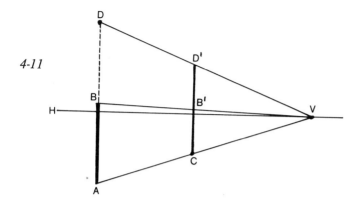

4-11

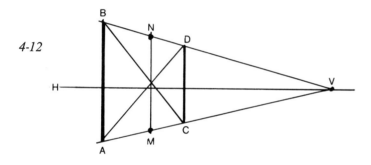

4-12

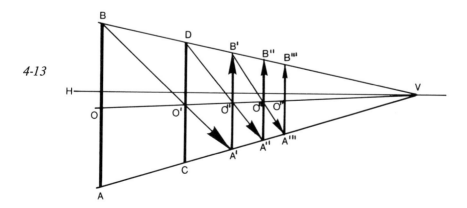

4-13

practical problem and abstract as much as possible. For instance, if you have the problem of rendering the perspective of a row of equally distanced but identical buildings of complex structure, the limit of abstraction is the vertical lines that will give you the perspective "rhythm" of these buildings.

In Fig. 4-12 we divided AC in two. But if AV is the path of an indefinite number of verticals continuing the "rhythm" of AC, then we can use the reverse method (Fig. 4-13). We can consider DC the middle vertical (MN in Fig. 4-12). Its middle O' will be the point of intersection of the former two diagonals. We need only the diagonal BO', which when extended to A' gives us the vertical $A'B'$. In order to repeat the operation indefinitely, we first trace the median line OV so that we will have this repetitive sequence of operations:

Given:	H line
	AB
	CD
Result:	AV
	BV
Trace:	O, thus obtaining $OA = OB$
	OV, cutting all verticals in half and giving O', O'', and so on
Then:	$BO'A'$ and $A'B'$ (obtain also O'')
	$DO''A''$ for $A''B''$ (obtain also O''')
	$B'O'''A'''$ for $A'''B'''$ and so on

Now look at the diagonals BA', DA'', and $B'A'''$ and recall the construction of a horizontal row of squares. There the diagonals had a unique vanishing point. However, the diagonals of identical vertical rectangles are parallel, so they must converge somewhere, and the illustration shows that they converge toward some point below the horizon level. As this point of convergence is generally poorly understood, we will devote a little time to clarifying another concept.

The Concept of the Vertical Horizon

Vertical *AB* (Fig. 4-14), as it is moved toward the horizon, covers a plane surface *ABV*, which is a very small portion of an infinite vertical plane. Line *AV* is the straight line belonging both to the vertical plane and to the ground plane, and it actually represents the intersection of these two perpendicular planes. You are accustomed to looking at an image so that the horizon appears as in Fig. 4-15. You have already studied, in Chapter 3, your eye's relationship to a considerable number of perspective events in this normal position. But what happens if you lie down as in Fig. 4-16? Well, no perspective rules will change, only

your horizon will become vertical. And let *us* see (in Fig. 4-17) how *you* see this horizon (we have simply rotated Fig. 4-16 by 90°). We mentioned in Chapter 1 (Exercise 24) that the horizon line is the only vanishing line actually experienced in nature. This is because the so-called earth plane is the largest material plane *we can see* vanishing. But besides seeing we are also capable, after so much training, of imagining. And to imagine the vanishing line of another infinite plane *that doesn't exist in nature* now becomes easier. So if we return to Fig. 4-14 and reason a little, we come to the following conclusions (Fig. 4-18):

- *ABV* is a small part of an infinite vertical plane.

- *AV* is the intersection between this vertical plane and the earth, and *V* is the vanishing point of *AV*.
- *AV* belongs to both planes; therefore *V* also represents the vanishing point of lines *AV*, *BV*, *A'V*, and an infinite number of parallel lines situated in the vertical plane.
- As *V* is situated on the *H* line and is the vanishing point of an infinite number of parallels determining one vertical plane, it follows that *V* determines a vertical line that is the vanishing line of this virtual, infinite, and vertical plane.
- *For each vertical plane determined by its intersection AV with the earth's plane, there is a vertical horizon line at the vanishing point V.*

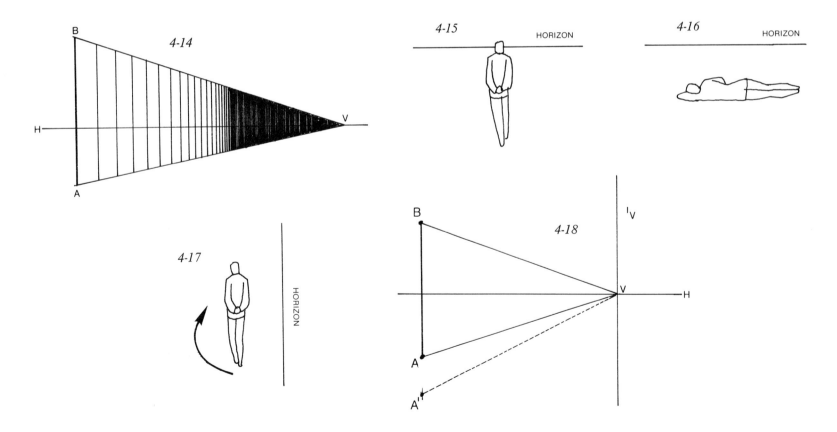

48

From the beginning of this section, V has been chosen arbitrarily. This means that we can have an infinite number of translation directions for a vertical AB, and hence an infinite number of vertical planes and an infinity of vertical horizons (Fig. 4-19). All these vertical horizons represent the limit of a plane rotating around an axis AB and are determined by the angle of rotation.

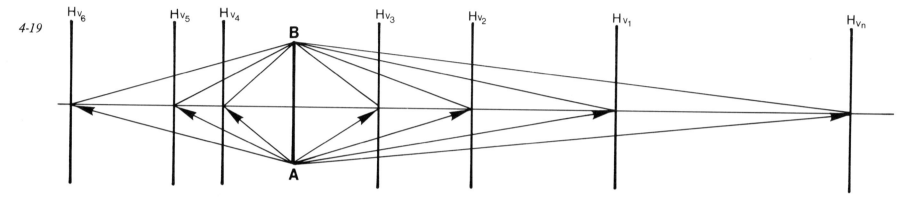

4-19

We return to the idea of diagonals. As we saw in Fig. 4-13, diagonals of equal rectangles (or squares) are parallel and converge toward a point situated below the horizon line. Now, since they belong to a vertical plane, all these diagonals must vanish on the vertical horizon line, and this will happen somewhere on HV (Fig. 4-20). Now we no longer need to construct the middle point on CD. It is enough to join D to V_H in order to obtain A', and so on.

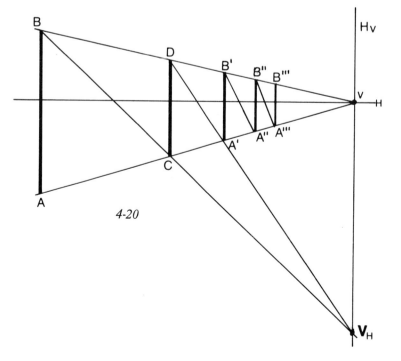

4-20

49

On any infinite vertical plane there are an infinite number of lines, which may be slanted rather than vertical, and as we know the vanishing line of this vertical plane, we also know that all these lines *must* vanish on it at some vanishing point (Fig. 4-21). The diagonal BC vanishes in V_H, together with *all* its parallels. The random line AR vanishes in V_{AR} as well as MP in V_{MP}. We realize that *all rules and methods we studied in Chapter 3 for lines and areas belonging to the earth's horizontal plane apply identically to the vertical plane.*

It is essential to understand the identity of the methods of constructing vertical planes and those of constructing horizontal planes, because of a considerable number of problems can thus be reduced to a minimum of operations. Suppose we have a vertical rectangle $ABCD$ situated so that the horizon line cuts it exactly at the middle (Fig. 4-22). Diagonal BC will vanish on the vertical horizon line H_V, at V'. Diagonal AD will vanish in V''. As the square is placed symmetrically with respect to the H line, $V'V$ and VV'' are equal. It is not only this particular position of the square (or rectangle) that will give diagonals vanishing in V' and V''; *all* equal squares, equal rectangles, similar squares, and similar rectangles situated in the same plane will have their diagonals vanishing at the same points (Fig. 4-23). Moreover, a similar square or rectangle situated in another vertical plane that vanishes at the same vertical horizon (i.e., is parallel to the first) will have parallel groups of diagonals that will vanish at the same vanishing point (Fig. 4-24). This helps us determine vertical walls equal to a given one with the help of diagonals.

It is interesting and important to keep in mind that *for equal and opposite angles (as in the case of diagonals of a square or a rectangle), the vanishing points are at equal distances from the H line.* So if we are given a triangle ABC in a vertical plane (Fig. 4-25) and wish to construct a symmetrical triangle BCD adjacent to it (as happens so many times with roofs and pediments), AC gives us the point of intersection

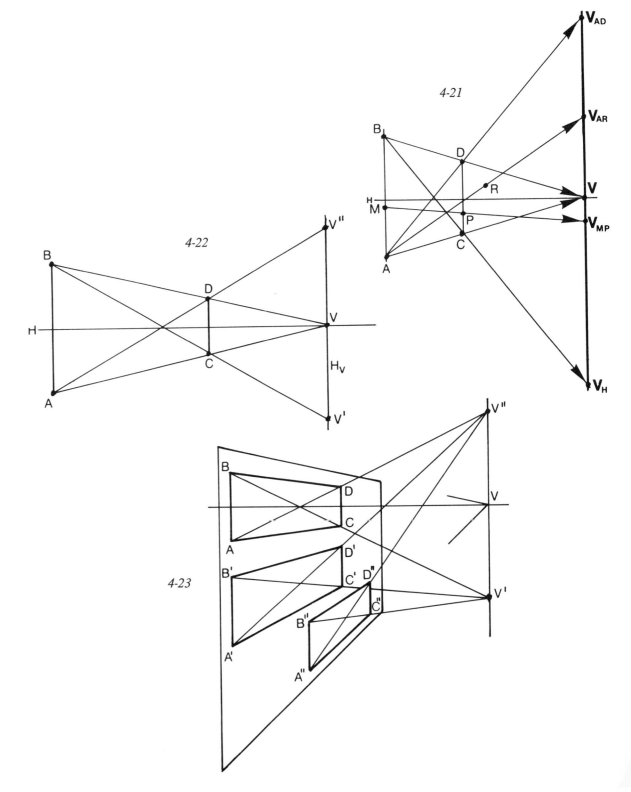

4-21

4-22

4-23

between the *H* line and the vertical horizon in *V*. Line *AB* gives us *V″*, and the distance *VV″* measured downward to *V′* from *V* gives us *BV′*, the other slanting side of the symmetrical triangle. The intersection *D* between *AV* and *BV′* completes the construction.

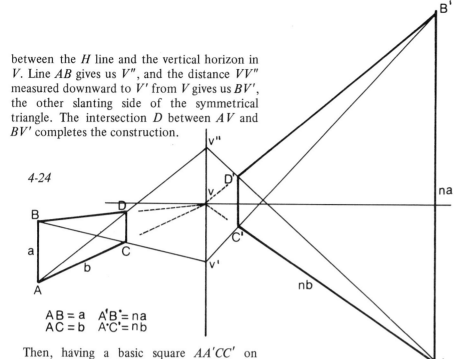

4-24

AB = a   A′B⁣·= na
AC = b   A·C·= nb

Then, having a basic square *AA′CC′* on which we want to raise a slanting lid (Fig. 4-26), if we already know one side of the lid *AB* that vanishes in *V′*, the other side *A′B′* will be obtained as the intersection of the straight line joining *A′* and *V′* with either the horizontal *BV″* or the vertical at *C′*. Now look carefully at the illustration and study the square *AA′BB′*. Suppose you trace the diagonal *AB′*. Can you say where its vanishing point is? Of course, this is as interesting a question as it is difficult at first glance. Let us solve it together in Fig. 4-27. Square *AA′BB′* is in a slanting position we have never encountered before. But being perspectively correct, this illustration shows that edges *AA′* and *BB′* vanish in *V″* and *AB* and *A′B′* vanish in *V′*. Well, as soon as we have *two* vanishing points of a rectangle or square, we know without doubt that these points *must* be situated on the horizon line of the square's or rectangle's unlimited plane. Therefore line *V′V″* (which is not shown in the illustration) is this slanting horizon line, and the extension of diagonal *AB′* will vanish at its intersection with *V′V″*. But we will talk more about these planes in Chapter 5.

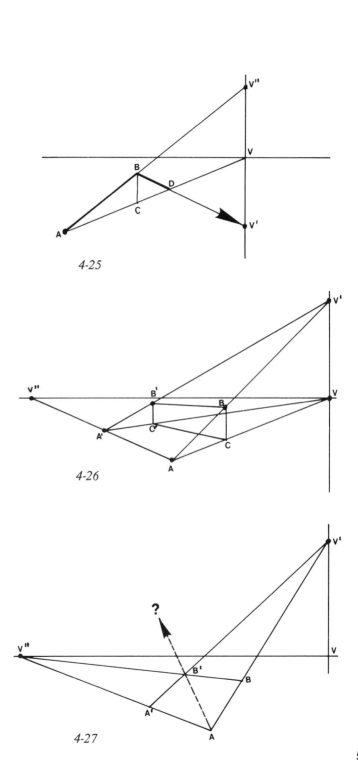

4-25

4-26

4-27

Let us return to Fig. 4-26. Square $AA'BB'$ (which, as we said, is a slanting lid) is represented abstractly here. Ordinarily it must have some thickness. So if we suppose that the thickness is uniform and measures AT (Fig. 4-28), then TS (parallel to AB) will vanish at V', as will any parallel to AB, not only in the plane ABC but in all parallel planes. We have come to understand that for each infinite group of parallels there is a vanishing point at infinity. As the number of parallel groups is infinite, the number of vanishing points in space is infinite as well. Although infinity cannot be defined, we can say that the totality of vanishing points in space form a sphere of infinite radius with the center at our eye. This is one of the ways of demonstrating that from the subjective point of view, each of us is the center of the universe!

Vertical Surfaces

We defined a vertical line at the beginning of this chapter as the trajectory of a point falling to the earth from any position in space under the influence of gravity only. A vertical surface can be defined similarly, as the trajectory of a horizontal line falling to the earth's surface under the influence of gravity, or as the trajectory of a vertical line traveling along a straight horizontal path toward some vanishing point. Both definitions are correct and profitable, depending on what type of construction we are dealing with.

To explain the uses of these definitions, let us look first at Fig. 4-29. A vertical wall, as we saw in Chapter 2, can determine other vertical walls of the same height through operations with vanishing points. Therefore, in this case, the image of the wall as the trace of a vertical line moving toward the vanishing point is more appropriate. In contrast, as shown in Fig. 4-30, a vertical wall can cut (intersect) another vertical (V) or horizontal (H) surface. This image applies mainly to the stage of construction of a perspective, where intersections between different planes occur frequently.

Naturally, the idea of intersection (cutting) is associated with the image of a knife moving downward. The differences between these two approaches to the definition of a vertical plane are only subtleties, because the final constructed plane will be the same in either case, but the imagination finds it easier to use one movement or the other according to the immediate needs of the construction.

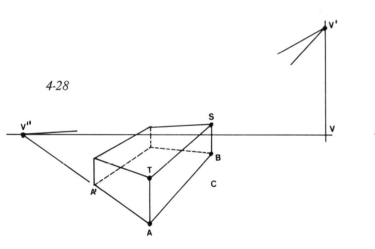

4-28

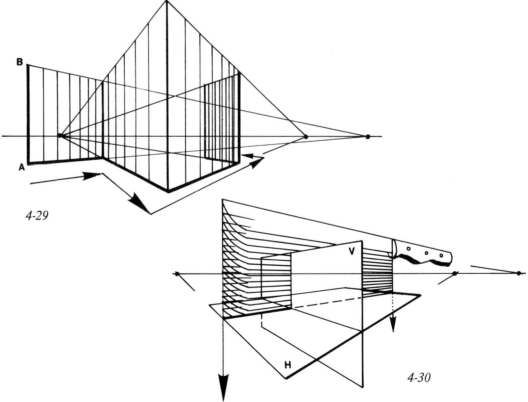

4-29

4-30

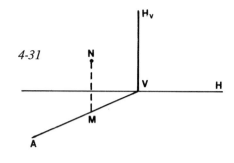

4-31

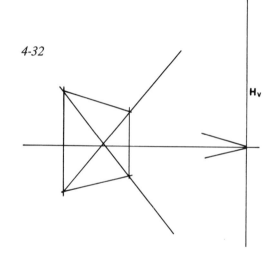

4-32

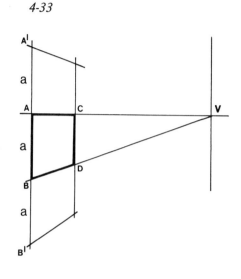

4-33

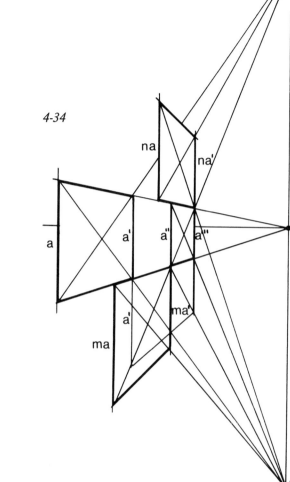

4-34

A vertical plane is completely defined by its intersection with the earth AV and its vertical horizon H_V (Fig. 4-31). If we insist on this definition, it is because we want you to preserve, memorize, get used to, and work easily with the concept of an infinite vertical plane and its vertical horizon. You must come to use a vertical plane as easily as you use the horizontal plane of the earth.

We can now study a few particular surfaces in the vertical plane, comparing their construction with similar constructions on the hori-

zontal plane of the earth.

Figure 4-32 shows a vertical square. Again it must be emphasized that before we know anything about measurable perspective, the square can only be an approximation. Knowing H_V, we can find the vertical vanishing points of the diagonals, and this enables us to perform all the additional constructions we studied for squares on the ground in previous chapters.

For instance, if we want a vertical row of squares above and below the initial square (Fig. 4-33), we repeat measure a on the frontal

vertical $A'B'$ and join points A' and B' to V. But when we build diagonally positioned (or "in-depth") squares (Fig. 4-34), the diagonals come into play, and for different-sized edges but the same vanishing diagonals, all surfaces obtained are squares.

In all these illustrations you can find exactly the same images you studied in the horizontal plane of the earth. It is like having it rotated 90°. So from here on, all problems involving surfaces on a vertical plane are solvable with the methods you know from the horizontal plane.

However, we must add a few words about a particular problem that often arises in drawing circles on a vertical plane, a problem that has much more to do with a shallow understanding of theory than with clumsy drawing (as is believed). As we have said, construction of a circle on a vertical plane requires exactly the same data as the same operation on the ground. If we have traced the square and obtained points *M* and *N* (Fig. 4-35), the circle can be traced. With time and experience, artists, illustrators, and renderers tend to make less and less use of the four intersection points determined by *M* and *N* and consider tangent points *A*, *B*, *C*, and *D* sufficient. This approach generally gives correct results—if the artist has,

besides experience, the necessary theoretical background. But the result can also be incorrect. In the case of drawing arcades, for instance (Fig. 4-36), the tendency of untrained renderers is to draw a perspective image like that in Fig. 4-37. As you can see, the arcades tend to fall out of the vertical plane; the error is due to an incomplete analytical understanding of the circle's perspective. Please reread Exercises 36 through 41 of Chapter 1 and Exercise 49 of Chapter 2. The illustrator's error consists in identifying the middle line *AB*, which determines the points of tangency of the upper and lower edges of the circumscribing square, with the highest point of the elliptically distorted circle. Naturally, the major axis of the ellipse is

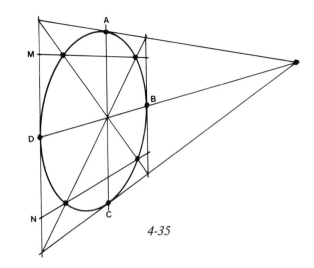

4-35

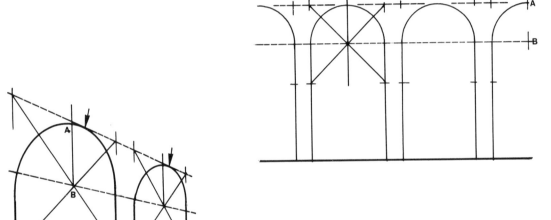

4-36

4-37

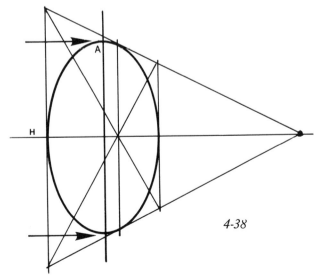

4-38

at the geometric middle of the ellipse. In the particular case when the circle is symmetrically positioned with reference to the *H* line (Fig. 4-38), the ellipse is vertical and its highest point *A* is slightly to the left of the perspective center of the circle. But when the circle is not placed symmetrically (Fig. 4-39), the resulting ellipse's major and minor axes slant and the circle's distortion is a slanted ellipse. To determine the slanting angle exactly in each particular perspective case requires a thorough knowledge of analytic geometry going much beyond the immediate needs of perspective construction.

We can summarize by saying that any perspective distortion of a circle is an ellipse, which requires careful sketching of the entire curve in relation to its circumscribing square or any other polygon. A more complex method for tracing a more accurate ellipse is the grid method shown in Fig. 4-40.

We divide the square vertically into a number of equal strips. The resulting verticals, as they intersect the circle, give us corresponding horizontal strips. The number of divisions is arbitrary and depends on the accuracy we require. As we know how to find these points in perspective, the problem is solved. The situation is even more obvious in the case of elliptical arcades (Figs. 4-41 and 4-42). Here the highest point *A* is clearly higher than the point of tangency *T*.

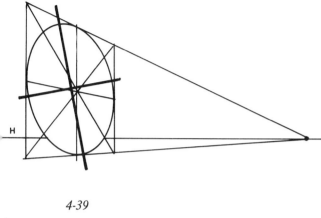

4-39

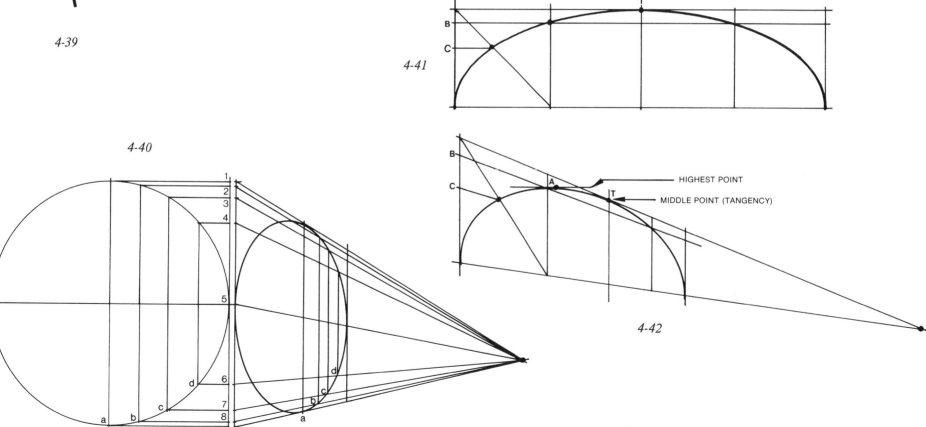

4-40

4-41

4-42

HIGHEST POINT

MIDDLE POINT (TANGENCY)

5. MOTION IN SPACE

The ability to draw in perspective depends to a great extent on mental training in visualizing motion. By motion we understand three types of change of position: (1) the change occurring when the object moves, or objective motion, (2) the change occurring when the observer moves, or subjective motion, and (3) the change occurring when both object and observer move.

We mentioned motion at many points in the earlier chapters. Now we will concentrate on the two first types of motion with regard to planes in space. And because imagining the motion of an indefinite plane in space requires a difficult mental operation, we will consider different plane surfaces in motion and consequently analyze the effects of motion on the indefinite plane to which the specific surface belongs.

Translation

Any two equal and parallel squares in space can be regarded as two different positions of a square in linear, objective motion. A square $ABCD$ on the ground (Figs. 5-1 and 5-2), moving vertically and preserving parallelism, will be found distorted in any instance $A'B'C'D'$ such that its vanishing points will not change. Each point $A', B', C', D', A'', B'', C''$, or D'' will be situated exactly above the corresponding point A, B, C, or D. The vanishing points do not change because if the square's sides always remain parallel to the original square's sides, they vanish at the same point.

We can say the same about a vertical square moving horizontally, either on two frontal rails (Fig. 5-3) or on two nonfrontal (vanishing) rails (Fig. 5-4). With fixed (stationary) vanishing points, any instance of the translating square can be obtained as in these illustrations.

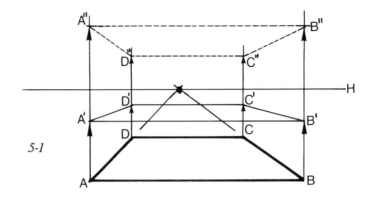

5-1

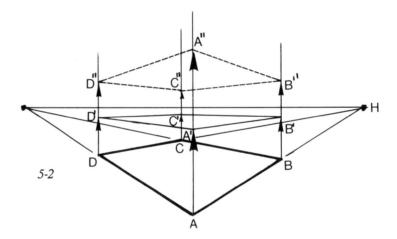

5-2

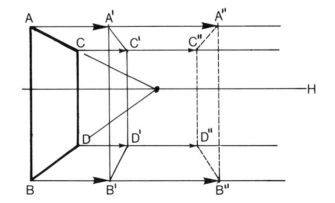

5-3

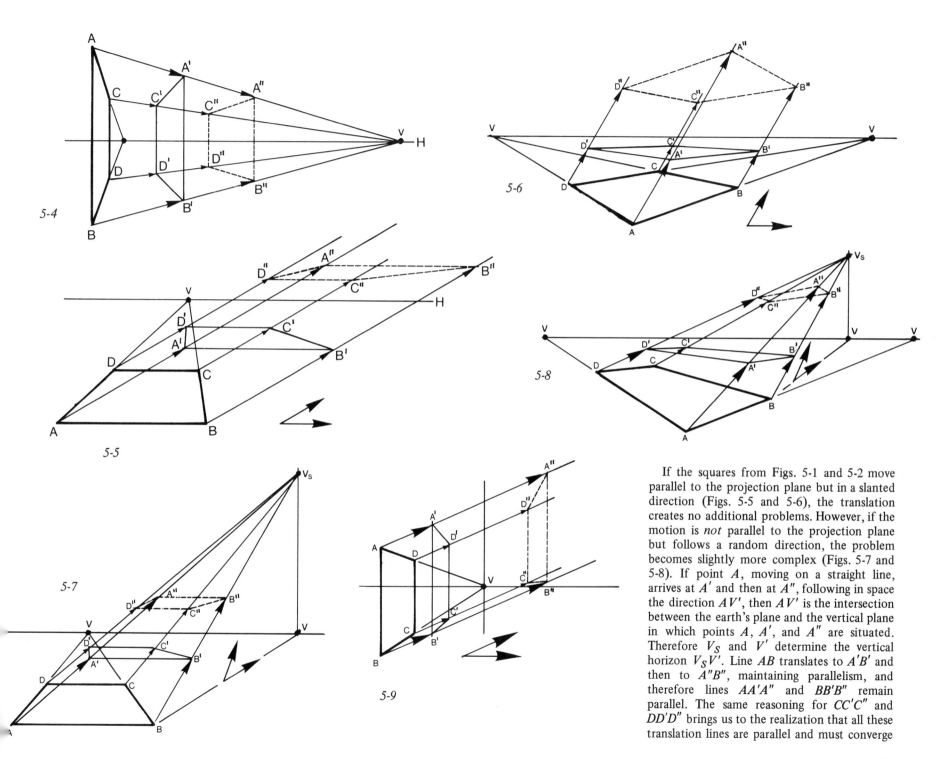

5-4

5-5

5-6

5-7

5-8

5-9

If the squares from Figs. 5-1 and 5-2 move parallel to the projection plane but in a slanted direction (Figs. 5-5 and 5-6), the translation creates no additional problems. However, if the motion is *not* parallel to the projection plane but follows a random direction, the problem becomes slightly more complex (Figs. 5-7 and 5-8). If point A, moving on a straight line, arrives at A' and then at A'', following in space the direction AV', then AV' is the intersection between the earth's plane and the vertical plane in which points A, A', and A'' are situated. Therefore V_S and V' determine the vertical horizon $V_S V'$. Line AB translates to $A'B'$ and then to $A''B''$, maintaining parallelism, and therefore lines $AA'A''$ and $BB'B''$ remain parallel. The same reasoning for $CC'C''$ and $DD'D''$ brings us to the realization that all these translation lines are parallel and must converge

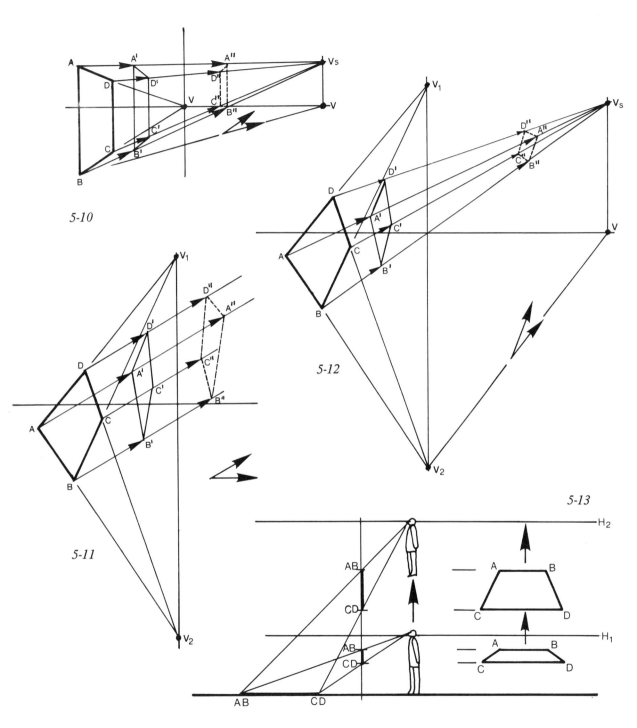

5-10

5-12

5-11

5-13

at the spacial vanishing point V_S. After the imaginary pyramid $ABCDV_S$ has been constructed, any instance of the square's translation will be easily obtained. Give careful attention to Figs. 5-5 through 5-8, because they indicate the basic structure of a perspective staircase and many other applications relating to slanting shapes.

Figs. 5-9, 5-10, 5-11, and 5-12 show similar translations for a vertical square. The explanations are basically the same as for Figs. 5-5 through 5-8. In summary we can say that for any translation in which the planes always remain parallel, the infinite planes will also remain parallel, so that their horizons (either horizontal or vertical) will remain the same.

Subjective translation is important for your ability to visualize. In mentally choosing the most appropriate viewpoint for your rendering, an understanding of the change of position of the eye-point, horizon line, and vanishing points as well as of the resulting different proportions and structures leads you to the proper choice of the observer's position. For instance, a vertical translation of your eye in relation to a horizontal square will lead to a transformation like the one shown in Fig. 5-13. As you can see, the two views of such a translation make no sense in one drawing. It is though a mere example of how the horizon line changes and the projection on the projection plane varies.

We can understand these changes better in separate, "cinematic" illustrations. For instance, a person crossing a road will receive the images shown in Fig. 5-14a, b, and c). While AB and the H line level remain constant, the Ey point moves from the right side of the road (Fig. 5-14a) to the middle of the road (Fig. 5-14b) to the left of the road (Fig. 5-14c). From this position the person takes an outdoor elevator and receives the images shown in Fig. 5-14d, e, and f. Here too, AB is constant and Ey doesn't move to the left or right, only upward. Figure 5-14d is the same as Fig. 5-14c, because the observer is practically at the same

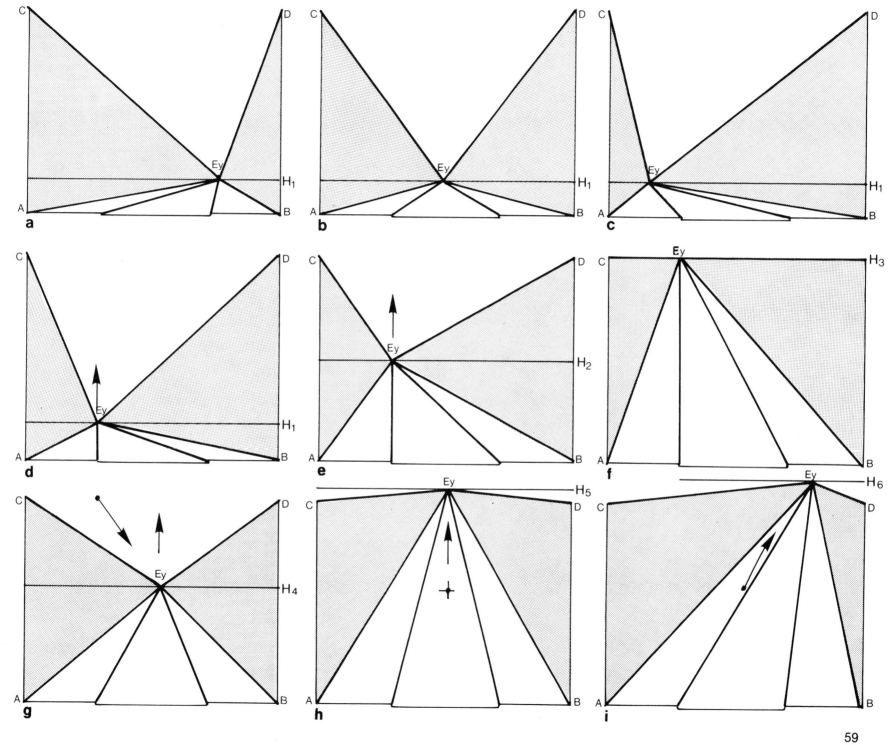

observation point as before. The elevator lifts him to the middle height (Fig. 5-14e), then to the top of the building (Fig. 5-14f), and the horizon line moves up with him. Once in the position shown in Fig. 5-14f, the observer can go down on a ladder toward the opposite side of the road (Fig. 5-14g) or fly above in any vertical (Fig. 5-14h) or slanting direction (Fig. 5-14i).

As long as a certain frame of reference (in this case the distance AB and the height of the buildings) is constant, the change of the observer's position in space determines a new horizon line level depending on his own eye level (the vertical component of the translation) and a new eye point (Ey', the horizontal component of the translation) and "drags" the whole construction toward it. So far, all this applies as well in situations where lines run toward *two* vanishing points. The eye motion will not distort the distance between the two points.

What happens in the case of "in-depth" translation? To answer this important question, let us recall the method of finding the vanishing points on the projection plane. Please return to Chapter 3 and study Figs. 3-16 through 3-24 again. The last one illustrates two nonparallel lines that intersect under the observer's feet, but it also illustrates the identical construction of two vanishing points on the projection plane. We are now ready to study this construction in a more accurate way, the way architects would use, by constructing also the plan of a structure (Fig. 5-15). The ground square $ABCD$ (or any shape in a plane or space) determines the direction of perpendiculars that go to two vanishing points (AD and BC to V_1 and AB and DC to V_2). As all parallels have the same vanishing point, a parallel to AD and BC starting from O (the observer's eye) will go to V_1 as well and will *intersect* projection plane PP-$P'P'$ in V_1', thus determining the projection of this vanishing point. The same reasoning holds for the other vanishing point. As you see, the plane drawing (Fig. 5-15b) looks much simpler than the one in Fig. 5-15a. One reason is that the

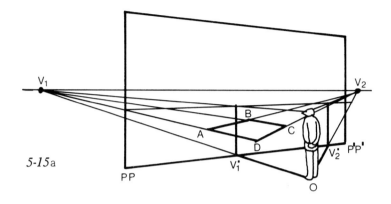

5-15a

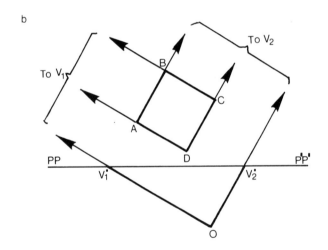

b

vanishing point construction is done with two construction lines (eye to V_1 and ground line to the same V_1), which, belonging to the same vertical plane, appear as only one line V_1O in Fig. 5-15b. Moreoever, in Fig. 5-15b there is no

H line and fewer construction lines. But Fig. 5-15b gives us the precision that doesn't exist in Fig. 5-15a, and when we come to measurable perspective, this will be the starting point for our work.

Now, Fig. 5-15 shows us a particular situation that can be altered "in-depth" in two ways:

1. Distance between observer and object is constant. Projection plane translates back and forth.
2. Distance between observer and object varies.

Without going into detailed construction, we will analyze how the perspective of a cube is affected by these situations, because a solid shows much clearer the occurring distortions (Fig. 5-16).

In case 1, the observer preserves the same distance and position in relation to the object. The recorded perspectives are the same, with exception of size. In case 2, the actual distance between observer and object is altered, so the distortions are different. It is too early to explain why, but these four cases are responsible for the "mood" of your perspective and your choice of position "in-depth" is perhaps the first and the most important decision you have to make in every particular perspective construction. While case 1 shows the irrelevance of the choice of the projection plane position in depth, case 2 shows the important relationship between subject-object distance variation, determining different vanishing points relation, hence a different "mood" expression.

If we make the theoretical assumption that an object is still observable from an infinite distance (for all objective and subjective cases), then either the object becomes so infinitely small in relation to the distance between the vanishing points, or the distance from the vanishing points to the object becomes so infinitely large (which is actually the same thing), that the vanishing lines of the object become practically parallel. Thus we have obtained the basic principle of orthogonal projection (*ortho:* "straight, right"; *gonos:* "angle"), used every day by draftsmen, architects, engineers, designers, and many other professionals. This assumption leads us to understand that orthogonal projection is a particular case of conical projection or perspective, namely, the case in which the eye of the observer is at an infinite distance from the object. All these translations can occur simultaneously creating an infinite number of instances or relationships between subject and object, new and various images that occur in every single moment of each person's life. This is the inexhaustible variety we have to choose from when beginning our construction. It is therefore of paramount importance to exercise our vision in understanding from the perspective viewpoint every single *observation* of our surroundings, when objects move, when we cross a street, travel in a car, rise in an elevator, take off in an airplane or merely move our head a few inches in any direction.

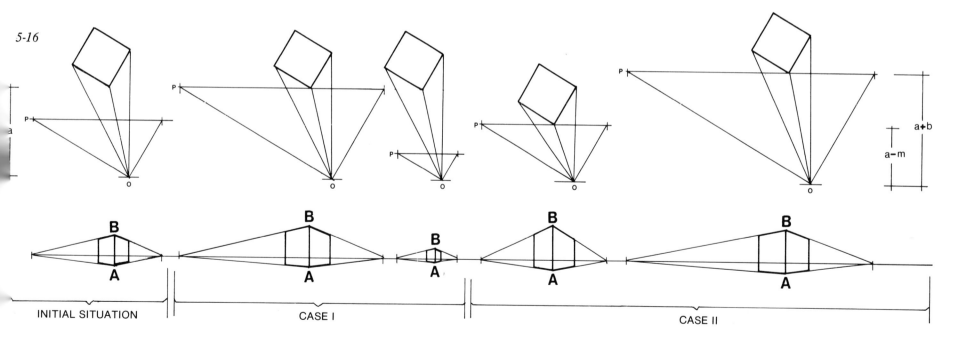

5-16

INITIAL SITUATION   CASE I   CASE II

61

Rotation

Rotation is any movement of a point preserving a constant distance to a fixed point, the center. Any rotation therefore describes an arc of a circle, and again, the movement can be objective or subjective.

Objective rotation assumes that the observer doesn't move, while the object describes some circular motion. In the case of a line, we can have two types of objective rotation (Fig. 5-17). The first type (Fig. 5-17a and b) preserves the distances *CA* and *CB;* the second type (Fig. 5-17c) preserves the *direction* of line *AB*, so that only one point *A* describes a circle with center *C*, while *B* describes another circle with center *C'* (*CC'* being equal to *AB*).

When objective rotation takes place in a vertical and frontal plane, the construction of the points can be easily done with a compass for every instance, just as in Fig. 5-17. In any other plane we must first determine the ellipses representing the distorted circular motions (Fig. 5-18). Figure 5-18a shows that for every new instance, *AB* will have a different vanishing point, while in Fig. 5-18b the vanishing point remains the same.

Subjective rotation assumes that the observer describes an arc of a circle around an object. This again makes no sense within one drawing but is an important exercise for your ability to visualize and choose the most appropriate angle for rendering an object or group of objects in perspective. The most frequent application of objective rotation in perspective, the rotation of a plane around one of its lines, helps us to understand slanted planes and slanting horizons.

Let us return to Exercises 59 and 60 of Chapter 2 (and their answers) and to Chapter 4 (the section on the concept of the vertical horizon) and review the incomplete statements and observations we made there. For this we will again take the case of the frontally rotating horizontal lid on the ground plane of the earth and study its rotation around a hinged edge *AC* (Fig. 5-19). In order to obtain *CD'*, knowing the given *AB'*, we use the additional point *M*. When

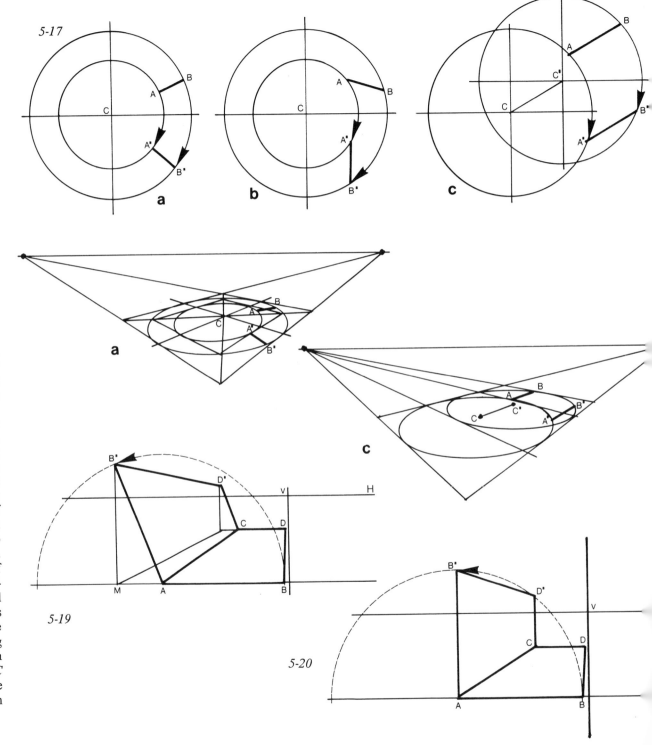

AB rotates only 90° (Fig. 5-20), we have an abstract vertical wall, which we have already studied. We have seen that such a vertical plane vanishes in a vertical virtual horizon, which is necessary for any other construction on this vertical plane. We have also seen that for every vertical plane there must be a vertical horizon line.

Now, returning to the rotation in Fig. 5-19, we realize that as the lid rotates around its edge to another angle, the whole infinite plane ex- tended from this lid rotates with it. As this plane must have a vanishing line, we can deter- mine it. We have one of its infinite lines, *AV* (Fig. 5-21), and one of its frontal lines, *AB'*. Since the horizon line of a plane is parallel to all its frontal lines, it follows that this slanting plane will vanish in a line passing through *V* and parallel to *AB'*, the line $H_S H'_S$. Thus we have determined the construction of a slanting plane and its slanting horizon. To make things simpler, let us take again a comparison. Sup- pose that the observer can *stand* on such a slanted plane, perpendicular to it (Fig. 5-22). For this observer, his floor, the slanted plane, becomes horizontal and all the laws and con- structions that apply to the horizontal plane of the earth remain valid. All lines not parallel to the slanted horizon will have vanishing points on this slanted horizon, and the first lines for which we can check this statement are the diagonals of equal rectangles (Fig. 5-23).

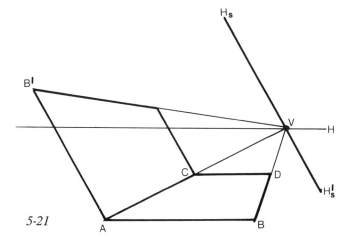

5-21

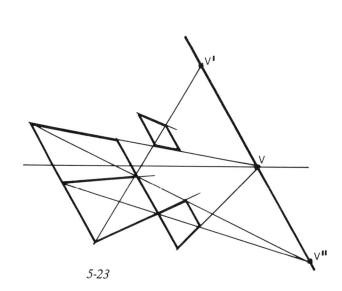

5-23

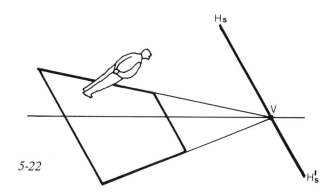

5-22

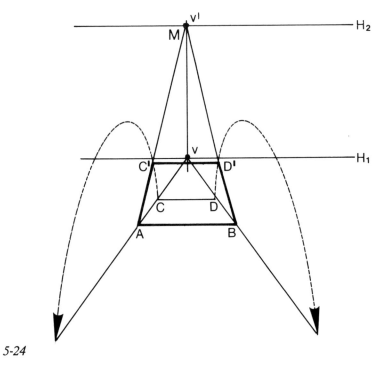

5-24

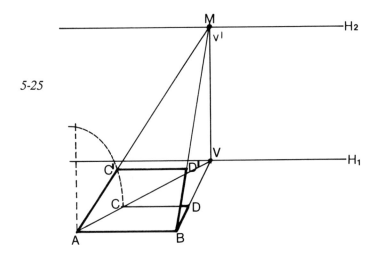

5-25

Frequently a square (or rectangular) lid must rotate around a frontally hinged edge (Figs. 5-24 and 5-25). If *AB* is the hinged edge and *CD* rotates in the direction shown by the arrow, parallels *AC* and *BD* will continue to meet at infinity on a vertical *VV'* at any point *M* that results from any instance of the rotation. As the infinite plane determined in every instance of rotation intersects the earth in the infinite extension of *AB* (which is frontal), its vanishing line or horizon line will remain parallel to the earth's horizon. The observer can say that we have a slanting plane but not a slanting horizon line. *However*, it is enough for the observer to rotate slightly (subjective rotation) for the image of a slanting plane and its horizon to change drastically. Let us analyze this statement.

Figures 5-24 and 5-25 are the perspective observation of an observer moving from the first position to the second. This subjective translation, which is parallel to *AB*, preserves the parallelism of the horizons and the lid's edges. It only changes the vertical horizon for every instance of the translation.

But suppose the observer starts *rotating* around point *B*, as shown in Fig. 5-26.* The following details must be recorded (Fig. 5-27):

1. The observer moves from *G* to *G'*.
2. The earth's horizon line remains the same.
3. Surface *ABCD* is no longer frontal but at an angle.
4. *V'* remains at the same height, *VV'*.
5. *AB* is no longer parallel to the earth's horizon but vanishes at *V''*.

---

*You might wonder why a simple translation "in depth" of the observer will not produce the same effect. It will not because *subjective* translation means a change in place, not a change in the angular orientation of the observer's eyes. If he moves "in depth" according to the broken arrow in Fig 5-26, the image of the rotating lid only becomes closer without changing the complexity of the structure. By rotation, the observer's eye moves from *V* to another *Ey* situated (in our case) at the left of *V*.

6. *C'D'*, being parallel to *AB* and *CD*, also vanishes at *V"*.

7. *BD'* belongs to plane *BVV' but also to plane ABC'D'*.

8. *AB* belongs to the earth's plane *but also to plane ABC'D'*.

9. *V'* and *V"* therefore are vanishing points of plane *ABC'D'*, and they are the two necessary and sufficient points to determine the horizon line *V'V"* of the infinite slanting plane extending from *ABC'D'* and intersecting the earth through *BV"*

This whole analysis serves one purpose, to demonstrate that subjective rotation is indeed subjective. The most unexpected thing has happened: We succeeded in changing a horizontal vanishing line into a slanting one. But is this so unexpected? Answer this question yourself by observing this simple, everyday occurrence: Before crossing a street, look frontally at the row of buildings on the other side. Considering the upper edge of the buildings as a frontal upper part of the lid, you will see it as horizontal. Then turn 90° to the left and then 90° to the right and look again at the same upper edge. In neither rotation does it remain horizontal; it runs toward a vanishing point on the horizon.

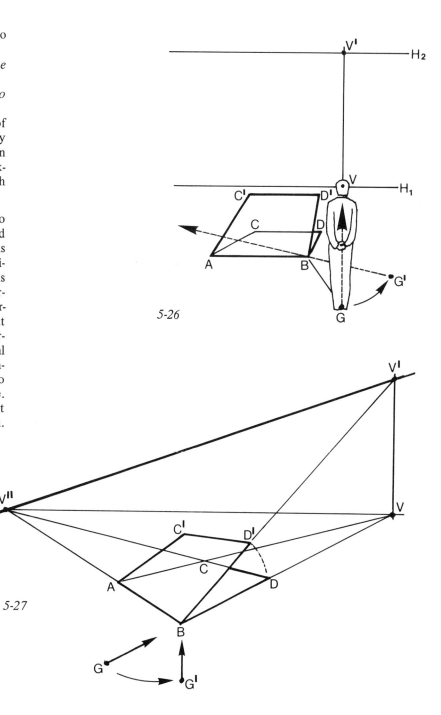

5-26

5-27

Vertical Lines on Slanting Planes (Perpendiculars)

Look at Fig. 5-28. To raise a perpendicular to the plane containing points A', C', B, and D (the rotated frontal lid) is simple. As long as the circle of rotation $AA'E$ is in a frontal plane, nothing is distorted, so the 90° angle that $A'B$ makes with $A'A''$ and BB'' remains the same. A vertical raised at any point of the slanted surface will be parallel to all the others.

The problem becomes difficult and creates visual barriers for the student when the rotation of the slanted plane does not follow a frontal circle. In Fig. 5-29 basic rectangle $ABCD$ rotates to position $ABC'D'$. Line BD' determines a vertical vanishing point V', which, together with V, determines the vertical vanishing line of plane BVV'. Since any vertical raised at B or D' belongs to the same plane, their extensions must vanish *on* VV'. Moreover, as BB'', DD'', AA'', and CC'' are parallel, they all must vanish at the same vanishing point V'' situated on the vertical horizon. Before handling measurable perspective, the distorted 90° angle $V'BV''$ (or the choice of the vanishing point V'') must be approximated in the same way we approximated it on the plane of the earth (see Figs. 3-27 through 3-30 again). Therefore verticals, or perpendiculars to non-frontal slanting planes, do *not* remain parallel in perspective, and for such constructions we will utilize more than two vanishing points. The vertical vanishing point V'' that we just described becomes necessary not only in cases of slanting planes but also when the observer is looking down from above the construction or standing on the ground looking up at high, surrounding shapes. This type of perspective is treated extensively in other manuals, some of which are listed at the end of this book in the section on "Further Readings."

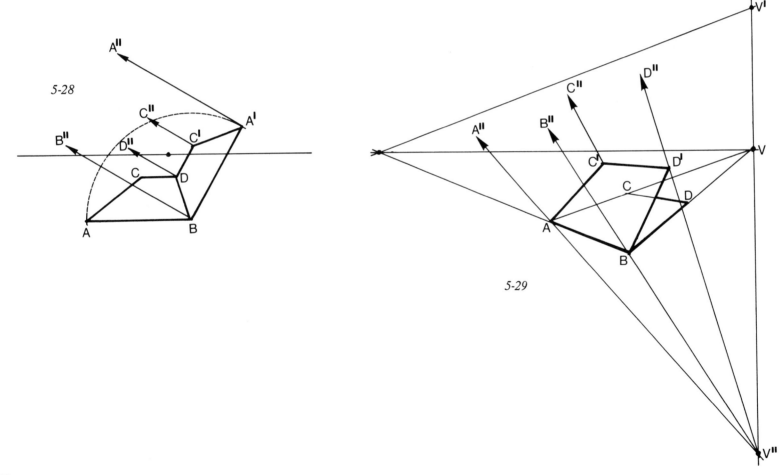

5-28

5-29

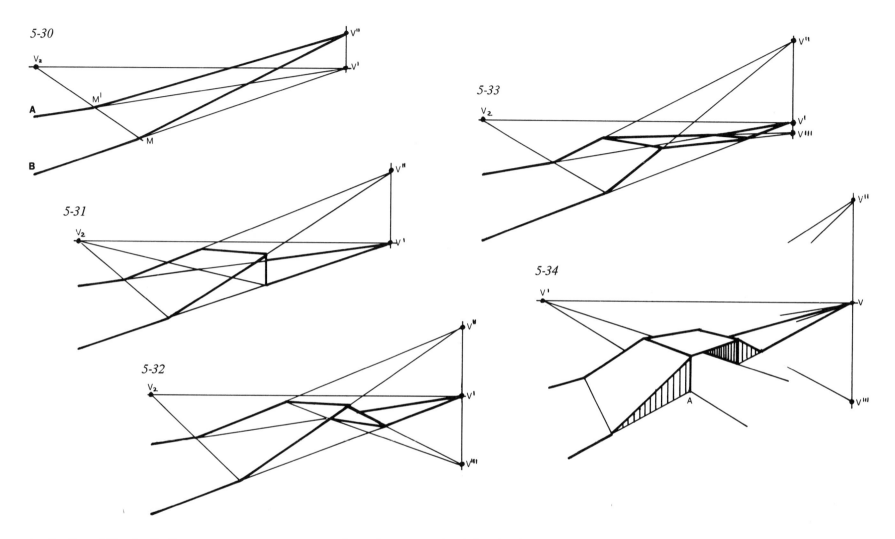

5-30

5-31

5-32

5-33

5-34

Application of Slanting Surfaces

The commonest and simplest instance of a slanted surface in perspective drawing is the changed level of a road (Fig. 5-30). Given a road AV' and BV' vanishing in V', suppose the road begins to slant upward at point M. Disregarding the angle at which the road slants, we determine V''. From M', which is the slanting point on AV' obtained with the construction of MV_2, we construct $M'V''$, and the

road continues upward indefinitely. Of course, the road cannot possibly stop here in reality, because it must return to the ground level. This can happen in three ways:

1. Abruptly vertical, as shown in Fig. 5-31.
2. Slanting at the same, symmetrical angle (Fig. 5-32).
3. Slanting down at a different angle (Fig. 5-33).

A road like the one in Fig. 5-31 is practically useless except for people like Evel Knievel.

Actually, such constructions appear frequently, but not as simple roads. For example, if at point A there is another road crossing the first one (Fig. 5-34), the drawing starts to make sense. Still, for such a raised crossroad you will need the return to earth, as shown in Fig. 5-31.

If the downward slant is symmetrical with the upward one, then as we have learned, $V'''V'$ will be equal to $V'V''$. Otherwise, the two vertical vanishing points are at unequal distances from V, depending on the angle variation.

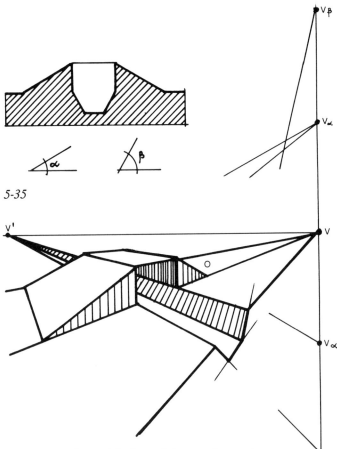

5-35

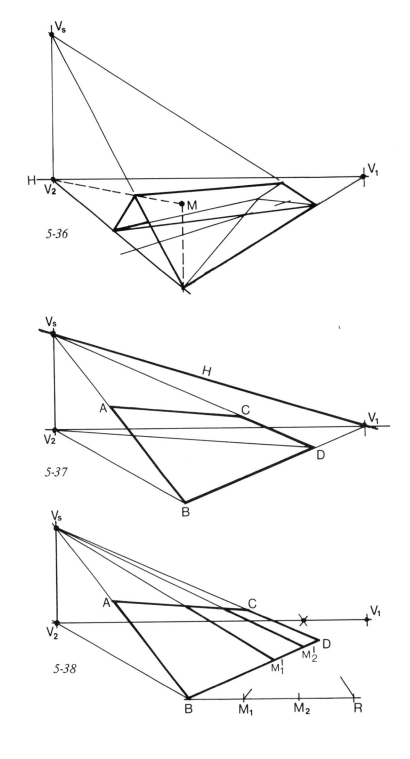

5-36

5-37

5-38

Suppose the original road is crossing not another road but a deep riverbed, as shown in Fig. 5-35. As you can see, angle β is much larger than α, so the vanishing points of the riverbed slopes will be much more remote than those of the bridge. (For now we are concerned with the principle, not with the exact dimensioning of sizes and angles.) Of course, ascending slopes vanish above the H line and descending slopes beneath it. "Ascending" and "descending" are relative conventions of the observer, because for another observer at O, ascending slopes would become descending ones and vice versa and another set of vanishing lines to another vertical horizon would be valid.

We have already studied several roof constructions, but now we will improve our ability to work with various aspects of slanted planes in a series of problems.

Problem 1. Given a rectangular base, raise on it a roof of height *M* with two symmetrical slanting sides. Figure 5-36 shows that we know what we need to about this problem.

Problem 2. Find the slanting horizon line of indefinite plane *ABCD* (Fig. 5-37). Rectangle *ABCD* vanishes at $V_1(AC$ and $BD)$ and $V_S(AB$ and $CD)$. Points V_1 and V_S determine slanting horizon H_S.

Problem 3. Divide rectangular roof *ABCD* into three vertical strips (Fig. 5-38). Divide *BD* into three by the usual method, obtaining M'_1 and M'_2, and join these two points to V_S.

Problem 4. Divide roof *ABCD* into tiles whose edges are symmetrically slanted according to its diagonals (Fig. 5-39). Extension of diagonal *BC* determines *V'*. Extension of diagonal *AD* determines *V''*. The division into five apexes (lower edge of the roof) is arbitrary.

Problem 5. Cut a rectangular window in the roof *ABCD* (Fig. 5-40). Unless we require precise dimensions or relative positioning of the window, the problem is as simple as introducing a rectangle in another rectangle on the horizontal plane of the earth.

The problems can be complicated to an indefinite extent. Our purpose here is to show that knowing special vanishing points and vanishing lines reduces such problems to the simplicity of construction in the earth's plane. We will learn more about intersections of roofs and slanting structures in Chapter 6.

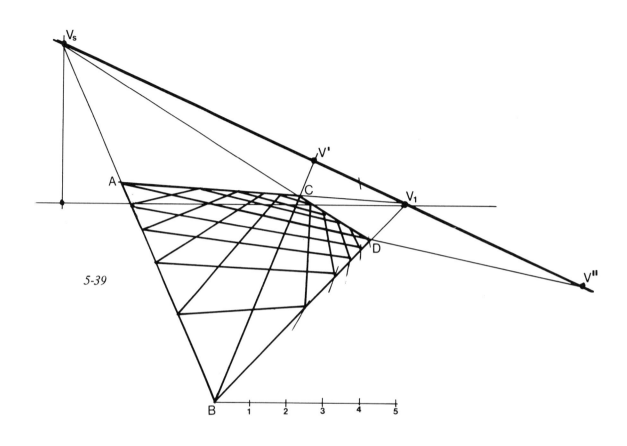

5-39

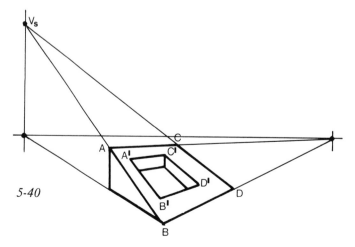

5-40

6. SOLIDS

Throughout most of the previous chapters we studied solids and their perspective representations and distortions. We are now ready to define solids the way we defined lines and surfaces. We said that a line is the trace left by a point in motion, whether this motion is straight or curved. We also said that a surface is the trace left by a straight line in motion, whether straight or curved. Now we can define a solid as the result of a translation or rotation of a surface. A parallelepiped will result from the straight-line translation of a rectangular surface *ABCD* between two points *A* and *E* (Fig. 6-1). When the initial *ABCD* is a square and the distance *AE* is equal to the edge of the square, the solid is clearly a cube. If the basic surface is a circle rotating around a point *O* in space so that the distance between its center and point *O* is constant and in every instance the circle and point *O* belong to the same plane,

the result is a torus (Fig. 6-2), the geometric abstraction of a doughnut. Actually, this description of the rotation, with its complicated condition, can be simplified if we say that the circle rotates around an axis belonging to its extended plane (Fig. 6-3). When we are talking about rotating surfaces, the rotation center is a line, not a point. (A door cannot rotate around a point; it needs two, and two points determine a line, the axis of rotation.)

Now, depending on the choice of this axis, we can obtain unexpected solids, and we will give you a few examples from the virtually limitless number of possibilities. Figure 6-4

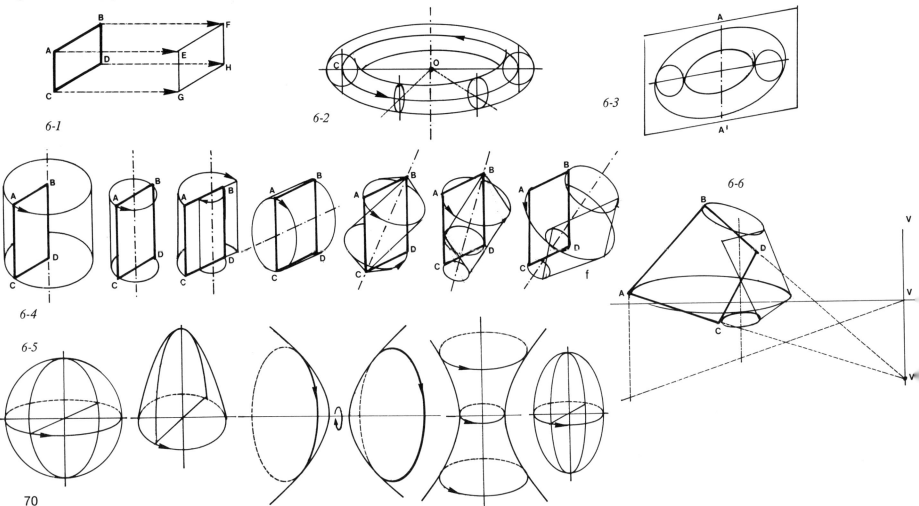

6-1

6-2

6-3

6-4

6-5

6-6

70

shows various rotations of one and the same rectangle, and Fig. 6-5 shows solids obtained by rotating conic surfaces (circle, parabola, hyperbola, and ellipse).

Each illustration should be self-explanatory. You should continue to explore this subject by translating and rotating triangles, making various choices for the axis of rotation. This will help you realize how many solids can be obtained from very simple, elementary surfaces.

This introduction into the world of solids has an important purpose: *In perspective drawing, understanding the basic generator of a solid simplifies its construction.* For instance, if you have to render in perspective the solid obtained in Fig. 6-4f, the first thing to do is to build the perspective of rectangle *ABCD* in a convenient position, then the axis of rotation, and then the perspective circles of rotation for points *A*, *B*, *C*, and *D* (Fig. 6-6). If the axis is vertical, the circles will be parallel to the earth, so their planes will vanish at the horizon line.

Understanding Solids

This section is dedicated to what we may call "Understanding Solids." Perspective drawing deals most often with more complex solids than those studied in elementary geometry, those resulting from intersections of elementary solids. As we studied elementary solids in Chapter 2, we are now ready to become familiar with different intersections, although a comprehensive study of these new (and more complex) shapes forms an entire discipline, called descriptive geometry. In this type of geometry plans and side and frontal views are used in order to determine the precise intersection of the solids involved, but here we will show a schematic plan only to show that for one plan there may be different intersections.

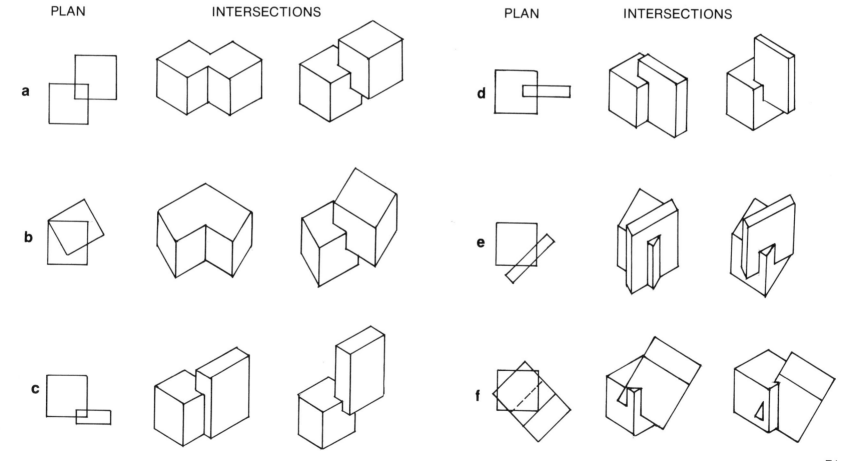

PLAN   INTERSECTIONS   PLAN   INTERSECTIONS

a

b

c

d

e

f

6-7

The plan is necessary because no perspective drawing of any intersection can be done without first drawing the perspective of the plan. The illustrations shown in Fig. 6-7 have no scale and no perspective construction. They are only intended to give you basic images of inter- sections you will meet frequently in your work. Most of these complex-looking structures can be easily rendered in perspective if you keep in mind that each separate surface must be inter- sected with another surface and that the whole construction is the result of a series of such intersections. However, intersections of the type shown in Fig. 6-7f, i, l, m, n, and o can- not be successfully rendered without a previous study of their intersections in descriptive geometry.

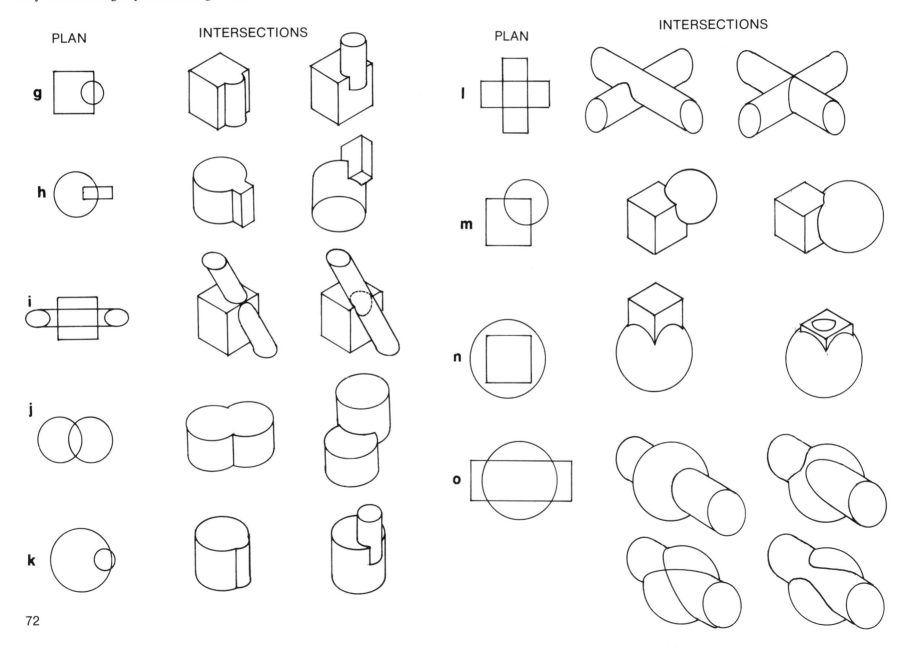

PLAN   INTERSECTIONS   PLAN   INTERSECTIONS

g

h

i

j

k

l

m

n

o

Other solids can be obtained by *separating* the shapes that were shown in Fig. 6-7 into the nonintersecting parts of the two solids and the common portion of their intersection. These are shown in Fig. 6-8.

a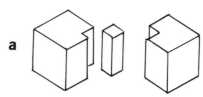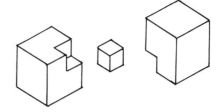

b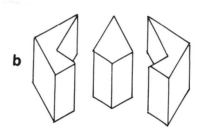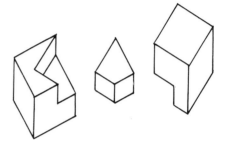

c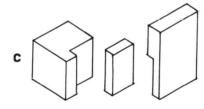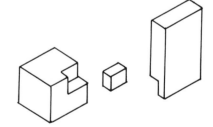

d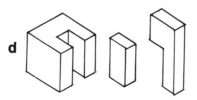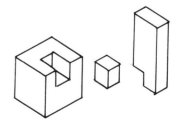

6-8

73

SEPARATED SOLIDS

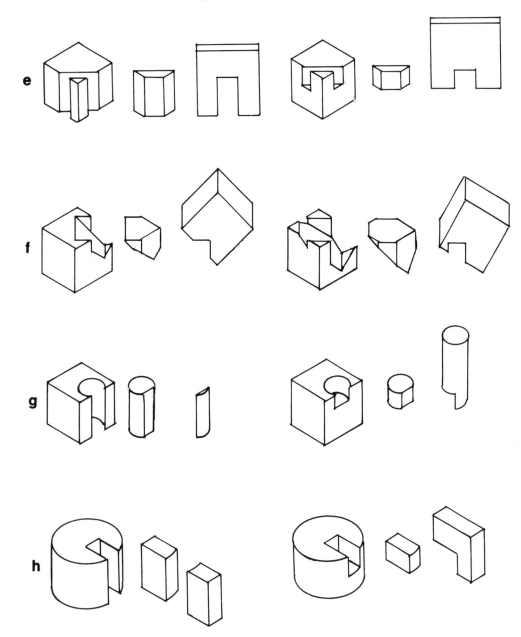

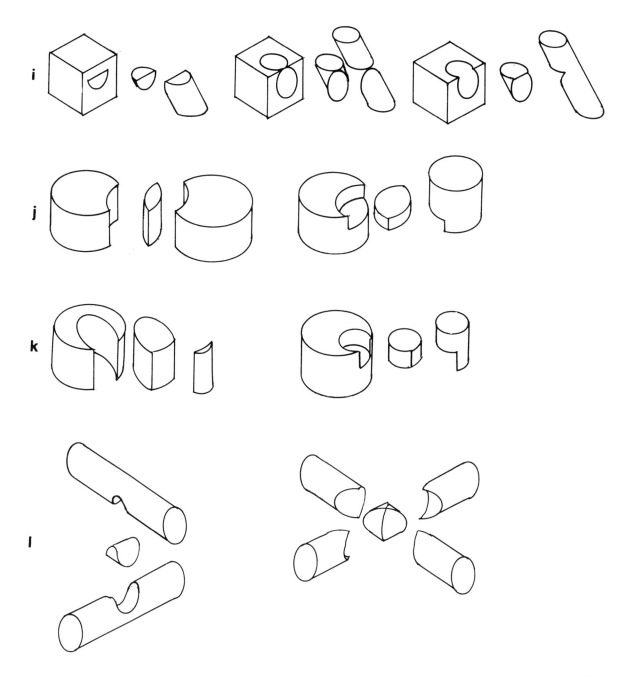

i

j

k

l

SEPARATED SOLIDS

m

n

o

Understanding solids is sometimes a difficult task. Intersections result in an infinite variety of shapes, some of which are studied in the discipline called *stereotomy*. Sometimes understanding these shapes requires mental effort even for those already trained in visualizing. In other cases the problem of understanding a solid derives from the difficulty of reading a blueprint. For instance, Fig. 6-9a shows plan and elevation of a cube with one circle on top and another on a side. The information is not complete, because some additional sections show how many possibilities there are (Fig. 6-9b). We now give a few similar problems to exercise your understanding of solids. All these exercises have answers at the end of the chapter.

1 Figure 6-10 shows a wire bent in various ways (wire is also a solid). Given the plan and elevation, find as many solutions as you can and sketch them in perspective. Remember that the wire is one continuous piece.

2 Given the plan and elevation (Fig. 6-11), sketch the perspective, knowing that the small squares are *not* holes.

3 Given two elevations, front and side (90°), show the solid in perspective (Fig. 6-12).

4 Given elevation, plan and side view, sketch the solid in perspective and explain it (Fig. 6-13).

From these exercises we infer that perspective drawing is not only a rendering tool but also an explicit mode of expression, a simple way of communicating the shape of a structure. Inventors, technicians, engineers, architects, artists, designers, and many other professional people exchange ideas by discussing freehand perspective sketches. The deeper one's knowledge of perspective, the more accurate and readable a sketch one can make.

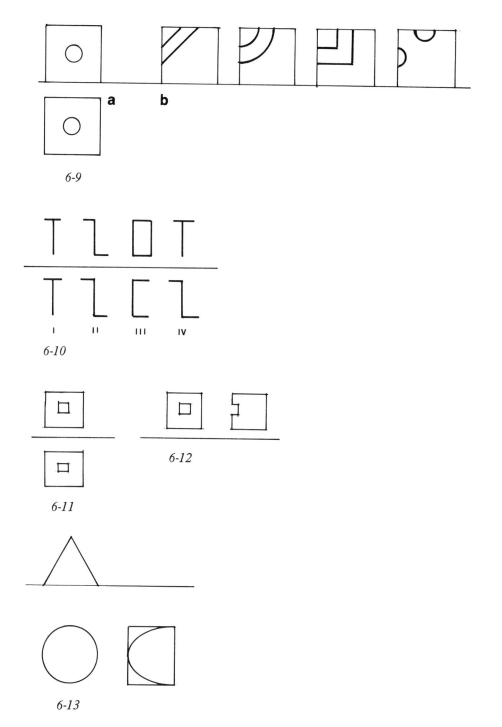

6-9

6-10

6-11

6-12

6-13

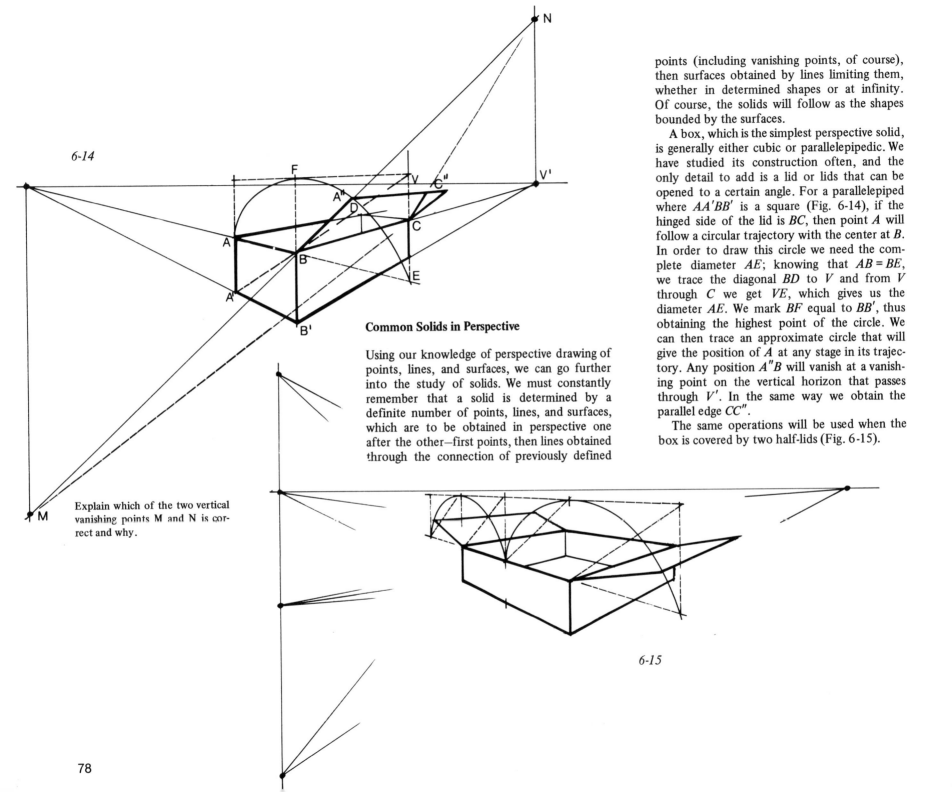

6-14

Explain which of the two vertical vanishing points M and N is correct and why.

points (including vanishing points, of course), then surfaces obtained by lines limiting them, whether in determined shapes or at infinity. Of course, the solids will follow as the shapes bounded by the surfaces.

A box, which is the simplest perspective solid, is generally either cubic or parallelepipedic. We have studied its construction often, and the only detail to add is a lid or lids that can be opened to a certain angle. For a parallelepiped where $AA'BB'$ is a square (Fig. 6-14), if the hinged side of the lid is BC, then point A will follow a circular trajectory with the center at B. In order to draw this circle we need the complete diameter AE; knowing that $AB = BE$, we trace the diagonal BD to V and from V through C we get VE, which gives us the diameter AE. We mark BF equal to BB', thus obtaining the highest point of the circle. We can then trace an approximate circle that will give the position of A at any stage in its trajectory. Any position $A''B$ will vanish at a vanishing point on the vertical horizon that passes through V'. In the same way we obtain the parallel edge CC''.

The same operations will be used when the box is covered by two half-lids (Fig. 6-15).

Common Solids in Perspective

Using our knowledge of perspective drawing of points, lines, and surfaces, we can go further into the study of solids. We must constantly remember that a solid is determined by a definite number of points, lines, and surfaces, which are to be obtained in perspective one after the other—first points, then lines obtained through the connection of previously defined

6-15

A house might be as simple as a cube or a parallelepiped, an intersection of two or more parallelepipedic solids, or any other intersection of a parallelepiped with a cylinder, a prism, or a pyramid, depending on the imagination of the architect. This is the main group of solids that appear most frequently in cityscapes or architectural renderings. To put these solids in perspective we must start with the plan (as shown in the "intersections" section of this chapter) and then elaborate the verticals in accordance with the rules we have learned. All exercises referring to divisions will be useful for doors, windows, and numerous details embroidered on the basic solids.

Let us take an example and build a perspective drawing step by step. Given the plan and front elevation of an architectural structure in modular dimensions we are told the following (Fig. 6-16):

1. The height of a floor is $\frac{1}{2}$ unit.
2. The observer stands at a height of 2 units.
3. He is situated somewhere on the dotted arrow AA'.

We are asked to reproduce in perspective his view of the building.

Remember that we have not yet studied measurable perspective, so the observer's position is flexible and the choice of vanishing points is approximate. So, before any attempt to start the perspective construction, we trace the horizon line—any horizontal line. Then we start the approximations: The first step is *necessarily* a mental one. By studying the plan and elevation, realizing what abstract solids are involved, and visualizing their intersections we must form an increasingly clear mental image of the structure. The exercises in Chapters 1 and 2 were intended to give you practice for this first critical encounter with the problem's data. It is at this incipient stage of analyzing the still undrawn perspective structure that you must use one of our suggestions: Imagine yourself in a helicopter flying around the building. This mental method yields several important benefits:

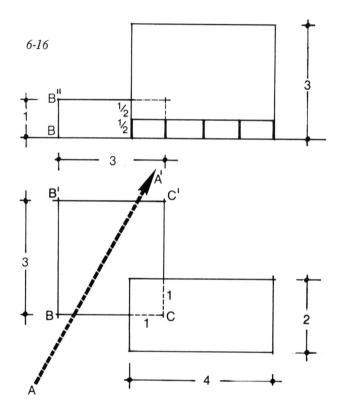

6-16

1. It gets you mentally acquainted with all the details of the building from all sides.
2. It gives you the proper height of vision required by the problem.
3. It gives you the flexibility of moving closer or farther and helps you choose the position where you will stop.

The results of this imaginary traveling should be translated into rough, light preliminary sketches which will help you reach the proper final rendering. We will think reason as follows: If the observer's view is directed along the arrow AA', the vanishing point of this arrow will be his eye-point projected on the horizon line. According to the location of this point (which we can mark on the horizon line *somewhere* toward its middle), we can infer where the two basic vanishing points of the structure will be, to the right and to the left of it. As *B* is a point of reference we see that it is situated to the left of *AA'*, as *BB'* vanishes closer to the eye-point than *BC*. Therefore we can mark the area of approximation of *B* to the left of the eye-point (Fig. 6-17). We can also mark the area of approximation for point *C'*, which is situated at the right of the eye-point (Fig. 6-18).

Now, if necessary, reread the section on "Surfaces on the Earth" in Chapter 3, and begin building square *BB'CC'*. We have established the eye-point; we established as well the projection on the earth of *AA'* (Fig. 6-19); and we approximated the position of *V* and *V'*. Now we make some attempts to build the first square on the ground. *Observe how AA' intersects the square.* The perspective construction of the same square must be built around the vertical *AA'*, with approximately the same relations preserved. After a few attempts we come to the most satisfactory square (Fig. 6-20).

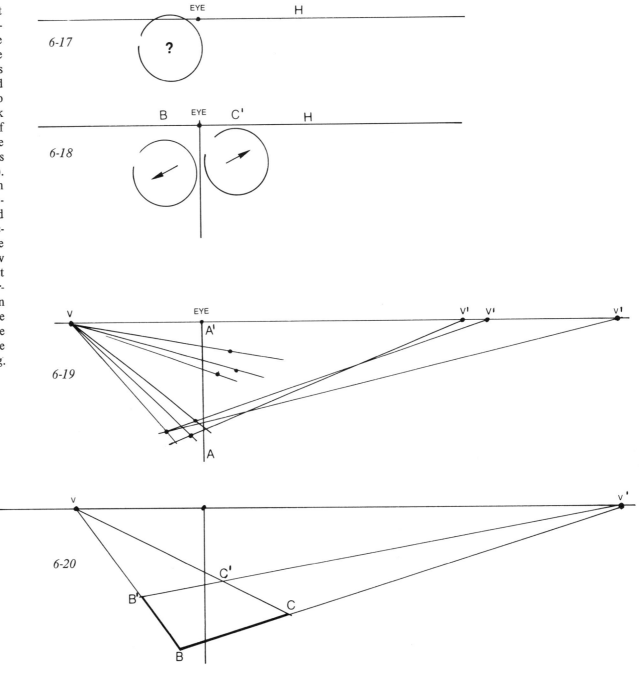

6-17

6-18

6-19

6-20

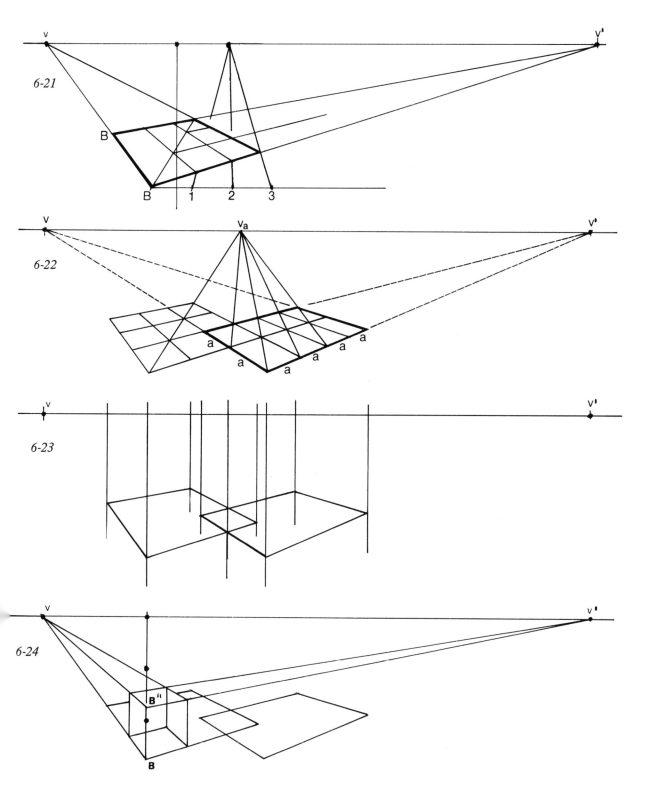

6-21

6-22

6-23

6-24

In order to complete the whole plan we must determine the module unit, so we divide the square (with one of the methods we know) into 3 × 3 smaller squares (Fig. 6-21). The next step is easy. The plan indicates the number of modules defining the other solid's plan (Fig. 6-22). Now if we raise verticals at every corner, we have established the perspective vertical limits of the structure, but now we must approximate the location of the whole structure according to the second specification of the problem, namely, the height of point *B* in relation to the observer's position (Fig. 6-23). For this we have to approximate the vertical value of the unit of measure. As this value is constant on one vertical but differs on another, we will return to point *B* and its first unit square and build a cube on it, with the same careful approximation we acquired during our study (Fig. 6-24). Line BB'' is the vertical unit for this particular location as well as for all verticals situated on the frontal line passing through *B*. Now, knowing that the observer's height is two units, we can find the precise vertical position of *B* by measuring down two units on the vertical BB'' from the horizon line.

It is possible, even probable, that our first construction of the perspective plan has been vertically misplaced because of a wrong choice of *B* in relation to the horizon line. In this case, having already all the vertical lines (Fig. 6-23), we *translate* the whole plan vertically according to the corrected position of *B* (Fig. 6-25).

The choice being entirely completed, we can build the whole perspective, beginning with the lower structure, then adding the higher one, with the help of vertical division into units (Figs. 6-26, 6-27). Observe that we have the type of intersection of two parallelepipeds we studied before. Also imagine the multitude of different perspectives possible when we change the relationship between plan and eye-point and the height of the observer. Imagine also the possibility of adding slanted roofs, changing one of the parallelepipeds to a cylinder, and any other alterations, additions, and changes you can think of.

In order to simplify our explanation, we have disregarded the distance between the observer and the structure. This additional specification determines the relative distance of the two vanishing points, leading to variations in angles of the horizontal lines of the structure. The same structure seen by a more remote observer will look as shown in Fig. 6-28. For an infinitely remote observer the vanishing points also go to infinity (right and left), the horizontal lines of the structure become parallel, and we transfer our drawing into the realm of orthogonal projection (Fig. 6-29). In this situation the location of a horizon becomes irrelevant.

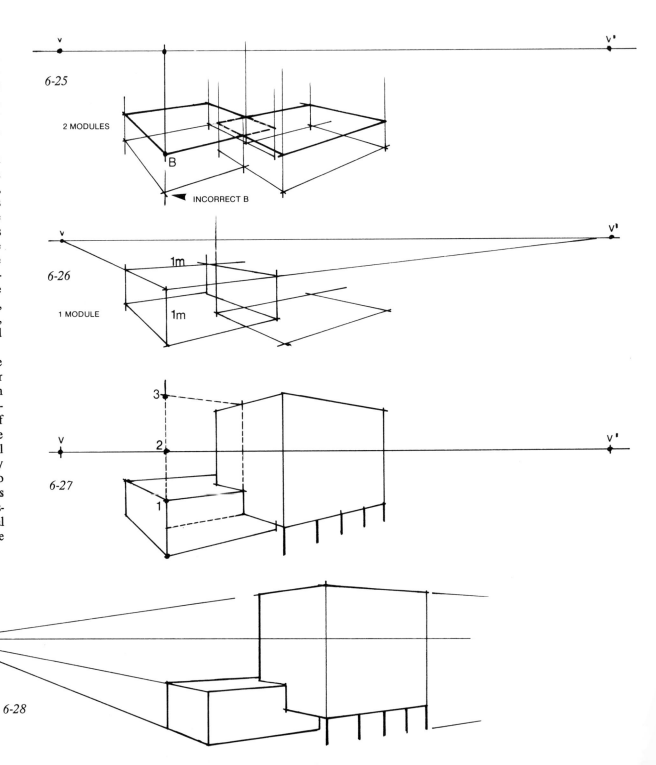

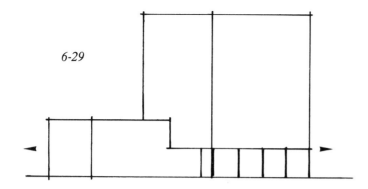

6-29

In addition to this step-by-step analysis of the perspective construction of two solids, let us remind you of some other structures that appear frequently in perspective problems. The *skyscraper* is ordinarily a vertically extended parallelepiped. Its construction requires no additional knowledge. If the plan and number of stories are given, we can immediately construct it (Figs. 6-30, 6-31). Notice that the roof (seen in transparency) looks enormous, a much bigger area than the apparent basic square. This is a distortion that will be discussed and corrected in Chapters 7 and 9.

The *tower* is generally a prismatic or cylindrical solid. We studied the cylinder in Exercise 98 of Chapter 2. If on top of such a cylinder we add a conical steeple, we obtain the basic specific structure of a mosque, which gives us the opportunity to study an additional exercise (Fig. 6-32). This time you have the plan,

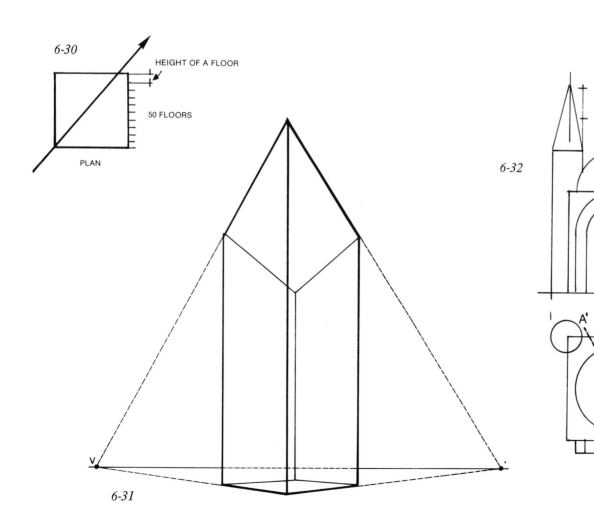

6-30

HEIGHT OF A FLOOR

50 FLOORS

PLAN

6-31

6-32

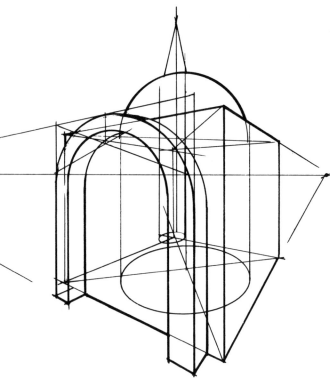

In such a situation we propose two solutions, based on the same principle:

1. Build the plan considering the eye level much higher than specified and then *translate* the vertical dimensions to the required position (Fig. 6-33).

2. Build the plan on a higher level and then return the vertical lines to the ground (Fig. 6-34). In both cases the key word is *translation*, and the choice is dictated by your particular aim.

the elevation, the unit dimensions, and the direction of the observer's eye, as well as the final perspective with all its construction lines, but you have no indication about the unit value of the observer's height. Carefully follow the complex network of lines, think out their meaning step by step according to the method we used in the previous construction, and find out at what height the observer's eye is situated. With more experience you will realize that our method is only one of many, and you yourself will find the most suitable methods to your vision, logic, and imagination, each method corresponding to a strategy particular to each problem. As an example, consider this question: What happens when the eye is situated on the ground level (i.e., the ground level and the horizon line are identical), so that we cannot build a plan on the ground?

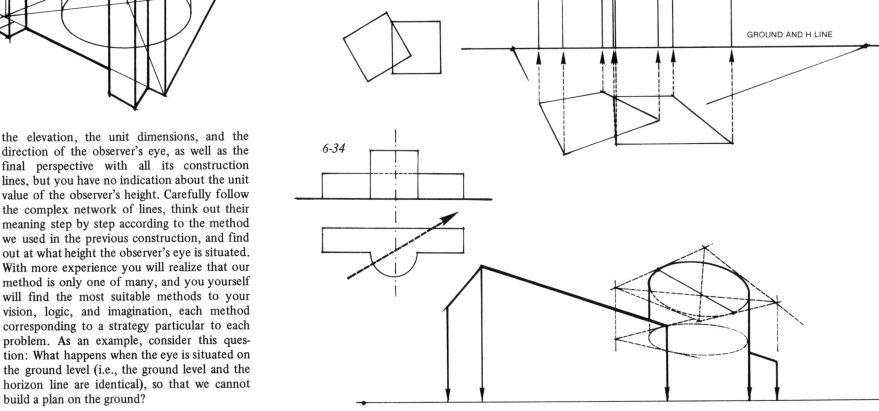

6-33

6-34

GROUND AND H LINE

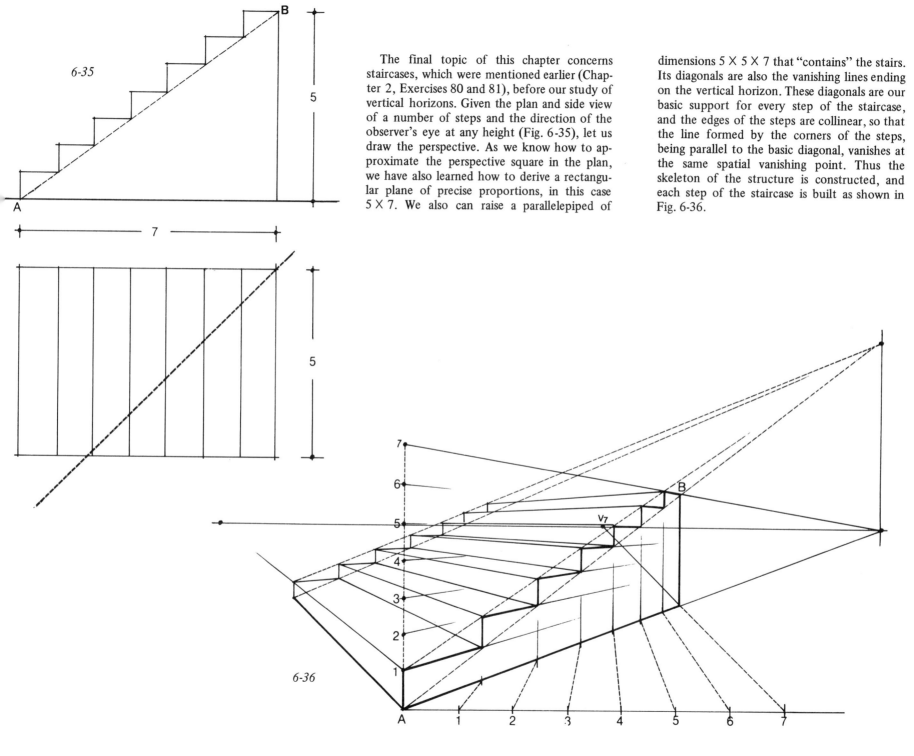

6-35

The final topic of this chapter concerns staircases, which were mentioned earlier (Chapter 2, Exercises 80 and 81), before our study of vertical horizons. Given the plan and side view of a number of steps and the direction of the observer's eye at any height (Fig. 6-35), let us draw the perspective. As we know how to approximate the perspective square in the plan, we have also learned how to derive a rectangular plane of precise proportions, in this case 5×7. We also can raise a parallelepiped of dimensions $5 \times 5 \times 7$ that "contains" the stairs. Its diagonals are also the vanishing lines ending on the vertical horizon. These diagonals are our basic support for every step of the staircase, and the edges of the steps are collinear, so that the line formed by the corners of the steps, being parallel to the basic diagonal, vanishes at the same spatial vanishing point. Thus the skeleton of the structure is constructed, and each step of the staircase is built as shown in Fig. 6-36.

6-36

An entirely different problem is the perspective construction of a spiral staircase. The problem is interesting and valuable because it helps us understand the interplay of many vanishing points. First let us analyze the plan and elevation of such a structure (Fig. 6-37):

Parallel lines AO, $A'O$, OG, OG' have the same vanishing point V_1.
Parallel lines BO, $B'O$, OH, OH' have the same vanishing point V_2.
Parallel lines CO, $C'O$, OI, OI' have the same vanishing point V_3.
Parallel lines DO, $D'O$, OJ, OJ' have the same vanishing point V_4.

The same statements can be made for the other four pairs of lines, where the vanishing points will be V_5 and V_6.

What we must do first, of course, is put our plan in perspective. Here we recommend that you choose your angle so that one of the diameters marking a pair of steps is frontal. This is not a trick but a way of making it easier to

reach vanishing points for some of the other steps. A step with a very remote vanishing point creates a very annoying situation. Only when the demand for a precise viewpoint is imposed, thus creating a situation in which no pair is frontal, must we accept the difficulty; in that case measurable perspective may be the only tool we can use. However, we are not interested here in measurements or the observer's height and angle but in handling multiple vanishing points for different spatial levels of parallels.

If H is an arbitrary horizon line (Fig. 6-38) and FF' the frontal diameter we chose, then we define the basic square $MNPR$ with the known method of approximation, taking into account that MP is one of its diagonals. The completion of this square plus its median lines gives us points M', N', P', and R', the points of tangency necessary for the construction of the circle circumscribing our dodecagon. (The plan shows that the number of steps in a complete circle is twelve, and the polygon with 12 edges is named a dodecagon.)

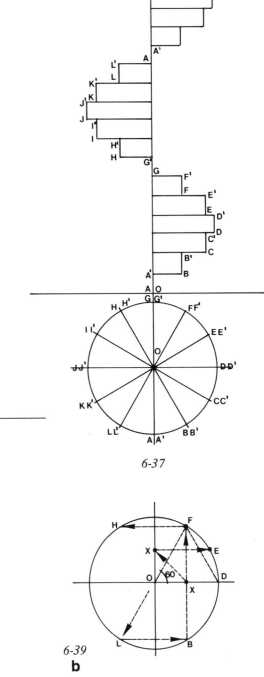

6-37

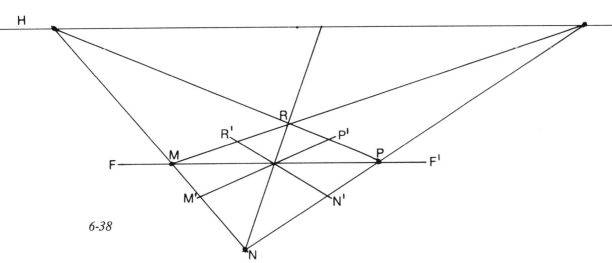

6-38

6-39
b

The intersections A, D, G, and J of the circle with the square's diagonals are the first four points of our dodecagon (Fig. 6-39a). By extending AG to the horizon line we obtain V_1, the vanishing point for all steps parallel to AO and OG. We also realize that V_4, the vanishing point of DO and OJ, is situated at infinity and is valid for all frontal steps in space. Now, in order to obtain the other eight points, which in our case are separated from each other by angles of 30°, we refer to the geometric property shown in Fig. 6-39b, where OFD is an equilateral triangle. We see that if we divide OD in two at point X and raise a vertical at X, its intersection with the circle determines the point F, and, following identical reasoning, we can determine all other points (see it first on the explanatory circle and then in perspective in Fig. 6-40).

Note: Obviously, if the number of steps in a complete circle is different from twelve, other geometric properties will be used for the construction.

The next step is to determine the vanishing points. This is a simple operation, consisting in the extension of all remaining four diameters to the horizon line (Fig. 6-41).

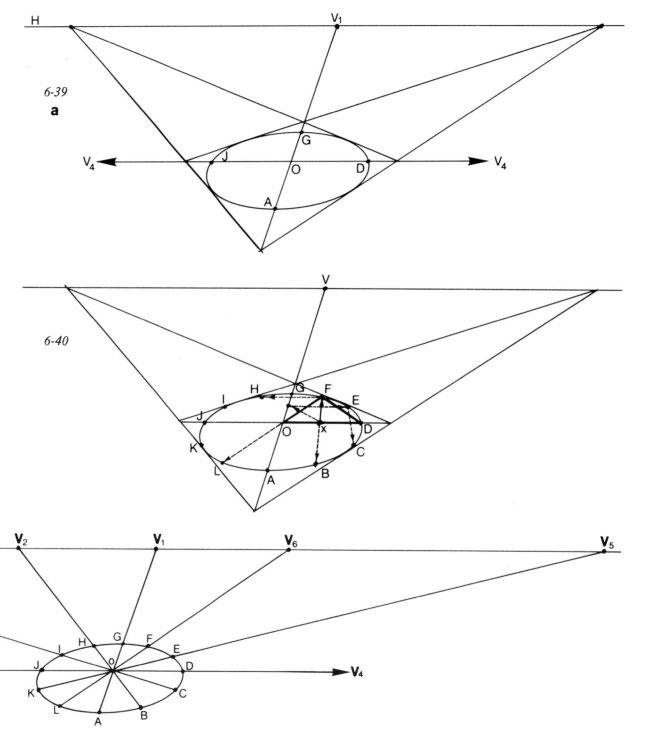

6-39 a

6-40

6-41

Now we can start building the actual steps. Observe that the straight edges of the dodecagon (AB, BC, etc.) each go to another vanishing point that has nothing to do with the V's we already found, but the information we have and the method we use will be sufficient for the vertical construction. We will first raise the vertical shaft OO' (Fig. 6-42). This is the axis of the whole construction, and on it we will mark the vertical units of the steps, as many as we want or need to build. The vertical unit is one of the four edges of the vertical rectangle of a step.

It becomes a very simple operation to complete each rectangle, having one edge, the opposite vertical limit (AA', BB', etc.), and its vanishing point. All that remains afterward is to join A' to B₁, B' to C₁, C' to D₁, and so on. If the basic plan is a dodecagon like ours, the operation of joining these horizontal lines, the horizontal faces of the steps, completes the construction. It is enough, however, to have the steps ending in arcs of the circumscribing circle to complicate our construction seriously. In such a situation, for every upper level we must draw again and again the basic circle in perspective distortion and retain the arcs $A'B_1$, $B'C_1$, and so on.

We have been discussing the abstraction of a spiral staircase. A real staircase would probably have a cylindrical shaft of a certain diameter intersecting with wooden, stone, metal steps of different shape, design, and thickness. These additional complications will increase the number of perspective drawing operations, but they will not change the basic method shown here.

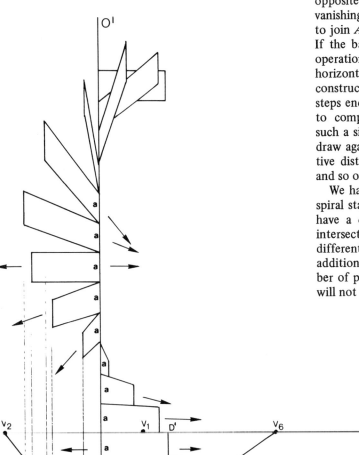

6-42

General Observations

It is inevitable for new perspective renderers or artists to make mistakes in their first attempts at freehand perspective construction. We might classify the *causes* of such mistakes into five groups:

1. Incomplete or wrong understanding of the structures to be rendered.
2. Insufficient visualization of the complex structure on the mental screen before working on paper.
3. Insufficient knowledge of (or lack of strategy in using) perspective methods.
4. Wrong initial choice.
5. Loss of orientation among the increasing number of construction lines.

You will realize even during your earliest attempts which group is particularly bothering you, what your weak point is. We all have one, and we must concentrate on it and work it out.

If your mistakes result from the first group of causes, do not start any visualizing or drawing before studying the structures, whether they are in nature, in front of you, in your imagination, or in blueprints. Observe them, analyzing every detail, make sketches of your imagined composition, and do not permit any detail to remain obscure. As we saw at the beginning of this chapter, many details that look complex are only elementary intersections. Then make your own sketches, *not* in perspective, to clarify the structure.

The second group is the most dangerous. This entire book has been designed as a guide against it, and the first two chapters provide the training you need.

The third group consists of the ordinary mistakes made by any professional who doesn't know his profession sufficiently. However, perspective drawing is a study based on a number of methods that can be used in accordance with the imagination of the renderer, enriched, combined, and replaced by other methods depending on his mental ability, training, experience, and inventiveness. You should think in advance about your general method, how to approach your problem, what to construct first and what later; in other words, plan your strategy.

The fourth is not a terrible class of mistakes, because it will oblige you only to take another piece of paper and start over again. A wrong initial choice might be, for instance, placing the horizon line too high for the rendering of a high-rise building seen by an observer situated at street level. Another typical wrong initial choice is that of the vertical square section of a prism (*ABCD* in Fig. 6-43), which when repeated laterally proves not to be a square. Regarding the infinite prism *ABCDV'* as of square section, we make the wrong initial choice of the square *ABCD*, which, when checked later in Section *A'B'C'D'*, proves to be rectangular. *ABCD* might indeed be misleading for anybody, not only beginners. Such initial mistakes are sometimes inevitable, but not dangerous.

Group five is again a dangerous maze. It requires great concentration during the whole process of rendering, a continuous link between your vision and your pencil, a light tracing of your construction lines, and a heavy, definite line for the final, structural lines. Seen in only one image, the complex operations of the problem worked out in Figures 6-17 through 6-27 look as shown in Fig. 6-44. It is a most disturbing image if you do not know how the step-by-step operations are carried out.

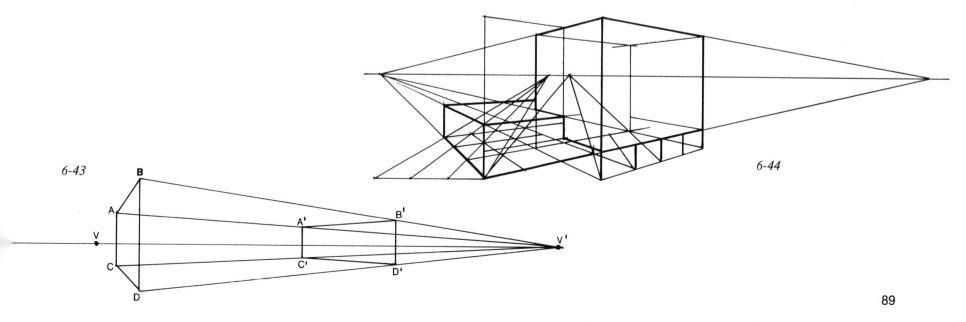

6-43

6-44

Answers

Problem 1. See Fig. 6A-1. The variations are much more numerous if we repeat some bendings.

Problem 2. See Fig. 6A-2. An additional side view would have clarified the problem.

Problem 3. See Fig. 6A-3. The misleading element is that the diameter of the cylinder and its height are given as equal. Therefore we immediately think of a cube and the effort of visualizing is jeopardized.

Problem 4. See Fig. 6A-4. This is a cylinder sectioned by two planes that are symmetrical about its axis.

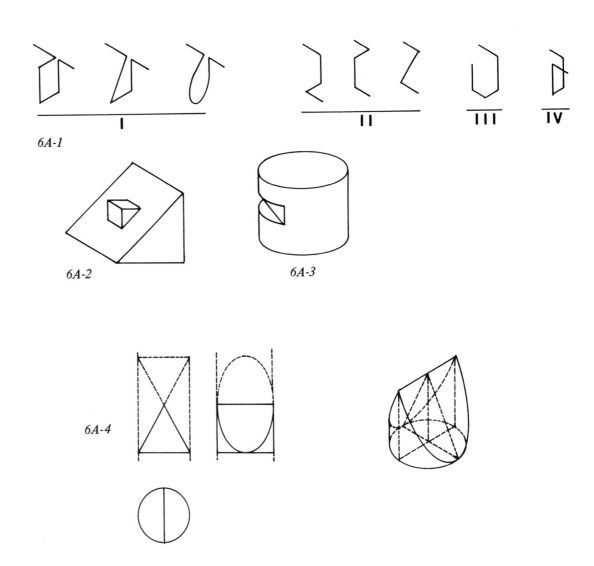

6A-1

I   II   III   IV

6A-2

6A-3

6A-4

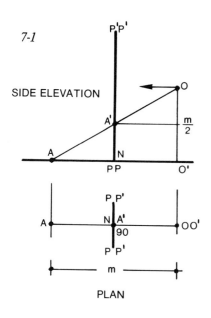

7-1

SIDE ELEVATION

PLAN

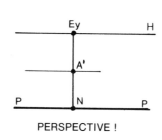

PERSPECTIVE !

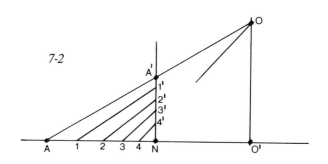

7-2

Eye, Object, and Projection Plane

A typical perspective problem is the following: Given the plan, elevation, and section (if necessary) of a structure, build its perspective as seen by an observer at height x, distance y, and angle z with respect to the structure. No approximation and no choice permitted.

Throughout the previous chapters we chose vanishing points, approximated the first square, approximated the vertical value of the measurement unit, and so on. Not very many initial choices were necessary, because we learned how to continue our constructions in a free but precise manner once we had made our choice and approximation. When the problem is given as above, the first steps must be as precise as the specifications and data with which we begin, and this requires a new method.

Remember that a perspective image captures a structure's light reflection converging toward the eye on a vertical projection plane situated between the eye and the structure (or object). In the following very simple exercise is concentrated the entire principle of measurable perspective: Given a point A on the ground, locate its perspective position on the projection plane for an observer m meters away, standing with his eyes at a height of $m/2$. The line joining point A with the feet of the observer is perpendicular to the projection plane (Fig. 7-1). The illustrations give you in plan and elevation the data of the problem *plus* the line that joins the eye with point A (AO). You need no more than this, because point A' (side elevation) is the precise location of the perspective A on the projection plane. Therefore, looking from the observer's viewpoint (i.e., in perspec-

tive), we raise the vertical segment NA', and we have completed our exercise.

Now, let us review some details. What is N? It is the point of 90° intersection between the line joining A with the observer's feet and the ground line PP of the projection plane. Therefore NA in side elevation and plan is the virtual line connecting the feet to the point A on the point's side of the projection plane. If you draw the line NA with a marker on the ground, then for each point of this line you will have the same process of piercing the projection plane (Fig. 7-2), so that in perspective the marked ground line NA will be seen as NA'. Remember this for the next exercise. Moreover, if in perspective we extend the vertical NA' toward the horizon, it is obvious that this line will end at infinity in the Ey point. And infinity is the horizon line at the level of the eye.

The next simple exercise is the following: Given the same point *A* on the ground, locate its perspective position on the projection plane for an observer *m* meters away with eyes at height *m*/2. The line joining point *A* with the feet of the observer makes a 45° angle with the projection plane (Fig. 7-3).

Although elevation (EL) and plan (PL) look familiar and understandable, (P) is a drawing that requires explanation, analysis, and deep understanding, because in the future examples and in your work with measurable perspective, (EL) and (PL) will no longer appear. (P) is a combination of (EL) and (PL), an overlapping of plan and elevation, obtained as shown in Fig. 7-4. Figure 7-4a shows a familiar image: the diagramatic representation of a point, an eye, and the perspective recording of this point on the projection plane. Nothing could be simpler. But, as you see, you can look at such a diagram from above (Fig. 7-4b) or horizontally (Fig. 7-4c), to see the plan or the elevation, respectively. Let us separate them as in Fig. 7-4b and c, and analyze:

(b)   *AO'* = plane projection of eye-point connection

   PP = intersection of projection plane with the ground

   Ey'O' = line defining the placement of point *Ey* on projection plane

   N = intersection of *AO'* with the projection plane line *PP*

(c)   *N* = same as before

   Ey = eye position on the projection plane, also defining the horizon line

   A" = point *A* seen on *PP* in elevation

Now we perform the apparently difficult operation in Fig. 7-4d, which in theory is quite simple but nevertheless complicates everything: We rotate the elevation until it lies on the plane as shown and realize that Fig. 7-4e is the same drawing as (P) in Fig. 7-3.

Now all we must do is reconstruct triangle *AOO'* projected and the similar triangle *ANA'*,

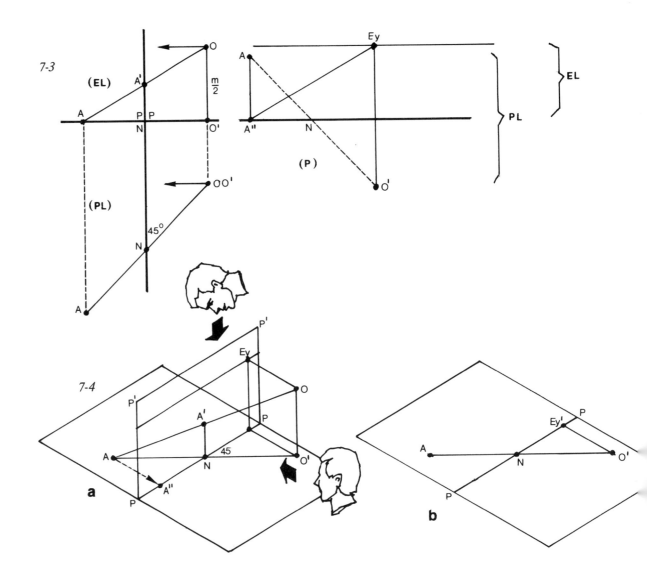

7-3

7-4

and the perspective A' of point A is finally obtained. Let us do it for the first time in correct and accurate measurable perspective (Fig. 7-5a, b, and c).

Triangle AOO' has three sides: OO', AO, and AO'. Point O is projected on the projection plane in Ey and O' in Ey'. Point A is projected in A''. Therefore in our elevation the triangle AOO' becomes $A''EyEy'$ (b). Look again at Fig. 7-4a and see that NA' is the vertical we need and A' is obtained as the intersection of this vertical with AO (in our last drawing, Fig. 7-5b, AO becomes $A''Ey$). Thus if we

raise the vertical at N (Fig. 7-5c), its intersection with $A''Ey$ is A', the perspective projection of A on the projection plane. So we have finished the exercise.

We must consider one more detail: If we extend NA' to the horizon line (Fig. 7-5d), we obtain the point V. What is this point? Look again at Fig. 7-4b and extend $O'A$ to the left (where the horizon of the earth's plane is supposed to be). Where the extension of $O'A$ meets the horizon line, we obtain the vanishing point of this line and of all parallels to it.

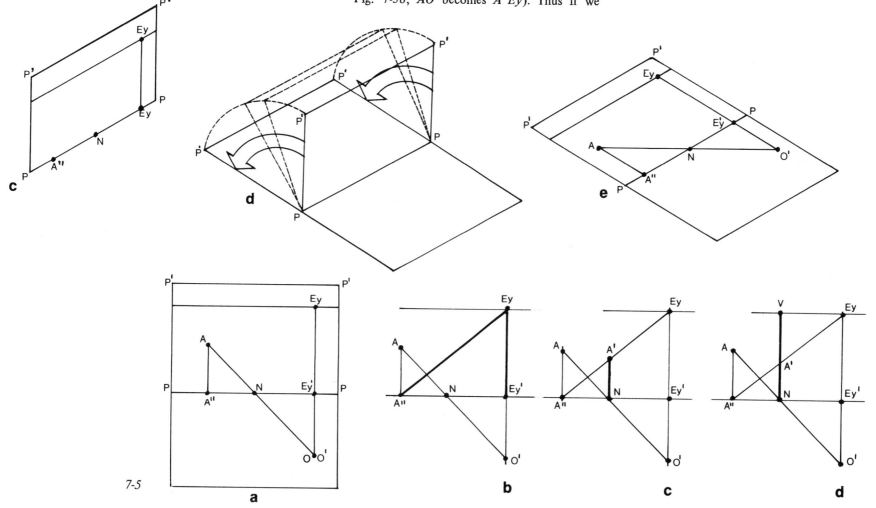

7-5

a   b   c   d

93

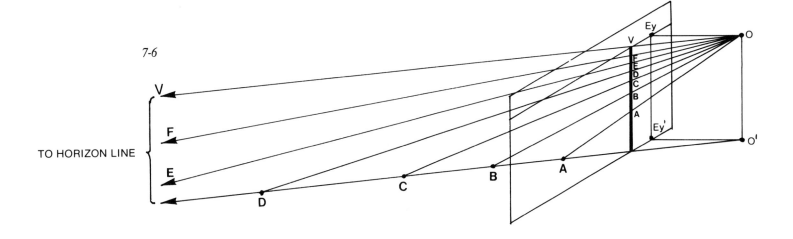

7-6

TO HORIZON LINE

Figure 7-6 shows that if instead of *A* we take *B* (in the same direction, of course), then *C*, and so on, lines *AO*, *BO*, and *CO* intersect the projection plane on the same vertical, at higher and higher points, until the line from the infinite point situated on the horizon line intersects the projection plane in *V*. Recall that we had a puzzling example of parallel lines coming vertically down from two different vanishing points in Chapter 3. We have seen that such vertical and parallel lines intersect in reality under the feet of the observer, and the preceding discussion explains the puzzle, showing that *any* vertical line (one that makes a 90° angle with the horizon line) passes under the observer's feet.

Surfaces

In the previous exercise, the line joining the observer and the point made a 45° angle with the projection plane. Of course, you have seen that the angle was necessary only for the initial construction of the data and was not necessarily involved in the actual perspective building of the point. That is, *any* point, no matter where it is situated, will be constructed in the way we have studied. So let us complicate our exercise a little and find the perspective rendering of *two* points on the ground. In order to make this exercise more interesting, let us say that the two points (*A* and *B*) and the observer's feet (*O'*) are the vertices of an equilateral triangle, that one vertex is situated on *PP*, and that the opposite side crosses *PP* and is divided by it in the ratio $\frac{1}{3}$ to $\frac{2}{3}$, as shown in Fig. 7-7. We also assume that the height of the eye is equal to the length of one side, *a*.

We will repeat the operations in the way we know, as follows:

1. Find *Ey* and the horizon line.
2. Point *B* is already in its place on *PP*. We do not have to find its perspective position.
3. As the previous exercise, *A* is seen by the observer along the line *AO'*, which intersects *PP* in *N*.
4. The triangle of vision is *A"EyEy'*, and its intersection with the projection plane is *NA'*.
5. Point *A'*, is the perspective of *A*.

Again, extending *NA'* to the *H* line and drawing a vertical parallel from *B* (Fig. 7-8), we obtain *V* and *V'*, the vanishing points of the two sides *BO'* and *AO'* of the triangle. The very strange and unexpected result of the exercise is that this particular triangle is so distorted in perspective that the complete triangle cannot possibly be seen by the observer in its entirety. (Do not forget that the observer, like a camera, has a limited field of vision and is not supposed, as in reality, to move his head or eyes. Of course,

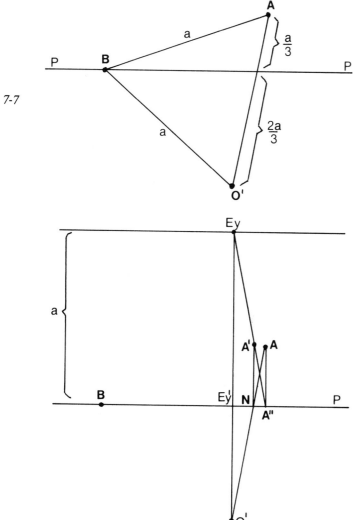

7-7

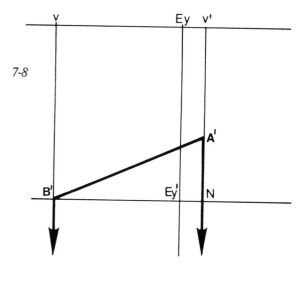

7-8

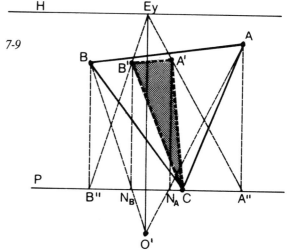

7-9

if he does move his head, he can see.) The observer will see $A'B$ clearly, but BO' and AO' will look like parallels to him. We already know why; in fact, we deliberately chose this unusual example in order to underline the extreme subjective distortion that can arise in our work.

Indeed, if we decide to draw the same triangle entirely disconnected from the observer's feet, beyond PP and touching it at C (Fig. 7-9), the problem becomes very simple, a threefold repetition of one-point process. Let us

consider equilateral triangle ABC in the given position, with C touching (for convenience only, we eliminate the third one-point process) and the O defined as in the diagram. Separately we determine B' and then A' while C remains the same in projection and in perspective. Our triangle therefore will be seen in perspective by the observer in the distorted manner shown with dashed lines. We know that the construction becomes complex and might discourage you, but we remind you that

1. This construction represents one process repeated twice.

2. If you reread the beginning of this chapter a few times, your vision will grasp the processes more and more easily.

3. Measurable perspective is a help and not an essential tool. We insist on analyzing the details only to give you a complete understanding of the first steps. After this our work will be much easier. Take heart, review the chapter thus far, and let us continue.

The Fundamental Square

In all the previous chapters we had only one main trouble. We constantly had to approximate *the first square*. After this first square was obtained, most of the other surfaces, shapes, and constructions were drawn very accurately with free perspective methods. This means that if we can build a square in measurable perspective, most (if not all) of the remaining steps of a perspective rendering can be done with methods we already know. So we will now study several instances of squares. But you already know that, after building one point, then two points (a line), then three points (a triangle), the problem of building the square (four points) is only an extension of the previous exercises, the fourfold repetition of one-point processes. We will only try to simplify the problem, not to uncover new difficulties.

Case 1. Ground square in random relation to *PP* and eye (Fig. 7-10). *A*, *B*, *C*, *D* become *A'*, *B'*, *C'*, *D'* after four one-step processes.

Case 2. Ground square in random relation to the eye but touching *PP* at one corner (Fig. 7-11). Points *A*, *B*, *C* become *A'*, *B'*, *C'*; *D* remains the same. We have reduced the operation to three one-step processes.

Case 3. Ground square with two frontal sides in asymmetrical relation to the eye (Fig. 7-12). Points *A*, *C* and *B*, *D* have common *N* and *N'*, respectively. The work is simplified.

Case 4. Ground square with two frontal sides, one touching *PP*, and the eye situated at its middle (Fig. 7-13). It is sufficient to locate *A' or B'*. Points *C* and *D* are *C'* and *D'*, being located on *PP*. Once we have *A'* (or *B'*), the opposite points are symmetrical.

After studying these squares, we can draw a few conclusions. First, it is always convenient to locate the surface to be rendered so that at least one of its points is on *PP*. This reduces

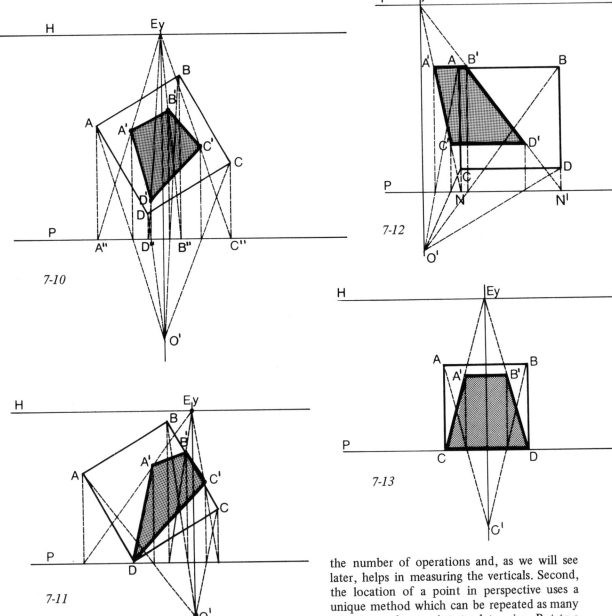

7-10

7-11

7-12

7-13

the number of operations and, as we will see later, helps in measuring the verticals. Second, the location of a point in perspective uses a unique method which can be repeated as many times as we have points to determine. But to a certain extent, this type of work becomes difficult and time consuming and clutters the paper with too many construction lines. It is therefore advisable to find a simpler and more comfortable method for any rendering that involves constructing more than a ground square.

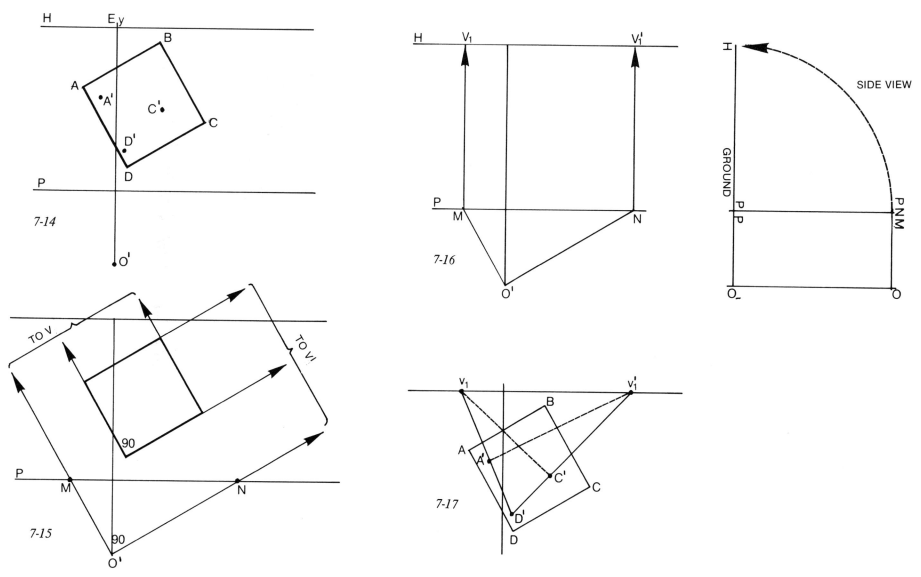

7-14

7-15

7-16

7-17

SIDE VIEW

So let us return to Case 1 and review it with another approach in mind (Fig. 7-14).

Let us find the perspective rendering of A, B, and C in A', B', and C', respectively, using the methods we know, and make some inferences: We have learned that groups of parallel lines go to the same vanishing points. Therefore AD and BC will go to one vanishing point and AB and DC to another. Of course, if we trace (in the plan) a parallel to AD and BC and a parallel to AB and CD from O', these two lines (which,

because of the properties of the square, form an angle of 90°) will also have the same two vanishing points (Fig. 7-15).

These lines, $O'V$ and $O'V'$, intersect the projection plane in points M and N. We know that the points M and N must be located on the horizon line, so if we rotate the projection plane onto the ground plane as explained in Fig. 7-4, we obtain the vanishing points of the square we used on the H line (Fig. 7-16). So, as we established points A', C', and D' before, we

can reconstruct our perspective square utilizing the vanishing points (Fig. 7-17). We construct the two pairs of vanishing lines (parallels), and at the intersection of $C'V_1$ with $A'V'_1$ we find point B'. This method seems to be more complicated than finding the four points of the square, but it is *the* method for complex structures that require finding more than four points. In order to illustrate this last statement, let us see how we go about putting in perspective a complex structure.

We will consider the plan of two separate structures (Fig. 7-18). We are given that A is touching PP and the eye is on the dashed extension of line BC, at a distance of 4 units from the projection plane (PP) and at a height of 7 units. In Fig. 7-19 the plan is shown with a thin line so that the final perspective (in heavy black lines) will stand out clearly. After constructing the data, we find the vanishing points. Since A is the same in plan and projection, we trace AV and AV', on which B' and C' can be found through the one-point process. After these two points have been defined, we no longer need measurable perspective, because all other points can be constructed with the free perspective methods we know.

Observation: You can see that angle $B'AC'$ is too acute and the distortion of the plan is rather unpleasant and unnatural. In order to correct this, let us repeat the construction of the data, this time in a side elevation and plan (Fig. 7-20). Unlike the eye (which constantly moves in all directions), but very much like a camera, the field of vision in perspective is limited to a certain angle within which dimensions are not exaggeratedly distorted. You can see that point O (side elevation), being so close to the plan from A to T and enclosing in the field the horizon line, scans a surface encompassed in a rather large angle α. Whatever is comprised only in an angle of 60° (i.e., between S and T) looks more normal in perspective. This applies in plan and also laterally, to the right and to the left of the Ey point. Our recommendation is that the distance and height of the observer should be so determined in relation to the structure to be rendered that the whole structure could be enveloped by a cone of vision not wider than 60° (Fig. 7-21). This is exactly the operation a photographer makes when aiming a camera. This recommendation is approximate and results from practical experiments. We will see in Chapter 9 that distortion is an inescapable problem in perspective, but within the indicated limits it can be tolerated.

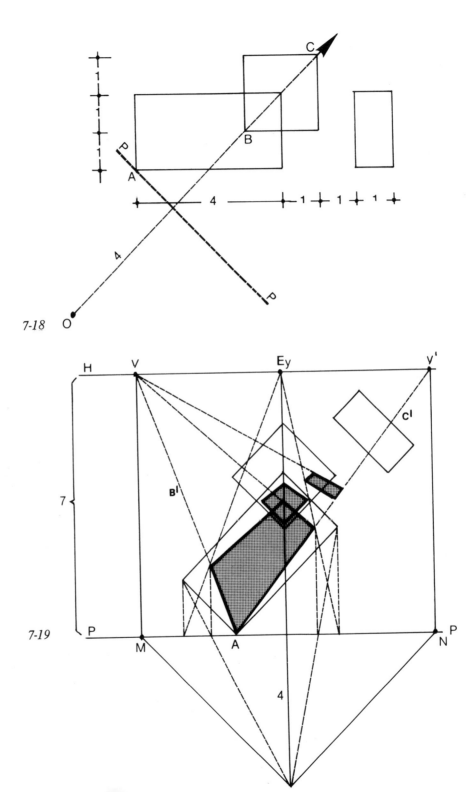

7-18

7-19

98

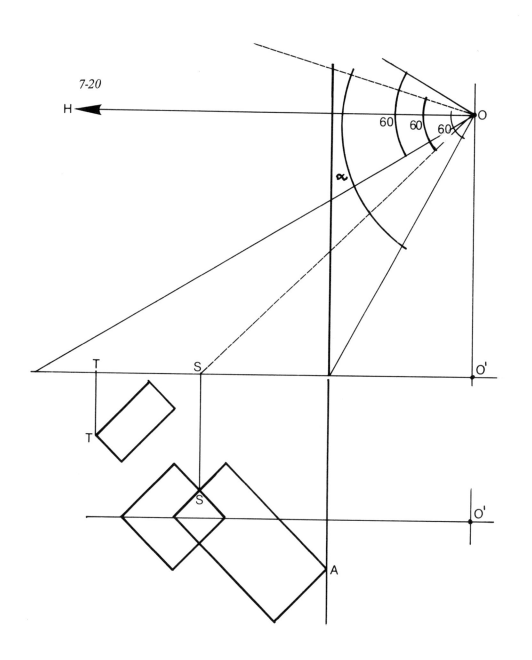

7-20

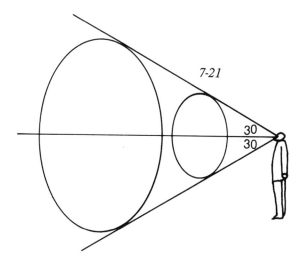

7-21

The Fundamental Cube

The problem of rendering solids in perspective (i.e., the addition of a vertical or third dimension to the plan) is much simpler than the construction of plane perspective. As we said, the most *comfortable* condition for constructing a perspective drawing is that at least one point of the plan should touch the projection plane. The second advantage of such a positioning is that, as we know, all dimensions within this plane are undistorted. This means that a structure whose plan touches *PP* has at least one vertical undistorted dimension. Suppose that a cube is given in plan in any relationship to the eye (Fig. 7-22). We build the perspective of the plan, basic square according to the method we know, with one small but useful exception: It is much simpler to trace diagonal *AC*, then a parallel *O'N* to it. Point *N* rotated on the *H* line gives *V"*, the vanishing point of the diagonal and all other lines parallel to it. So if we have traced *AV* and *AV'* and then located either *B'* (or *D'*) and traced *B'V'* parallel to *AV'*, then its limit is obtained at the intersection *C'* of *B'V'* with *AV"*. You might find it surprising that we call this a simpler method. For only one square, indeed, this method gives no substantial advantage, but when the plan indicates square-based complex surfaces, this third vanishing point becomes indispensable. But let us return to our initial purpose, namely, building the entire cube. In this particular case *A* touches *PP*, so raising a vertical at *A* (and therefore on the projection plane) means raising an undistorted frontal dimension (Fig. 7-23). The completion of the cube falls under the methods of free perspective.

Even if the cube does not touch the projection plane, we learned in Chapter 4 how to extend one of the lines until it touches it. Once we have determined this vertical measure, all others represent no problem. Actually, we can now see that with convenient initial specifications, measurable perspective is reduced to the precise construction of "the first cube."

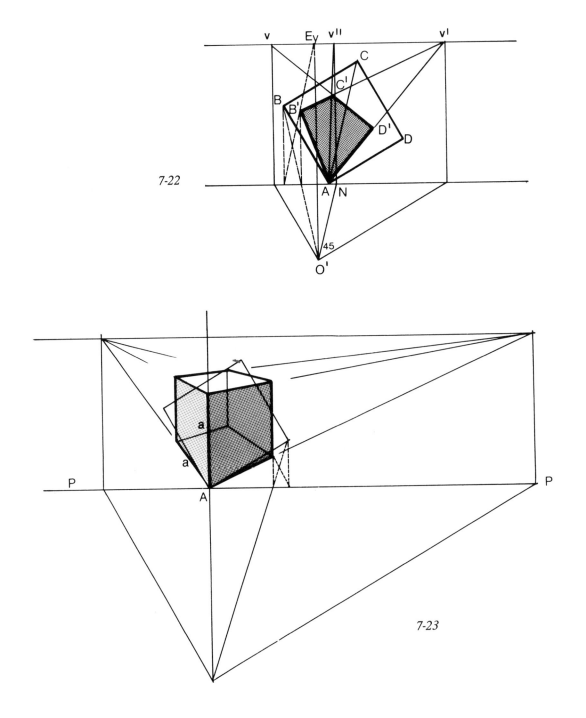

7-22

7-23

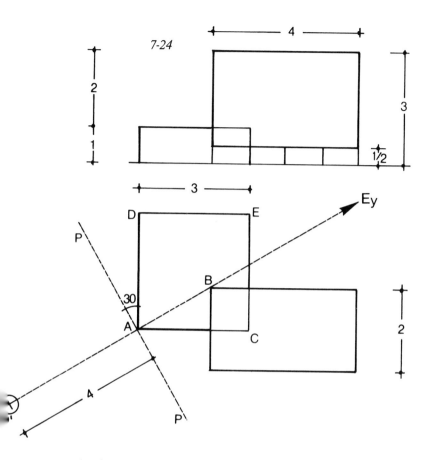

7-24

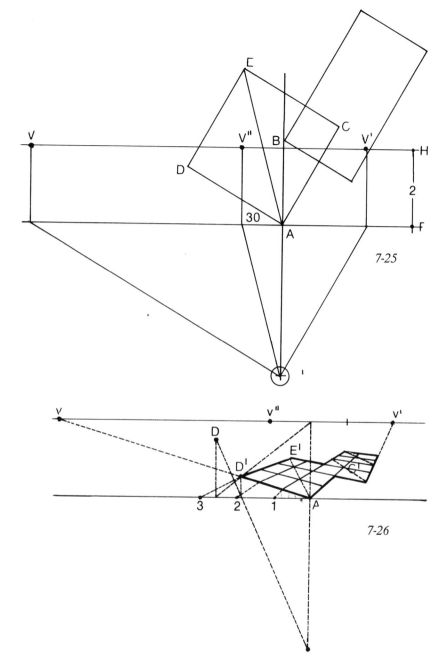

7-25

7-26

At this point let us again take the problem given in Chapter 6, Fig. 6-16, and build the structure with precise data (Fig. 7-24):

1. Point *A* touching *PP*; 30° angle between *AD* and *PP*.
2. Line *O'Ey* perpendicular to *PP* and passing through *B*.
3. Distance from *O'* to *PP* is 4.
4. Height of *O* is 2.

(Do not forget that this choice is one of an infinity of possibilities. We recommend that after studying this example you create your own exercises by changing the position of *PP* and the distance and height of the observer, and then start again with other structures.)

We first trace the plan data in perspective construction position (Fig. 7-25) and find the vanishing points *V*, *V'*, and *V''* (vanishing point of the diagonal of square). Then we find point *C'* (or *E'*) and complete the square *A'C'D'E'*

(Fig. 7-26). Using *V''* and tracing the diagonals, we complete the perspective rendering of the plan. Then at *A* we raise the real unit values of 1, 2, and 3 and continue the vertical structure as in Chapter 6 (Fig. 7-27).

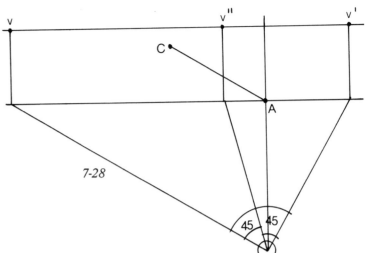

7-27

7-28

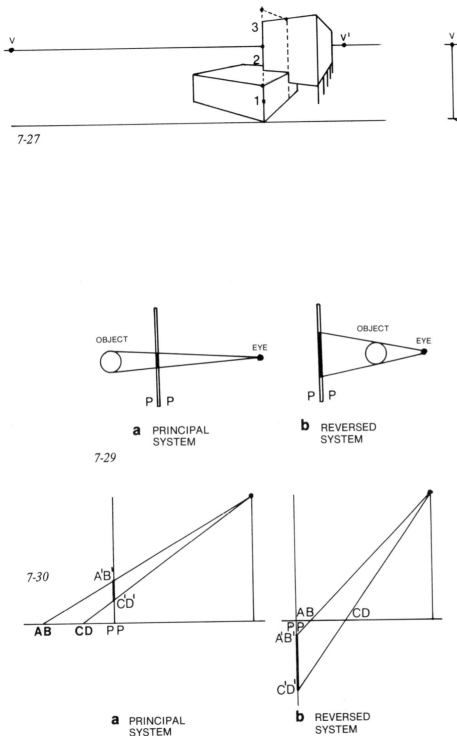

7-29

a PRINCIPAL SYSTEM

b REVERSED SYSTEM

7-30

a PRINCIPAL SYSTEM

b REVERSED SYSTEM

We intentionally separated the construction process into three diagrams so that the great number of construction lines would not become confusing. Superimposing the final perspective drawing above the plan creates a lot of confusion. And as we know that only the first cube is necessary in measurable perspective, we advise you to use the minimal number of data when tracing the initial plan. For instance, in our case it is enough to take the position of O' (from Fig. 7-24) and then trace the angles of the square to determine the vanishing points. Then place A on PP and C or E and construct the rest (Fig. 7-28).

Another detail to know is that what counts for the final perspective is the relationship between object and observer. Whether the projection plane is closer to the eye or to the object affects only the *size* of the final image, not any of the structural proportions. (Think of the projection of a slide when you move the screen closer to or farther from the projector.)

Indeed, our initial definition of perspective suggests that the image is captured by the projection plane situated between object and eye. But we can accept theoretically (and then verify practically) the possibility that the object is situated between the eye and the projection plane and that its points, instead of being captured by this plane, are projected on it

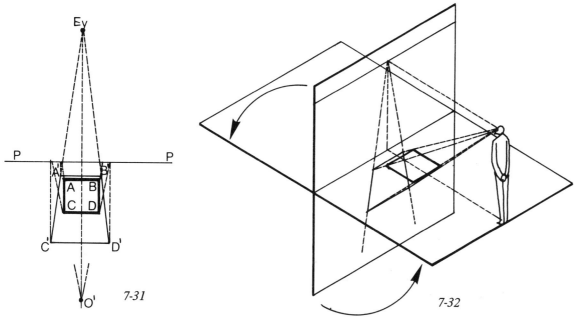

7-31

7-32

In general, measurable perspective, about which you now have sufficient information to be able to use it, is to be employed only when scientific exactness is required. Even with the best data and choice of position, the image obtained will never compete with reality, primarily because reality is perceived with two eyes and a photographic or perspective rendering is a flat, two-dimensional extract of reality. It is always preferable to have a mental idea about the image we want to obtain and *then* to specify the most appropriate data.

Before ending this chapter we will complete an exercise that remained unsolved in Chapter 2 (Exercise 74), where we were looking for the distorted length of a rotating door at any point in its rotation (Fig. 7-33). If WW is the plane of a wall and DD_1 is the door opening, then the door will rotate around D_1 (let us say). For a point A, which can be anywhere on the circle, we must find the proper perspective. The problem is as simple as finding the perspective location of three points D, D_1, and A, and we know how to do this. Once A' is found, the height of the opened door is determined with the vanishing point of $A'D_1'$.

(Fig. 7-29). This second approach is preferable when the object is too small to be reduced even more. But here, only additional knowledge of descriptive geometry helps the construction process. This particular procedure goes beyond the purpose of this book and could be learned by you in further readings about descriptive or projective geometry. In order to show you the difficulty, we will take the example of a ground square situated in the reverse position (Fig. 7-30a, b). You are familiar with Fig. 7-30a, in which square $ABCD$ is captured by the projection plane in $A'B'C'D'$. In the reversed system, any ground surface will be projected *from* the eye underneath the ground level onto the virtual extension of the projection plane. The drawing will look as shown in Fig. 7-31.

This strange-looking image is obtained by the same process of rotating the projection plane 90°. And as Ey remains on the upper, real side of the projection plane, the virtual, underground side has the opposite rotation (Fig.7-32). You can see that the principle is as simple as in

the initial system, but the construction process requires considerable visualization, an effort very seldom necessary.

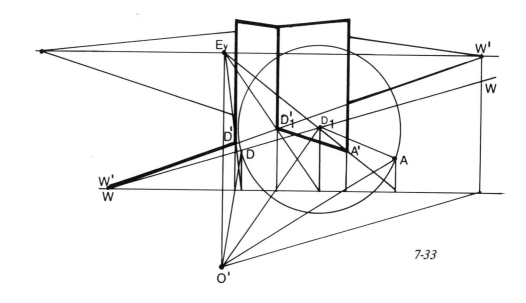

7-33

8. THEORY OF PERSPECTIVE

Thus far we have studied *how* perspective drawing is done. Having the necessary knowledge of perspective processes, we must go a little beyond the perspective study itself in order to answer a few philosophical, scientific, and artistic questions, so that we will also be able to understand *why* we draw in perspective, *how* to approach it, and *what* the difference between scientific and artistic perspective is.

We are told that Mozart used to say that when he created a symphony he heard it in his mind suddenly, in its entirety. This condensed-time phenomenon is very difficult to understand for those who do not have Mozart's musical gifts. But we might gain some understanding of how an architect can suddenly see in his mind a complex architectural structure. Such a structure has no time dimension and might be encompassed by three-dimensional imagination. Hendrik Van Loon writes in his book *History of Arts* that the most important step in the design of an architectural monument occurs when the architect sketches it for the first time on the back of his cigarette box. We believe that this is the second step; the first and most important one is the mental vision, without which there can be no sketch.

But mental vision is also the result of prior mental processes. A great amount of visual information is received every second by the eye, but only part of it is recorded in our memory storage. Only visual information (i.e., objects and events) that has a certain impact upon our life raises our interest and is stored for future use. However, the same object or event can have a different impact upon different individuals. Let us elaborate on this thought: Suppose that an artist, an engineer, and an architect look at a building. The artist's impact is mainly emotional: The beauty or ugliness of this building impresses him. He will record the colors of the building, their relationship within light and shade, the proportions of the general structure and its details, in other words the elements that enhance the artistic value of the building. The engineer is more interested in the logical design of the structure, in the way its designer solved the problems of resistance of materials. His recorded mental image is similar to the artist's image, but his point of view and thus his mental record differs. The architect is in the midway. His memory will record the geometry of the ensemble, its function, the relationship between the building and its environment, and other elements which together raise his professional interest. There is however no precise separation between these three types. The artist is not only an emotional perceiver devoid of logical analysis, just as the engineer can be also emotionally impressed by the aesthetics of the building. Many architects are also painters or engineers or both. Beyond the professional formation of an individual, a large number of subjective and objective factors contribute to the elaboration of the mental image that will be stored in his memory. What characterizes the artist and the designer is the ability to "filtrate" and elaborate his memory data in order to obtain a new, original mental vision he intends to render and communicate to others. The artist elaborates the data through a process determined primarily by emotion, the engineer by reason, the architect by both.

Perspective is not only our natural way to perceive things but also our fundamental method of processing mentally visual data. The ability to visualize differs from one individual to another. If our first two chapters are dedicated to improving your ability and our book is entitled Understanding Perspective (not Understanding Perspective Drawing), this is because prior to drawing your mental vision must be trained to process accurately your future works.

If now, after studying the previous chapters, you can juggle with points, lines, shapes, solids, infinity, and distortions on your mental screen, you still lack the means of approaching the problem of composing them into an expressive and meaningful perspective drawing. For this, we must make several points:

First, you should decide whether you are primarily the rational or emotional type. Depending on the answer, your tendency will be to express yourself in rigorous measurable perspective or free perspective, respectively. A scientific mind needs accuracy and exactness, whereas an artistic one needs freedom extended sometimes to great (however emotionally motivated) distortions.

Second, we have seen that emotion is prevalent in the artistic type, but it pervades the scientific as well. Before attempting to come to any vision, try to analyze your goal, to understand *why* you have to express yourself, *what* impresses you emotionally about your subject, and *what kind* of feeling you want to communicate to those who will look at your work; in other words, what is your message? These questions and their answers provide you with the means of approaching the problem.

A different situation occurs when you are the perspective renderer working for an architect. In this case you are like a soloist interpreting the work of a composer: You must study his blueprints, understand their three-dimensional complexity, and, most of all, understand the architect's emotional canvas and the logical structure that determined his design. When you come to your own vision (not necessarily identical with his), the perspective composition is virtually determined.

Third, we know that when an actor on stage must *express* anger, he normally does not *experience* the feeling. He has an inborn talent for expression, for understanding almost intuitively the expression of anger even without the actual feeling, and he has learned the technique of materializing this expression, of acting. Like the actor, you train your ability to visualize, then you learn perspective drawing methods for the relationship between the emotional observer's reaction and its subject. For example, very distant vanishing points create a peaceful feeling, in contrast to close vanishing points, which produce acute angles and enhance a dramatic feeling. A view from above determines a feeling of vastness and grandeur, a view from the ground level a feeling of gigantic or overwhelming environment. The variations of such techniques are limitless, as are the feelings obtained. We see that the observer's position in relation to his subject is fundamental in expressing an overall feeling. When shades, shadows, and color (which will be studied in the last chapters of this book) are added, perspective drawing can be a powerful means of emotional communication.

Do not forget that artists and architects project on their mental screen a complete idea in which there is no separation between structure, shadow and color.

Finally, we must stress an elementary matter: We have the tendency to avoid imagining things we do not understand. In other words, an incomplete understanding of visual processes jeopardizes our freedom to create whatever we intend to. In a sense, it is easier to design a semicircular arcade, than to render it in perspective where the notion of ellipse and a detailed study of it is necessary. The renderer having too little understanding of the problem will either give up the subject, or produce a clumsy construction, as shown in Chapter 4.

Perspective drawing rules are the technical tools for translating your mental vision onto paper. Their discovery, at the beginning of the 15th century, was a result of painters' need to produce accurate landscapes and townscapes. Prior to this period, painters worked with little understanding of perspective. Observation and empirical inferences were not sufficient for accurate construction, but the artistic vision of many painters was able to compensate for this lack through color and balanced composition (Fig. 8-1).

8-1. Fra Angelico and Fra Filippo Lippi. The Adoration of the Magi *(1085). (Photo courtesy of National Gallery of Art, Washington, D.C., Samuel H. Kress Collection.)*

2. *Vredeman de Vries.* Imaginary City. *(From* Perspective
* *Jan Vredeman de Vries, published by Dover Publications,*
c.)

After Filippo Brunelleschi's discovery of the mathematical basis of perspective, many artists, captivated by this revolutionary technique, began painting and engraving perspective views for the sake of using perspective and for the pleasure of handling and mastering its laws (Fig. 8-2 and Fig. 8-3). Both examples are built on two major vanishing points (the central eye-point and the left-right infinity point), although we observe secondary pairs of vanishing points in the octagonal base of the central fountain (de Vries) and the spatial vanishing point of the slanted roof (Fig. 8-3). The simple, almost rigid observer's point of view is enough to obtain the feeling of elegance, of linear accuracy they were endeavoring to convey. The names of these works indicate the painters' aims.

It was only normal that after this period of learning, understanding, and practicing perspective in a purely formal, rigid, and scholastic manner, artists of great skill would develop more detailed and complex perspective relations between images and produce astonishingly rich and realistic views of Europe's townscapes (Fig. 8-4, Fig. 8-5, and Fig. 8-6). In these three examples we can see the artist's attempt to understand, reflect, preserve, and communicate not only the image of some particular place but also the special emotional impact this place has on him. Constable faces the cathedral; his view encompasses a quiet, pastoral scene. The vanishing points are so remote from each other that the perspective seems almost orthogonal. Hence there is a feeling of calm, uneventful life, underlined by the static figures in the lower left corner of the painting.

8-3. *Master of the Barberini Panels (Giovanni Angelo di Antonio).* The Birth of the Virgin. *(The Metropolitan Museum of Art, Rogers and Gwynne M. Andrews Funds, 1935.)*

If we take two points A and B on the earth's surface and rotate lines around them, we obtain two overlapping fans (Fig. 3-9), which make no particular sense or have no particular meaning or relationship. But when two vanishing lines, one from A and the other from B, end (or vanish) at the same point on the H line, the relationship between A, B, and V (Fig. 3-10) makes sense. In this case AV and BV are parallel, because two parallel lines *meet* at infinity and V is their point of intersection. This statement is valid not only for a pair of lines but for *all* the lines (an infinite number of them) that converge in V. So we obtain (Fig. 3-11) an upside-down fan, illustrating the group of parallels vanishing at a particular point. If we have two vanishing points on the H line, two fans representing two groups of parallels will be defined (Fig. 3-12). We can have an infinite number of vanishing points on the H line, each associated with an infinite number of parallels.

We know from geometry that two parallel lines *intersect* at infinity and that two non-parallel lines intersect in one point. Let us select from Fig. 3-12 a few examples in order to understand the perspective meaning of different pairs of nonparallel lines. Figures 3-13a, b, and c each show two nonparallel lines and their intersection point, the first very remote, the second closer, the third even closer. Figure 3-13d shows two parallels, and Fig. 3-13e two divergent lines, both instances showing no intersection point. These last two cases baffle our eyes, because for a moment we cannot understand the contradiction between drawing and theory. These pairs of lines *must* intersect in any situation! They do intersect, and there is no contradiction, but in order to understand what happens we need an additional concept that is fundamental in perspective drawing.

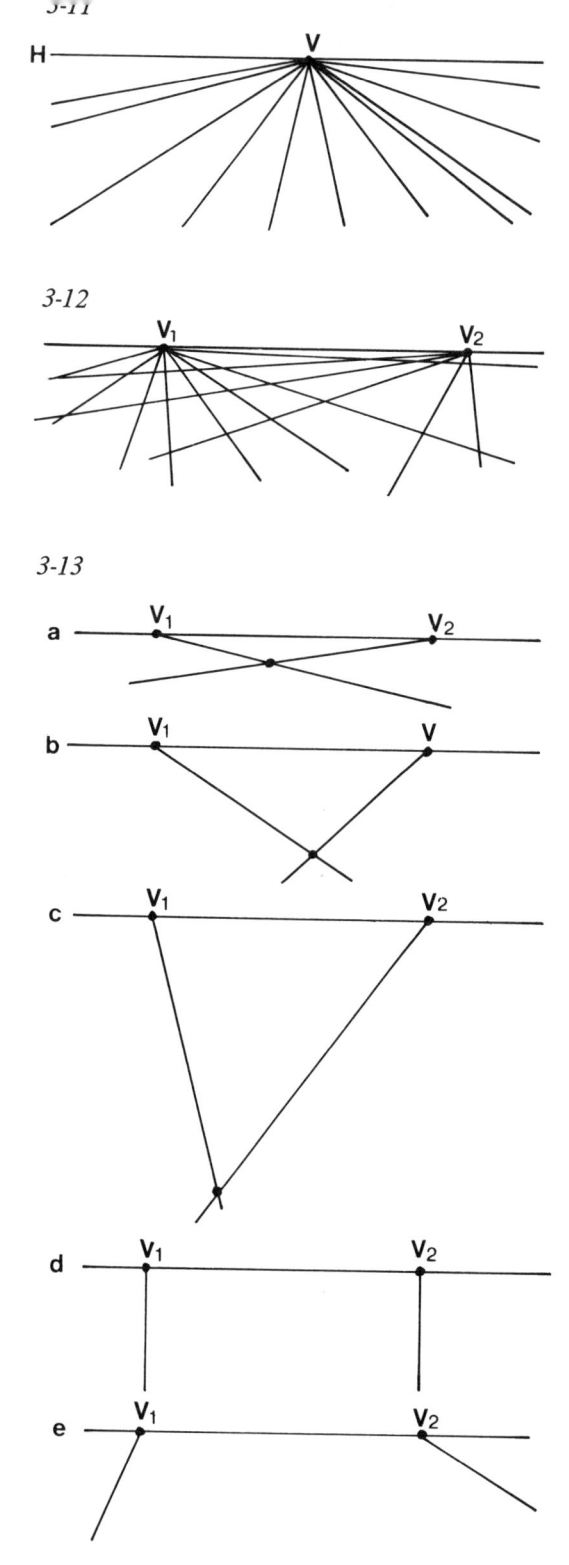

3-11

3-12

3-13

a

b

c

d

e

3-9

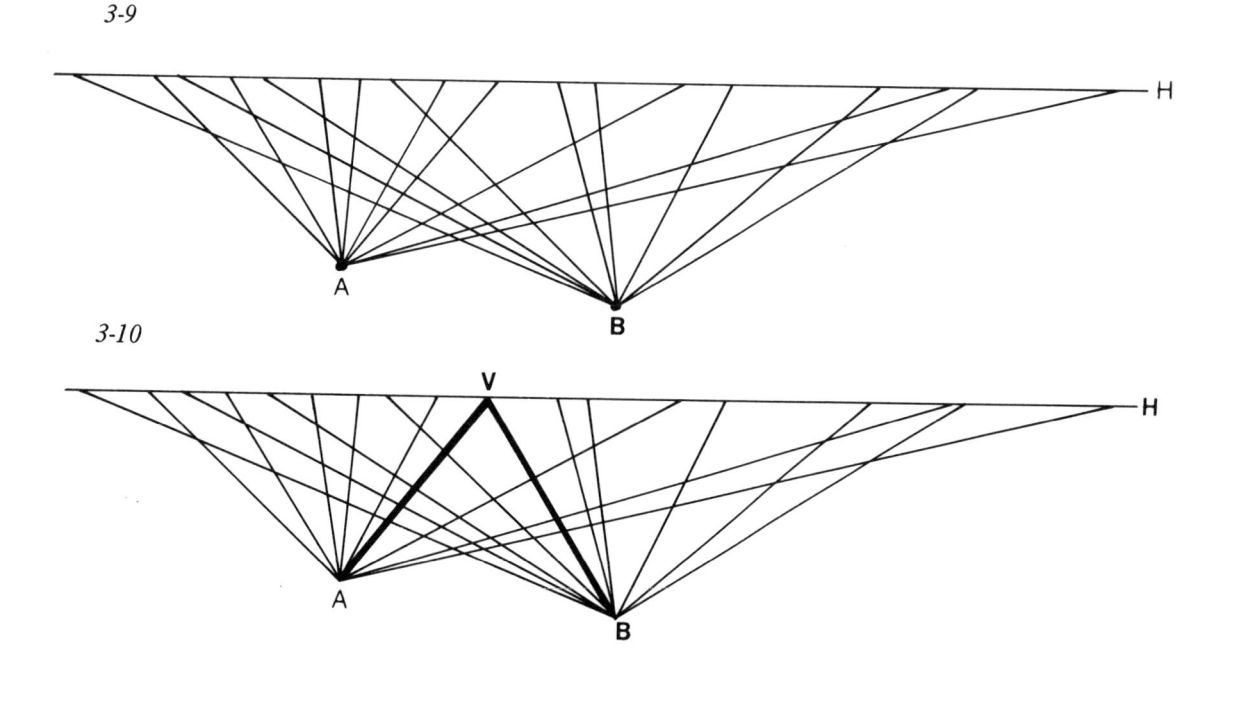

3-10

The Projection Plane Concept

The process of drawing involves a flat surface on which the drawing can be done. This flat surface, a plane (generally a piece of paper), will be the battleground for a considerable number of points, lines, constructions, measurements, and corrections that will result in the desired drawing. Now imagine how much all this work is simplified with a camera, which when focused on a number of objects can retain their perspective shapes and relations without any perspective drawing effort. Geometrically speaking, all cameras work in the way the eye works (Fig. 3-14). The lens of the camera (or eye) reverses the image, which is unreversed before reaching the lens. By interposing a transparent sheet of flat material between the eye and the object, we can easily draw on this sheet the precise contours of the object behind it (Fig. 3-15).

If you try such an experiment on a glass panel with a marker, you will realize that such a copy directly from nature requires you to use only one eye. Each eye records a slightly different image, without which perception of depth is impossible. So the first inference is that perspective, like photography, gives us a one-eye view, a two-dimensional record of our surroundings. Let us see in a sequence of diagrams how this projection plane works.

Figure 3-16 shows an observer looking toward the horizon. The eye of the observer and the horizon point toward which he looks define an infinite line. The parallel to this line on the ground and the eye line belong to a vertical plane *EyEB*, and this plane moves with the observer whenever he moves to the right, left, front, or back. Obviously, when the observer looks toward a different point *V* on the *H* line, the plane *EBV* is also vertical, but for the moment we will not analyze this plane further.

In Fig. 3-17 we introduce between the observer and the horizon line a vertical, transparent screen. Plane *EyEB* and the screen intersect, as any two nonparallel planes do, in a straight

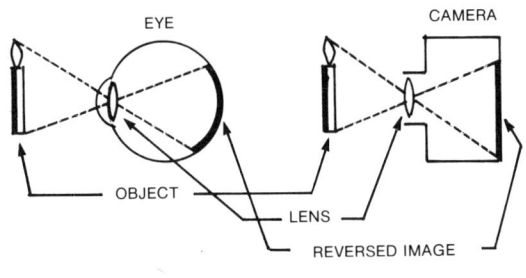

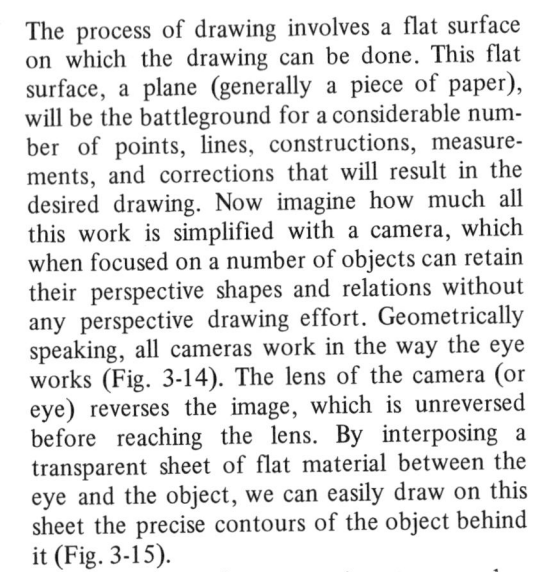

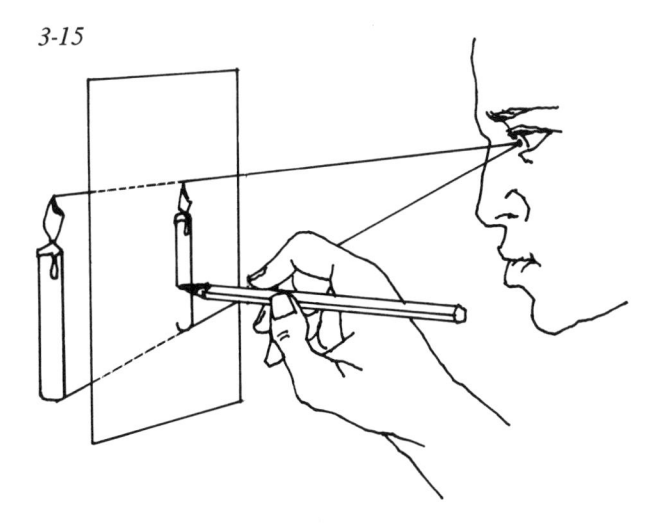

line; in this case, as both planes are vertical, the intersection is a vertical line. This vertical line is the one and only tool that can help us locate on the screen the points and lines we see behind it. This is because for every two intersecting planes we have an intersection line, and any line coming from an object to the eye must intersect the screen exactly where the intersection line of the two planes meet this object-eye line. Line *IG* represents the vertical intersection of the two planes, and the intersection of *EyE* with *IG* is *where we see the eye-point, on the horizon, on our projection plane.* Obviously, obtaining this point enables us to trace the

8-4. John Constable. Salisbury Cathedral from the Bishop's Garden. *(The Metropolitan Museum of Art. Bequest of Mary Stillman Harkness, 1950.)*

8-5. Canaletto. The Thames and City Seen from Richmond House. *(From Goodwood House by courtesy of the Trustees.)*

The majestic grandeur of Canaletto's London is conveyed by the contrast between the dominant height of St. Paul's Cathedral and the almost linear, horizontal expansion of the city. Like a photographer, Canaletto either is impressed by an image *or* is trying to find the most suitable position as observer in order to convey his feelings about the city. Perhaps a religious feeling generates the whole conception, because the cathedral, being the central element, seems to appear as the unique link between sky and earth, between God and man. While the cathedral is the focal point of the perspective, the Thames River and the foreground promenade, with major construction lines running toward definite vanishing points, underline the horizontal vastness of the city and its remoteness. Try to imagine the composition seen by an observer situated at the same distance but at the level of the cathedral dome. The whole effect just described would be lost and replaced, perhaps, by a totally different one.

Turner captures the image of the active Canal Grande in 8th century Venice. He, as the observer, situates himself on the water. He stands quite above the normal human height. An observer at a normal height would catch the townscape architecture but not its human energy. This energy is underlined by the closeness of the artist: a central point of view with steep, rapidly vanishing parallels, almost suggesting a central explosion point. Both artist and viewer become part of the scene and live the atmosphere of the moment. A large amount of detail transports us into the historical environment depicted.

111

8-7. *Salvador Dali.* The Temptation of St. Anthony *(1946).*
(Musées Royaux des Beaux-Arts de Belgique.)

8-8. *Eduardo de Chirico.* The Anxious Journey *(1913), oil on canvas, 29¼ X 42 inches. (Collection, The Museum of Modern Art, New York. Acquired through Lilli P. Bliss Bequest.)*

These examples only begin to show the place of perspective imagination in classical art. Artists remained faithful to realistic perspective until recently. While architectural rendering, being a precise mode of communication (let us say information), continues to be realistic, many twentieth-century art movements introduce new ideas generated by philosophical and psychological attitudes toward the phenomenon of life. Life is not only what we know, say some psychologists; beyond what is real, conscious, and palpable there is the world of dreams and the subconscious. For the artists of our time these theories are a challenge; they feel the *need* to depict the newly discovered world of the unknown, beyond physics and realism. Metaphysical and surrealist art have appeared in response to this need. Again perspective plays a fundamental role in artists' vision.

Salvador Dali, in his surrealistic *Temptation of St. Anthony* (Fig. 8-7) shows the saint facing his imagined temptations. In order to represent these figmentary evils as threatening and crushing, Dali utilizes an infinite horizontal plane of the earth, on which depth is stressed by the quick vanishing of the human size. Compared to the little human silhouette, the monstruous animals (entirely out of any real scale) are terribly gigantic, and their slanting legs indicate motion toward the saint.

Eduardo de Chirico's *Anxious Journey* (Fig. 8-8), like many of his other works, is the result of too many philosophical and literary influences to be properly analyzed here. However, in order to achieve a complex theatrical feeling, a "dream" realism, where objects happen to be together and become symbols of mysterious moods, de Chirico disregards realistic perspective, creating for each object another independent and invisible horizon line, with absurd vanishing lines.

8-9. M. C. Escher. Relativity. *(Escher Foundation, Haags Gemeentemusem—The Hague.)*

Finally, artists can be challenged, impressed, and influenced by scientific and mathematical concepts and, wishing to illustrate such concepts, arrive at new ideas substantially structured on new perspective combinations. M. C. Escher deals with relativity, infinity, and the curvature of space, besides many, many other concepts. In an elaborate perspective based on three vanishing points (Fig. 8-9) Escher suggests that the ideas of up, down, left, and right are dependent only on the context, that they are relative; if the observer concentrates on one of the staircases, then the two others can be defined in relation to it, and even so a staircase can be double-sided or lead upward or downward according to the standing position of the figures. All this is done with the help of an imaginative system of three vanishing points, situated at the three vertices of an equilateral triangle (much beyond the borders of the image), and at any time two points belong to the same plane while the third is spatial. In any relative position, this duality continues.

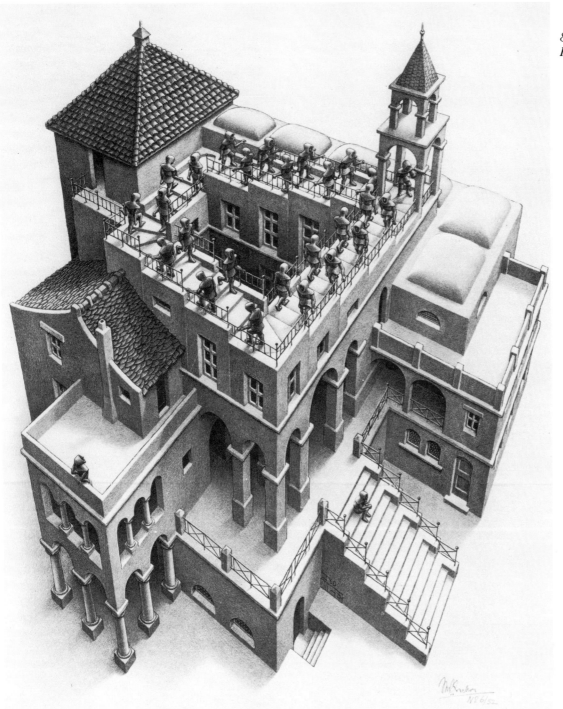

8-10. *M. C. Escher.* Ascending and Descending. *(Escher Foundation, Haags Gemeentemuseum—The Hague.)*

Escher elaborates the idea of infinity or endlessness in his work "Ascending and Descending" (Fig. 8-10), where monks moving in opposite directions continue their steps endlessly, even if the stair seems to be continuously ascending *or* descending. The artist uses a purely perspective illusion in order to obtain the illustration of his concept. This illusion can be easily explained if we follow its construction (Fig. 8-11). The normal descent of a stair-slope (we can eliminate the steps) in relation to a horizontal plane $ABCD$ (dashed line) will start from an upper level A', passing through B', C', and D' and arriving under A in A'', thus completing one flight. Instead, Escher continues the line $D'A''$ toward its spatial vanishing point Vs, until it intersects line $A'B'$ in S. The rest is elaboration. Escher also creates splendid images of curved space, a concept we will discuss in detail in the next chapter.

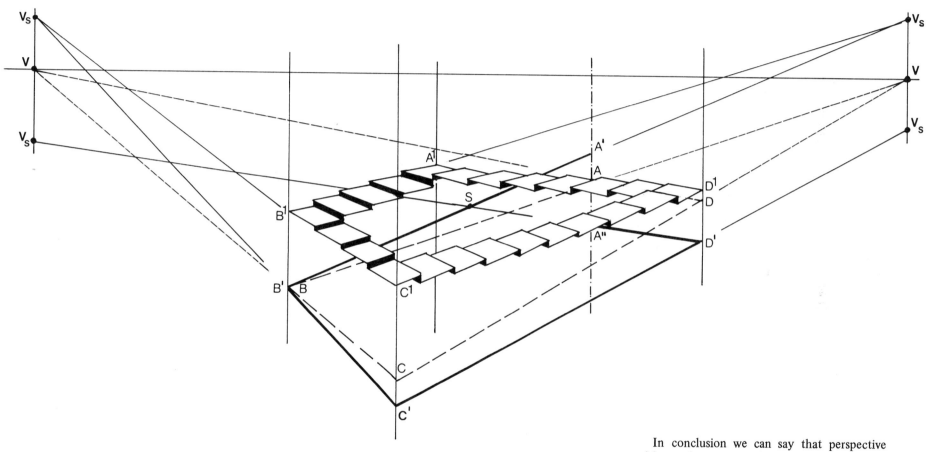

In conclusion we can say that perspective vision undergoes a continuous process of adjustment to the ideological determinants of creation. And before ending this chapter, we will give you another type of "exercise," a most difficult one and certainly the most rewarding one if you solve it: Find your own philosophy, your own idea about life, your own visual answer to universal problems. Of course, we have no answer for you!

9. SPHERICAL PERSPECTIVE

Both perspective drawing and photography suffer from undesirable distortions, which stem from our technical inability to render in two dimensions the complex perceptions of our eyes. One type of distortion, which has been corrected in photography but not in perspective drawing, is the missing sensation of depth. As we know, the three-dimensional perception of our environment is possible because the brain combines the two different images of the same view received by our two eyes and translates this combination of views into three-dimensional information. Each separate image is two-dimensional; unlike fish, birds, and other animals that have eyes located on the sides of the head, humans and the higher vertebrates, with forward-looking eyes, receive less of a visual field but a deeper understanding of space, a stereognosic vision (*stereo* means "solid" in Greek).

The process of receiving the two-dimensional images is shown in Fig. 9-1, in plan and perspective. This is what actually happens when we look at a cube alternately with the left and the right eye. However, if the images received look like the ones shown, it is very difficult to know whether we are looking at a cube or merely two walls. We need additional information,

which can be obtained either through observation of the object from various angles, or through the "definition" of the object (e.g., if the image shows the details of a building, we will infer that it is a cube). In general,

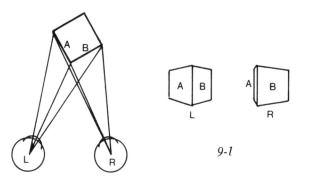

9-1

thought elaborates data with the help of stored, inherited, and preacquired information. This is why we can compensate for the missing third dimension in photography, painting, and perspective drawing with the "idea" of depth already stored in our visual memory. And for the same reason we have difficulty in understanding a spatially two-dimensional image that is unfamiliar or totally new.

In order to correct this problem, photography, imitating human vision, uses cameras with two objectives, obtains two stereoscopic images, and lets each eye perceive one of them through different technical devices. Perspective drawing does not necessarily have to deal with three-dimensional renderings, because ordinarily the subject deals with buildings with quite a number of details familiar to our memory. Only in very particular situations where unusual shapes lead to no visual associations might a stereoscopic rendering be desirable. But the process of making two perspective drawings from two slightly different points of view is so time consuming and unrewarding that the renderer will probably prefer to submit an additional perspective view of the object from an entirely different angle rather than a stereoscopic drawing.

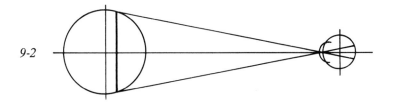

9-2

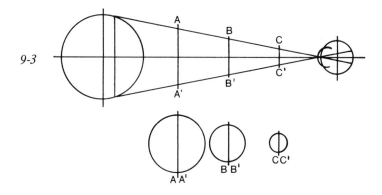

9-3

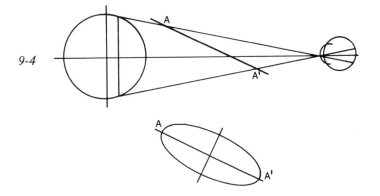

9-4

The second and much more important type of distortion derives from the basic principle of perspective construction itself. As we have seen, we construct a perspective image on the vertical projection plane situated between the observer and the subject. However, a single example will show that this system not only is theoretically wrong but also leads to considerable distortions. We mentioned in a previous chapter that the perspective image of a sphere is always a circle. This happens because no matter where the sphere is and what its diameter is, the eye will receive its image conically, as shown in Fig. 9-2. The cone of projection envelopes the sphere tangentially, has its apex in the eye lens, and forms an opposite cone that ends on the retina, creating the upside-down image of the tangential circle of the sphere. As long as we cut the cone with a plane perpendicular to the cone's axis, the section will be a circle (Fig. 9-3).

If we return now to our perspective vertical projection plane and place the sphere so that the line joining its center to the eye's lens is perpendicular to the projection plane, the projection cone will intersect it in a circle. But if we move the sphere laterally so that the connecting line is no longer perpendicular to the projection plane, the section of the cone will be slanting, an ellipse. But according to what we have already said, this is not possible in true perspective, where a sphere is always seen as a circle (Fig. 9-4).

Consequently we can extend this observation to any solid shape that becomes distorted whenever its projection is not perpendicularly sectioned by the vertical plane. Thus we can conclude that the image obtained on this plane is *not* a perspective image as we see it but a distorted *section* of the projection lines.

As we can see from Fig. 9-5, the smaller the angle of intersection between the projection lines and the projection plane, the more disturbing the distortion. We have come to the unpleasant realization that the only correct projection is the one for the single point that is connected with the eye by a line perpendicular to the projection plane! Of course, the distortions of objects comprised within a reduced visual field, although real, are so small that they can be neglected, and so for centuries it was possible to draw perspective renderings fairly accurately. However, the distortion becomes annoyingly noticeable when we deal with extensive lengths or heights of objects that approach the edges of the projection plane. In such cases we obtain floor tiles so elongated that they no longer give the image of squares as the central ones do, cubic objects that become elongated parallelepipeds, and rooftops so acute that they do not correctly represent the basic section of the building (Fig. 9-6). There are countless examples of such distortions, and in order to correct them we must return to the study of the eye.

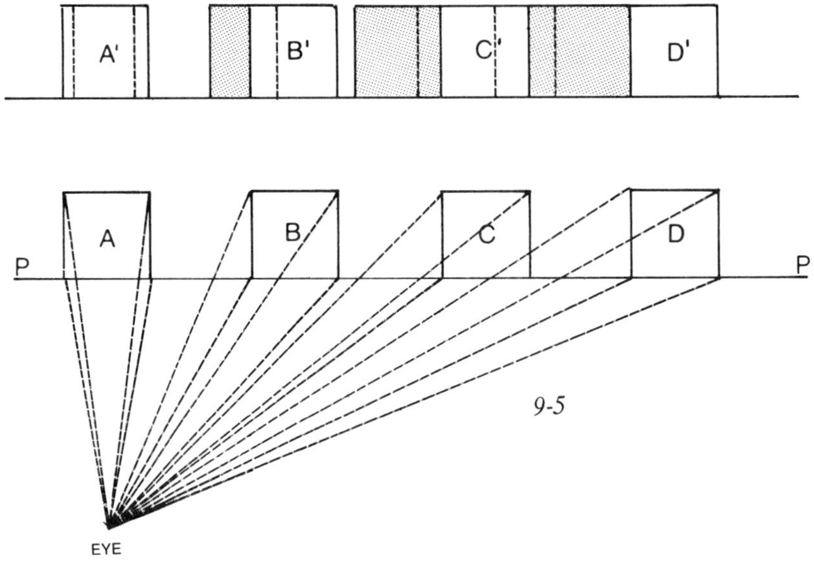

9-5

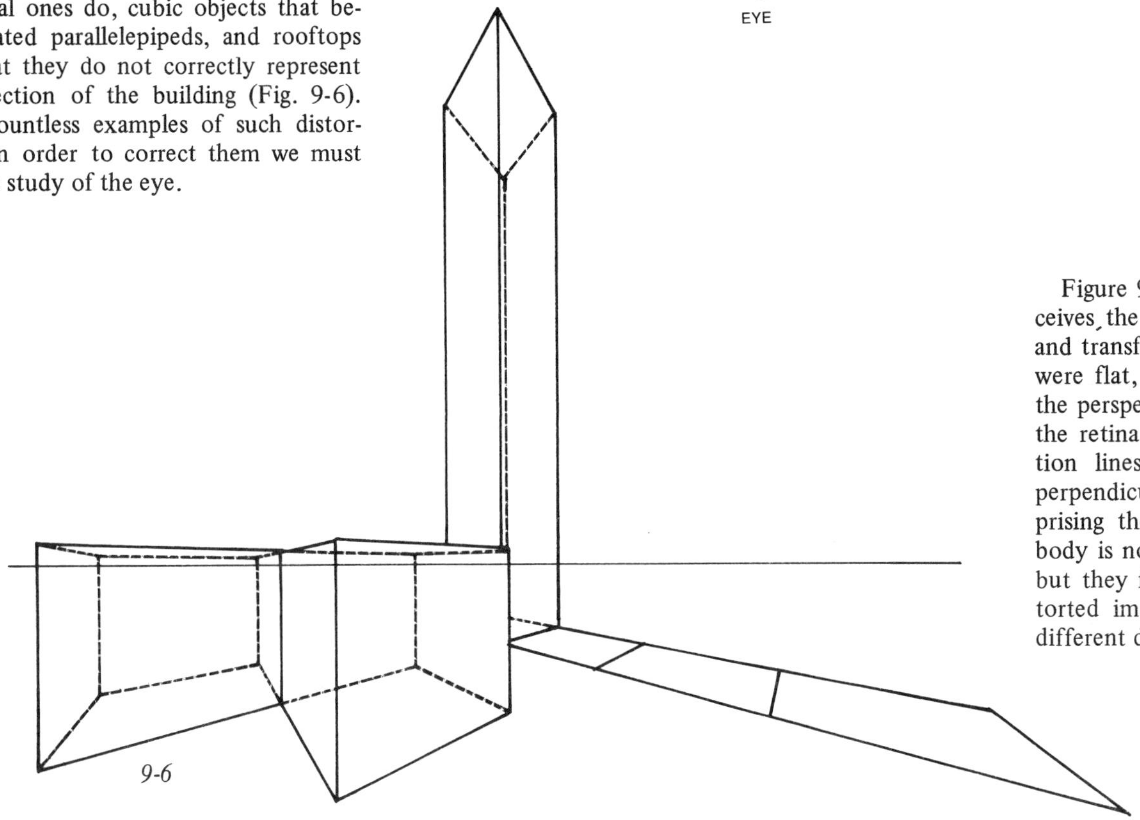

9-6

Figure 9-7 shows how the lens of the eye receives the images that make up the visual field and transfers them onto the retina. If the retina were flat, our image would be as distorted as the perspective images on paper. But as we see, the retina surface is spherical, and the projection lines coming from outside are almost perpendicular to it. The system of lenses comprising the cornea, the lens, and the vitreous body is not situated at the center of the sphere, but they function together to obtain an undistorted image and allow the eye to adjust to different distances to the objects seen.

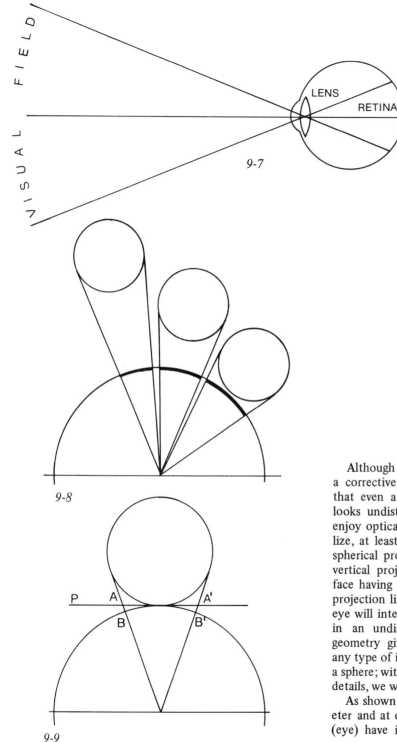

9-7

9-8

9-9

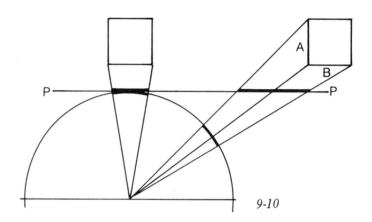

9-10

Although modern cameras are provided with a corrective system of lenses, which work so that even a photograph obtained on flat film looks undistorted, perspective drawing cannot enjoy optical corrective devices. But it can utilize, at least theoretically, a new concept; the spherical projection surface. If we replace the vertical projection plane with a spherical surface having its center in the eye, then all the projection lines coming from the objects to the eye will intersect the sphere radially and result in an undistorted image on it. Descriptive geometry gives us precise methods of finding any type of intersection of projection lines with a sphere; without going too much into technical details, we will analyze a few examples.

As shown in Fig. 9-8, spheres of equal diameter and at equal distances from the viewpoint (eye) have identical projections. More remote spheres have smaller projections but as their axes remain perpendicular to the projection sphere, their projection remains circular in any case.

If a projected sphere goes through the classical vertical projection plane and through the projection sphere (Fig. 9-9), we can compare and see that the spherical projection is slightly smaller than the plane one.

Figure 9-10 shows that spherical projection, unlike the flat-screen projection, will preserve undistorted, correct ratios of size of two identical objects (cubes in our case) at equal distances from the classical projection plane PP' but at unequal distances from the projection sphere. Compare the distorted projection of faces A and B on PP' with the correct projection on the sphere.

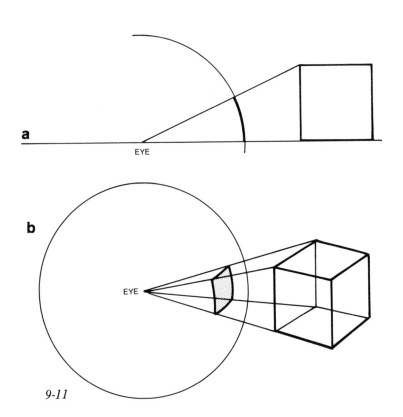

9-11

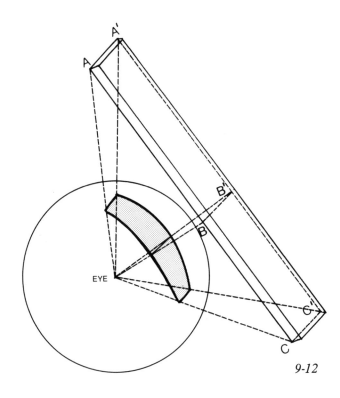

9-12

Figure 9-11a shows a lateral view of the projection of a cube and Fig. 9-11b a figurative image of the projection on the sphere. Note that *all straight lines in space become segments of circles in projection.*

An easily performed experiment will substantiate the preceding statement (Fig. 9-12). Take an ordinary 12-inch ruler and hold it in front of one of your eyes, about 5 inches away, so that its middle is more or less in front of the eye. Without moving your head, roll your eye up and down on the ruler. You will immediately realize that real perspective works in accordance with the statement above. The closest part of the ruler, *BB'*, has the largest projection, while the most remote, *AA'* and *CC'*, have the smallest. As every projection of a straight line on the sphere focuses at its center, it follows that the projection of a line will be an arc of a great circle of the sphere. This is because every straight line outside the sphere, together with its center, defines a plane that intersects the sphere in a great circle. Thus we see that spherical perspective might be called universal or integral perspective, because it gives a comprehensive, undistorted image of reality. Moreover, it integrates the perspective based on two vanishing points with that based on three vanishing points. The experiment in Fig. 9-12 can be repeated, with more striking results, when you are standing close to a multistory building (Fig. 9-13).

Spherical perspective shows us that our per-

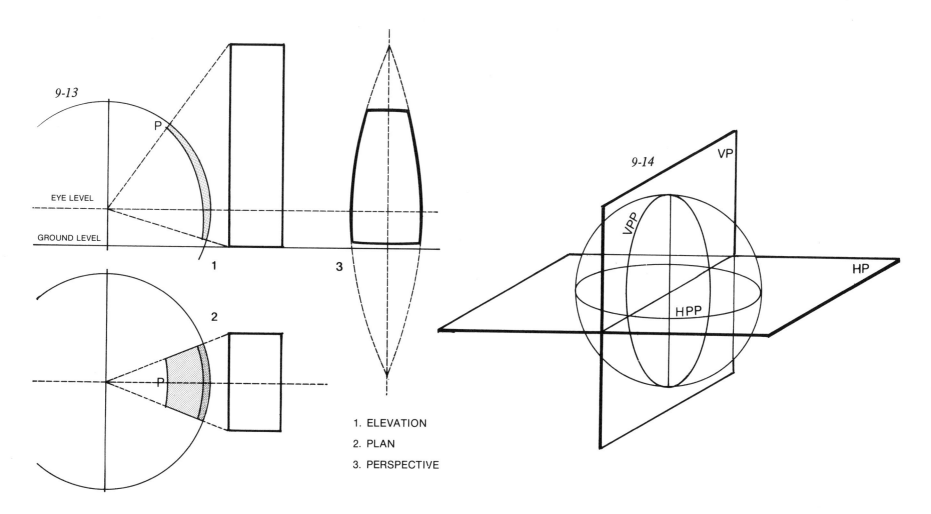

9-13

EYE LEVEL

GROUND LEVEL

1

2

3

9-14

VP

VPP

HP

HPP

1. ELEVATION

2. PLAN

3. PERSPECTIVE

ception of the environment is curved. We are generally not aware of this curvature, either because the objects we perceive are outlined by very small segments of curves, easily confounded with straight lines, or because the curvature belongs to a great circle of considerable radius and thus is not perceptible, or for another reason that we will analyze a little later. In any case, the more remote the object, the larger the radius of the projection sphere and thus the straighter the projected lines. We realize now that spherical perspective is the general answer for any perspective distortion, while plane projection is a particular case in which the projection sphere is (incorrectly) regarded as having an infinite radius.

Let us now examine how the eye works. We have seen that the eye level corresponds to the equator of the projection sphere. and we also know that this equator is the horizontal circle that appears to our eye as a straight line. We can also realize that the only vertical line that appears as a straight line is the one that crosses the equator perpendicularly through a point directly in front of the eye. Although these two projections are also great circles, an eye that looks straight forward without moving will perceive the point of intersection of these two perpendicular circles, but a horizontal motion of the eye within the horizontal plane or a vertical motion of the eye within the vertical plane will perceive the horizontal or vertical lines, respectively, as sections of these planes (Fig. 9-14).

This is all right in theory, because in reality even if we try to discipline our eye to move as described above, we find it difficult to do so. Actually, the eye, in its endeavor to grasp an image, makes numberless discrete jumps (called *saccades*) in all directions. It will be enough to give one example (Figs. 9-15 and 9-16) in order to understand the richness and variety of information accumulated by the retina and sent to the brain. Whenever there is a display of objects in front of our eyes, we *look* at the whole image, but we *see* only one detail at a time and then turn our attention to another point of interest. Each shift of attention determines a slight movement of the two eyes. In Fig. 9-15a, a pair of eyes looks at a prismatic building of square section. The eyes concentrate on the vertical intersection between the two visible planes (walls) of the building, *A*. In this case, as the projection lines go through the center of the eyes, their projection on the retina will represent the section line of the unique vertical plane that appears straight in projection. Edges *B* and *C*, being projected laterally, will appear curved, bent toward *A*, as seen in Fig. 9-15b.

But the next moment, the attention switches to edge *C* (Fig. 9-16a), and the eyes concentrate on this vertical, thus bringing it onto the unique central vertical plane. The result is that in this second situation edge *C* becomes a straight line (vertical), while edges *B* and *A* both bend toward *C*, as seen in Fig. 9-16b. Observe tall buildings from the street level. Fig. 9-15b is immediately confirmed. For Fig. 9-16b, an untrained eye might have difficulty in observing that edge *C* is actually straight, but if you cover edges *A* and *B* with your hand, *C* will appear straight. We can continue experimenting and observing the projections of a multitude of lines and curves in accordance with the motions of the eye, but this is a study beyond the interests of perspective drawing. So far, we cannot understand why eyes see this way, why so many different shapes of the same object are necessary in order to determine their geometry, but it becomes clear that the binocular vision is not only a device for depth appreciation but a far more complex tool of knowledge.

Let us now analyze some other advantages of spherical perspective. The horizon line is invariably situated on the sphere's equator, and

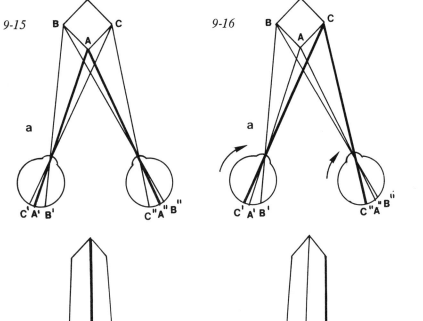

9-15

9-16

a

b

B A C

B A C

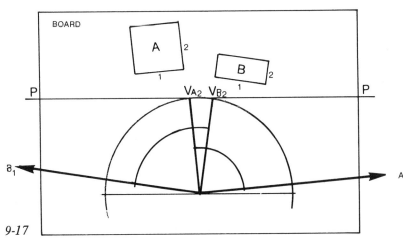

9-17

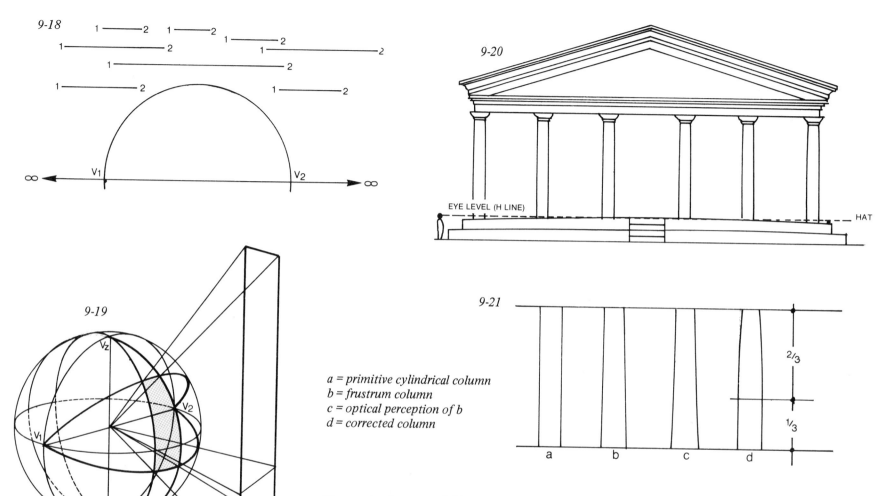

9-18

9-19

9-20

EYE LEVEL (H LINE)

HAT

9-21

a = primitive cylindrical column
b = frustrum column
c = optical perception of b
d = corrected column

2/3

1/3

a   b   c   d

the vanishing points of all lines parallel to the earth's surface are situated on this equator. Unlike the projection plane, which was stable, the whole sphere moves up and down according to the height of the eye (the sphere's center). The principle of determining the vanishing points remains the same, but now they remain at equal distances from the center (Fig. 9-17).

The great advantage of this unvarying distance is that we no longer have the problem of "inaccessible" vanishing points. Take, for instance, the group of horizontal lines that are also parallel to the classical projection plane. In classical perspective the vanishing points of this group of parallels are located at the right and left infinite points on the horizon line. In spherical perspective, the vanishing points are on the equator and divide it in half (Fig. 9-18). Thus all members of this group of parallels will be projected on the sphere as segments of the great circles rotating around the diameter determined by points V_1 and V_2 on the sphere (Fig. 9-19).

Similarly, all verticals will be projected as segments of the great circles rotating around the diameter determined by the two points V_Z (zenith) and V_N (nadir), like meridians through the poles.

An interesting example of a historical use of spherical correction is provided by ancient Greek architecture. When, some decades ago, a group of architects and archaeologists went to Greece to study the details and proportions of the old temples, they were unable to understand the secret of such marvelous proportions, until one of the members of the group left his hat on the left corner of one of the steps of the

Parthenon and found that he could no longer see it from the opposite corner (Fig. 9-20). This observation revealed that the steps curved upward slightly, toward the center of the building. The ancient Greek architects, who did not enjoy the knowledge of theoretical perspective but had a great sense of proportion and sophistication, felt the need to correct our perception of a straight line, which actually appears as part of the great circle bent downward as long as it is situated under the horizon line.

It is also known that the curvature of the Greek columns corrected the sensation that a simple conical column looks thinner toward its middle. This curvature is used only in the upper two-thirds of the column, perhaps because the architects wished to emphasize or exaggerate the impression of height given by these columns. In either case the Greek architects made empirically based corrections in perfect accord with spherical perspective (Fig. 9-21).

The curved perception of space haunted artists in the remote past. The fifteenth-century French painter Jean Fouquet, in his work *The Emperor at St. Denis* (Fig. 9-22), paints tiles and buildings in accordance with eye's curved perception. In *The Building of the Temple* (Fig. 9-23), Fouquet bends the verticals of the temple toward the exterior and, misinterpreting his own observations, leaves the building on the left undistorted.

9-23. Jean Fouquet. The Building of the Temple. *(Bibliotheque Nationale, Paris.)*

9-22. Jean Fouquet, The Emperor at St. Denis. *(Bibliotheque Nationale, Paris.)*

So far, so good. But after building the correct projection of a group of objects on the spherical projection screen, we meet the same unsolvable problem faced by makers of world maps, namely, the two-dimensional representation of a spherical image. For it is impossible to flatten a spherical surface. The only practical, but very rare and improbable, occasion to make a spherical projection occurs when we have to render a spatial image on the interior of a spherical cupola; and this only works for a viewer situated at the center of the sphere. However, spherical perspective is of considerable interest because it leads to better understanding of our perceptions and allows us to correct the distortions appearing in classical perspective.

In cases where distortions are really exaggerated and avoidable, we can employ a compromise method, by using cylindrical projection screens (either vertical or horizontal) when the height or width of our rendering goes beyond an acceptable visual field. This approach works because cylinders can be flattened and, if we measure the projection points on cylinders as arcs of circles from a point of reference or place a grid in degrees over the surface of the cylinder (in plan), we can easily locate the construction on a plane surface. The result of such a two-dimensional construction will have quite an odd appearance, as shown in Fig. 9-24; but if you enlarge the figure five times (either by photography or by redrawing) and curve the sheet so that you can form the half-cylinder considered in plan, then place your eye in the center of the cylinder at the level of the viewpoint, the curved lines will straighten and the perspective will be correct.

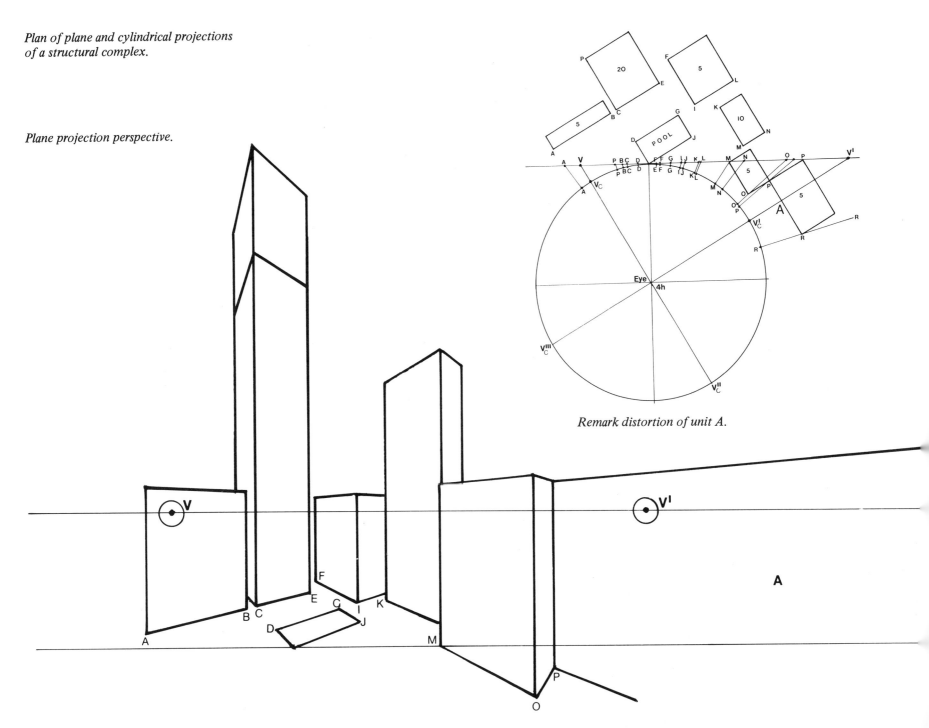

*Plan of plane and cylindrical projections
of a structural complex.*

Plane projection perspective.

POOL

Eye
4h

Remark distortion of unit A.

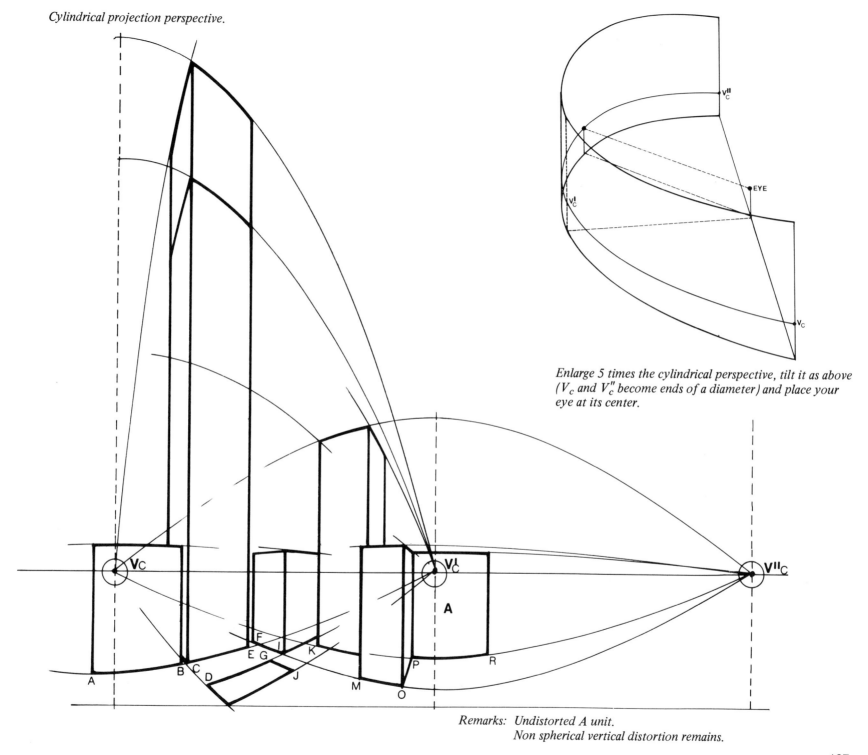

Cylindrical projection perspective.

Enlarge 5 times the cylindrical perspective, tilt it as above (V_c and V_c'' become ends of a diameter) and place your eye at its center.

Remarks: Undistorted A unit.
Non spherical vertical distortion remains.

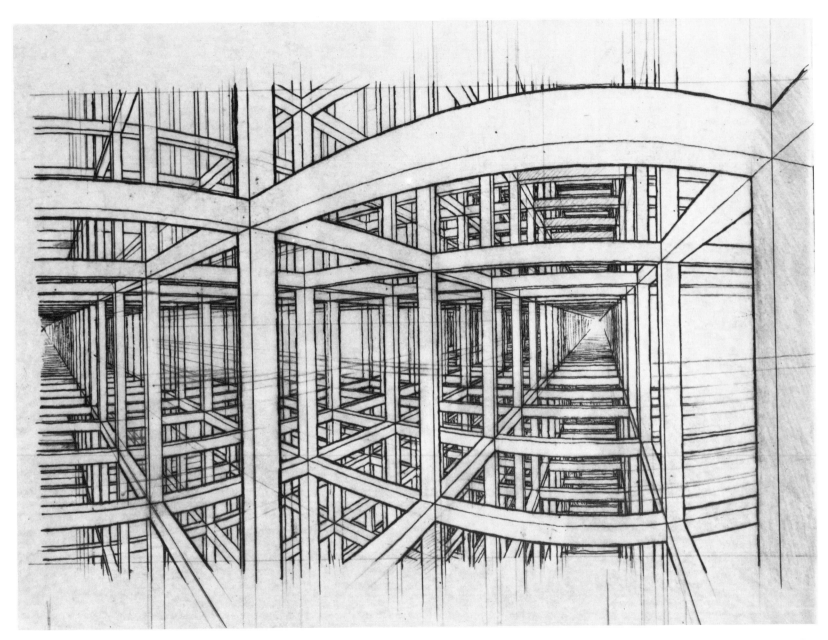

9-25. *M. C. Escher.* Study for House of Stairs. *(Escher Foundation, Haags Gemeentemuseum—The Hague.)*

M. C. Escher develops cylindrical perspective empirically, and for an entirely different purpose. He realizes that the eye records long, straight lines as curves and, situating himself on the axis of a cylinder, finds that the virtual line joining his eye to each point of the straight line intersects the cylinder in an ellipse. Unfolding the cylinder, he obtains studies like the one in Fig. 9-25, whose elaboration amounts to the finished lithograph *House of Stairs* (Fig. 9-26). The message transmitted through this unreal perspective has a purely intellectual origin and has a delightful impact, especially on people well trained in rational disciplines.

Cylindrical perspective has already been used for panoramic views. Because of its lack of distortion, it can be successfully utilized for completely circular murals representing landscapes surrounding the tower of a viewer, a group of buildings surrounding a plaza (seen from inside in all directions), the interior of an architectural space, or any other subject requiring a 360° view.

But in any of these cases, including plane projected perspective, only one point in space, the initial eye viewpoint of the observer, will permit a completely accurate, comprehensive, and undistorted analysis of the circular, partially circular, or plane perspective drawing. Again, we emphasize that perspective drawing is a unique experience of the observer.

9-26. M. C. Escher. House of Stairs. *(Escher Foundation, Haags Gemeentemuseum, The Hague.)*

10. ELEMENTARY NOTIONS OF SHADOWS

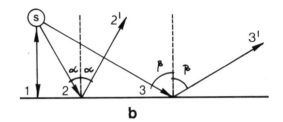

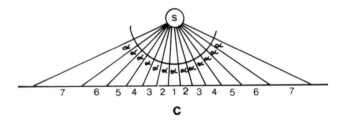

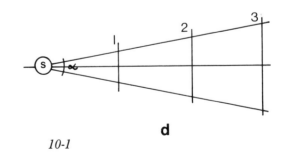

a

b

c

d

10-1

Behavior of Light

Before studying this chapter, please return to Chapter 2 and read *all* exercises and answers from Exercise 121 on. It is important that you do this even if you studied them before.

We may define the subject of this chapter as the study of the perception of the relationship between solids and light. We will need to understand the following points:

1. There is no optical perception without light.
2. The visible world is composed of solids. (In perspective drawing, what interests us about, say, a body of water is its geometric—solid—shape.) The pure line is a theoretical abstraction; even the thinnest thread is a three-dimensional solid.
3. Every solid is defined by a certain number of plane or curved surfaces.
4. Every plane or curved surface receives a certain amount of light (see Exercise 134 of Chapter 2), depending on its angle and distance from the source of light.
5. Our eyes perceive a particular plane or curved surface according to the amount of light the surface reflects directly toward them.
6. Our eyes perceive the difference between two surfaces by virtue of the *difference* between the numbers of photons reflected by each (intensity of light) and wavelength (color of light, to be discussed in the next chapter).

So far we have treated perspective drawing as a linear construction leading to a linear result. In order to obtain a more realistic rendering of our environment, we must make a mental adjustment and return from abstraction to matter, where a line is simply a border between two intensities of reflected light. With this way of visualizing, of understanding the relationship between light, matter, and eye, the line as such disappears and is entirely replaced by adjacent surfaces. However, the basic rules of shadow geometry will be studied in the abstract, linearly.

But first let us become acquainted with some general notions about light behavior. In Chapter 2 we studied the difference between light coming from a point source at close range and sunlight. The first radiates from a center in all directions, and the second, although it radiates in exactly the same way, is so remote that the beams reaching the earth are considered parallel. When the close-range light (Fig. 10-1a) falls on a surface, each beam makes a different angle with it. Experience shows that light is reflected by the surface at an angle equal to the angle between the line of incidence (of the coming beam) and a line perpendicular to the surface, called the *normal* (Fig. 10-1b). When the beam is perpendicular to the surface, the angle be-

130

tween the beam and the normal is zero, so the reflection will go straight back toward the source of light (case 1). Angles α and β (cases 2 and 3) will produce different symmetrical reflections. If we consider that for a given angle α between two beams (Fig. 10-1c) there is an equal number of photons, then the number of photons in case 1 covers a smaller area of the surface, the same number of photons is spread over a larger area of the surface in case 2, and an even larger one in case 3. This observation is in agreement with everyday experience: The light of a bulb close to a table is more powerful at the center and decreases as the distance between the bulb and the table increases. This statement is also verified if we move a screen closer to or farther from a bulb (Fig. 10-1d); the same number of photons (same angle α) is spread over a smaller or larger surface.

The sunlight beams make constant angles with a surface (Fig. 10-2a). Therefore the reflection preserves the same angle for every beam (Fig. 10-2b) on a flat surface. When the surface is broken (Fig. 10-2c), the reflections can be considerably scattered (minutely broken surfaces such as tracing paper or matte glass reflect light uniformly from their surfaces). For a curved surface (Fig. 10-2d) the most intense light reflection (I) is at the normal to the surface, and the reflection makes a larger angle according to the angle of incidence (II and III). When the beam touches the surface tangentially (at a 90° angle to the normal), the reflection will also make a 90° angle and the beam will continue on its path (180°). This is also the point (IV) where no more photons will touch the surface; it is the border between light and shade. For a particular surface (Fig. 10-3a), beam I will be reflected normally, beam II will mark the border between light and shade, and Point III will mark the strongest reflection. The surface between II and IV receives no light, so it will be shadowed. This explains why such surfaces (Fig. 10-3b) have stronger contrasts between light (III) and shadow (II–IV).

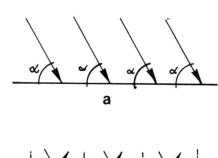

a

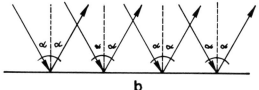

b

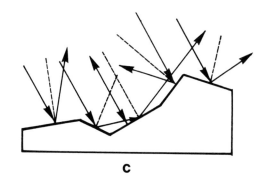

c

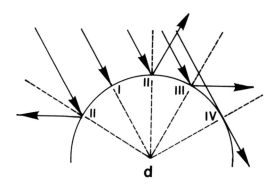

d

10-2

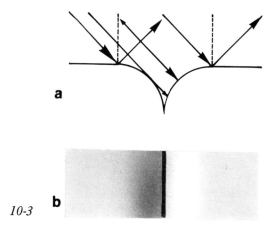

a

10-3   b

131

Another physical aspect of the relationship between light and surface is absorption. We have seen that a colored surface absorbs all photons of different wavelengths except the one reflected. Black absorbs all wavelengths, and white absorbs none. However, even white surfaces will absorb, if not a certain *quality* of wavelength, a certain *quantity* of photons (the photoelectric effect is due to absorption). Without this absorption the reflection of sunlight during the day would blind us. Even mirrors are absorbent, although their absorption is hardly observable with the naked eye.

Suppose a light beam coming from some source hits a surface *A* (Fig. 10-4). The beam will be reflected. Then another surface, *B*, will receive this reflection and reflect it again and again until, at the end of *B*, the beam will be reflected freely. In this process a number of photons have been absorbed. If we reduce only the distance between *A* and *B* (Fig. 10-5), there will be a greater number of reflections and therefore a greater number of incidences where light is absorbed. The final beam will be poorer in photons than in the previous situation. If we reduce the distance between *A* and *B* to a millimeter, the number of absorbing incidences increases so much that the resulting beam becomes almost invisible (Fig. 10-6). Moreover, the angle of incidence of a beam coming from the source determines the number of reflection and absorption points and therefore is a factor of change in intensity of the emerging beam (Fig. 10-7). Two beams of equal intensity but different angles, α and β, will result in stronger and weaker beams according to the number of reflection and absorption points.

These observations are necessary if we wish to draw in perspective a situation where two opposite walls determine a certain spatial relation to the source of light. It is clear that in such situations an observer situated at *O* will perceive shades diminishing in intensity from *A* to *A'* and from *B* to *B'*. Thus we have come to the next problem: the relationship between light behavior and the observer.

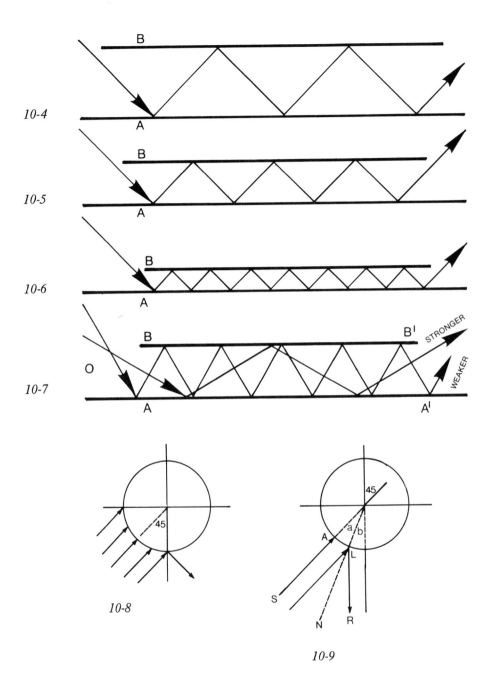

10-4

10-5

10-6

10-7

10-8

10-9

Basically, the eye receives two types of light:
1. Original light, from looking at the source.
2. Reflected light, from all other objects in the environment.

As perspective deals primarily with the environment, our main concern is reflected light (the number of photons reaching the retina) when we are dealing with light, shades, and shadows, and our main concern is combinations of wavelengths when we are dealing with color. For us to perceive the environment it is necessary that photons reach the retina; a beam of light itself is invisible! We cannot see a light beam in space devoid of matter, but when there is dust in space, each particle of dust is hit by light and reflects it, and some photons bombard our retina. We say that we see a painting on a wall, but what we actually see is the reflected light. The painting absorbs different numbers of photons according to the tone painted and absorbs certain wavelengths according to the chemical compound of a certain color. What remains is reflected in all directions, and some photons reach our retina. The most luminous surface of an object therefore is not the surface reflecting most photons but the one so positioned that the eye directly *receives* the most reflected photons.

A clear example of the subtlety of such determination is the relationship between light, architectural columns, and the eye. Suppose sunlight hits a column at an angle of 45° to the position of the observer (Fig. 10-8). It is obvious that the most powerful reflection is at point A. However, this beam of light is reflected directly back toward the source. We must find the beam that is reflected parallel to the observer's eye direction, and this is a problem in geometry (Fig. 10-9). The point appearing as most luminous is L, at the intersection of a light beam with the bisector NL. The reflection angle α is equal to β. As LR, the reflected beam, does not come directly into the eye and SA, the incident beam, determines the most luminous point, the whole area is the most powerfully illuminated one for the observer.

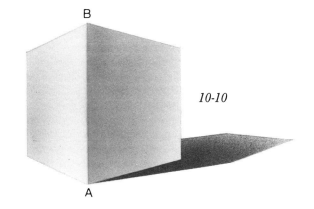

10-10

When we are facing a cube, our retina defines the two visible surfaces (Fig. 10-10) by adding contrast around the edge AB. The sunny side will look brighter near AB and the shaded one darker. The shadow will be stronger than the shade, which is supposed to receive some reflected counterlight from the ground. The same reflected light gives brilliance in the shaded "ceiling" areas (Fig. 10-11). The same amount of light, reflected from two walls to the eye, will have different intensity depending on the distance (Fig. 10-12). This is because the light reflected by wall B scatters more than the light from wall A does *and* because the atmosphere creates an optical cushion that grows thicker with the distance.

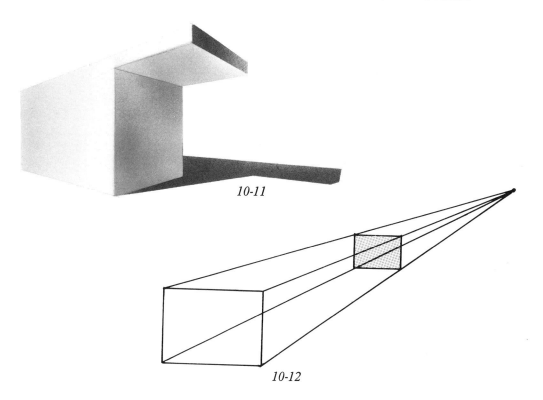

10-11

10-12

Short shadows are strong and clearly outlined (Fig. 10-13). Long or remote shadows tend to fade away. This happens because (1) the air cushion with its molecules, dust, and water vapor plays the role of a semitransparent curtain and (2) the light from the sky, reflected at a distance on and by the ground, counterbalances the darkness of the shadows. Small holes (like windows) have too little light to reflect from inside out. Moreover, the contrast with the surrounding walls tends to give the impression of blackness. It is generally not advisable to use complete black for shadows, because any dark gray will permit additional structures within the shadow. This will enhance the general transparent quality of your rendering. There are so many possibilities for incident beams, reflected beams, angles of surfaces, and eye positions that a complete study of the relationship between light, object, and eye is impossible. Much of one's understanding of such relations results from continual visualization, observation, and experience. Thus we will leave this topic and return to our basic subject, the geometric borders between light, shade, and shadow in perspective drawing.

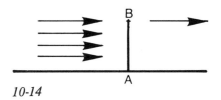

10-14

10-13

A Stick in the Sun

We studied elementary notions of shadow from a close-range source of light in Chapter 2, Exercises 142 through 156. Our main concern now will be the parallel beams of sunlight. As we know, light from the sun comes to us at an infinite number of angles, beginning and ending the day parallel to the plane of the earth (at sunrise and sunset). A vertical stick on the ground will therefore cast an infinity of shadows during a sunny day. At sunrise and sunset it will cast an infinitely long shadow (Fig. 10-14). How is this situation rendered in perspective? Suppose we face the sunrise and see the stick (Fig. 10-15). For convenience the sun is considered a point. It looks like a vanishing point, and it actually is one for all its parallel beams. As we know, parallel lines in space converge in perspective, so the stick's shadow will be seen as extending indefinitely toward us. This shadow is a line that never ends in theory, because the shadow of point *B* is parallel to the ground.

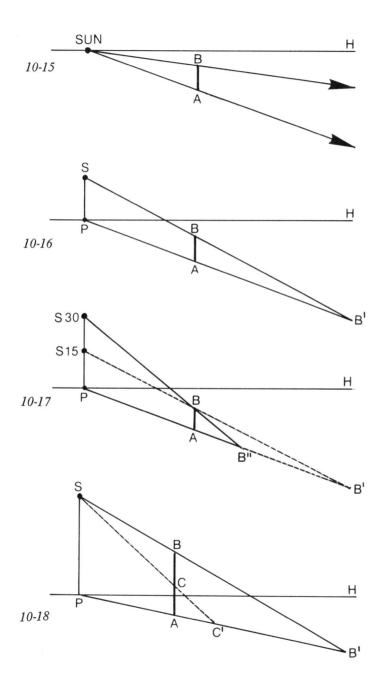

10-15

10-16

10-17

10-18

What happens an hour later when the sun has risen 15° above the horizon line, as in Fig. 10-16? (Of course, you know that the earth rotates 360° in 24 hours, thus traveling 15° per hour, but this specific angle is used only to make the example more concrete.) Three points determine a plane, and points A, B, and the sun determine a vertical plane. This plane intersects the earth in a line AP. Since the sun is theoretically regarded as situated at infinity and the horizon line is also a vanishing line for the plane of the earth, P is the sun's projection on the horizon line. Look carefully: The virtual line SP looks like something we have met before—a vertical horizon! Indeed, the sun is, as we said before, the vanishing point of all its parallel beams, so now, after rising in the sky, it has become a spatial vanishing point. The whole construction is reduced now to finding a slanted line BB' that joins the top of the stick AB to the ground. The sunbeam will touch B and continue traveling until it touches the line of intersection between the ground and the vertical plane PB'.

An hour later, the sun has risen another 15° above the horizon line, its beams making an angle of 30° with the flat surface of the earth. Using the same method, we find that nothing new happens except that the shadow will be shorter (Fig. 10-17), ending at B''.

We urge you to make your own observations, using a stick or a pencil and the sun, to verify our statements practically and to get used to the formation of shadows. Then take any kinds of squares, boxes, and other solids and see the variation of the light and shadow in different instances. You should also take note of a very simple but essential detail (Fig. 10-18). For a point C on the stick there will be a shadow point C' on the ground. *Inversely*, any point C' on the ground shadow corresponds to a point C on the stick. The idea of this inverse operation is quite simple, but you will see later that it is essential when we wish to establish the shaded side of some solids.

Let us now generalize the method of shadow construction. We will use three sticks instead of one and build their shadows separately by the same method (Fig. 10-19). Sticks AB, CD, and EF will have shadows AB', CD', and EF', respectively. Suppose we build beams BD and DF (dashed lines). The shadows will be B'D' and D'F' (also shown as dashed lines, on the ground).

The next step will be to consider, instead of lines, two walls ABCD and DCEF (Fig. 10-20). The shadows of these walls need no comments or explanations.

In conclusion, for the construction of a shadow cast by *any* point, we need two directions: that of the beam itself (or the beam's angle with the ground), and that of the ground line (the intersection of the vertical plane with the ground).

The sun continues to travel, reaching places beyond our projection plane or framework. So the sun is out of our reach, and its projection might go behind the observer. How can we build a shadow for such a situation? (We emphasize that most architectural perspectives are lighted this way.) In this case, we reason as follows: The sun is in constant motion; therefore its shadows are always changing. To find a very precise angle for a precise moment and a precise position of the observer is absurd (although such a shadow can be built with measurable perspective). Let us *choose* the most advantageous instance of the shadow at one particular point and then construct the complete shadow ensemble accordingly (Fig. 10-21). For the stick AB, we decide that we want a shadow AB'. This is enough for the purpose of obtaining our two construction points: All the shadows determined by the parallel beams of the sun for each point, stick, or other vertical line must run to a vanishing point V. Moreover, the actual sunbeams are all parallel to BB', so their spatial vanishing point V_S must be on the vertical horizon VV_S of the vertical plane ABB'. After establishing V and V_S, we can construct any and all shadows on the earth cast by any objects for a particular location of the sun. We can construct shadows for every point of an object if we have its projection on the earth so that the point and its projection form a vertical stick.

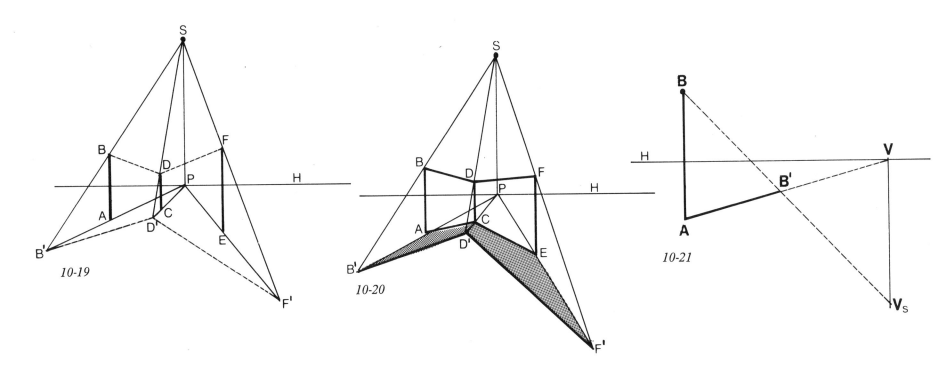

10-19

10-20

10-21

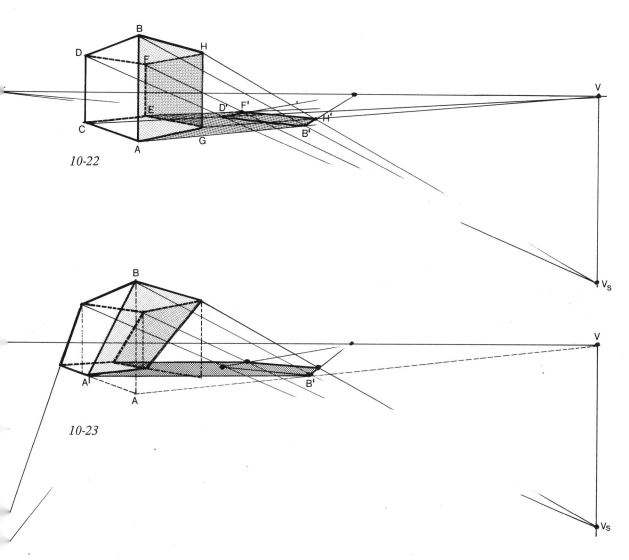

10-22

10-23

We are now ready to construct the shadow of a cube (Fig. 10-22). We use four identical steps for the four vertical edges (which we called sticks before) AB, CD, EF, and GH; any one of them can give us the desired initial construction of V and V_S. The shadows of the other three sticks need no further explanation. Points B', D', F', and H', the ends of the shadows AB', CD', EF', and GH', mark the shadow of the square $BDFH$.

It is interesting to observe two things:
1. The virtual shadow region (umbra) of the square $BDFH$ is a prism, which is sectioned by the earth. When we speak of the virtual shadow of the square $BDFH$, we are making an abstraction of the other sides of the cube. As the square is parallel to the earth, its shadow will be identical. This is not true when the shadow falls on a vertical or slanted surface, and we will study such situations later. In any case, recall

and develop your mental vision of prismatic shadow regions sectioned in various ways.
2. Shadow $AB'H'F'E$ shows us the corresponding separation $ABHFE$ between the side of the cube receiving light and the shaded one. In many simple cases it is easy to perceive this border directly, in others not. For the latter cases, we will return in some exercises from the cast shadow to the structure, in order to find the outline of the shades.

Let us now return to the cube, preserving unchanged the upper square $BDFH$, and translate the square $ACEG$ so that the cube becomes a slanted prism (Fig. 10-23). The shadow of square $BDFH$ remains the same, but this time the shadow of edge $A'B$ will be $A'B'$. We infer that for a slanted stick, the shadow of the upper point can be constructed with the help of a virtual vertical projection AB of that point (Fig. 10-24).

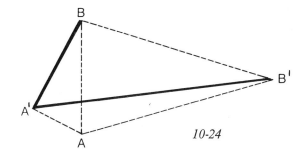

10-24

Consequently it becomes extremely simple to build the shadow of a pyramid (Fig. 10-25). As all four slanted edges of the pyramid meet at the apex, its vertical projection on the earth will determine its shadow. The pyramid's shadow is constructed in this way no matter what polygon forms its base. Therefore a pyramid whose base has an infinite number of sides (one definition of a circle) becomes a cone, and its shadow is found as in Fig. 10-26. As we do not have a precise edge to separate light from shade, we determine the shaded side of the cone by finding the tangents to the circle from point A'. What are the shaded side of the cone and its shadow when the cone stands upside down? In Fig. 10-27 we find first the section of the circle's shadow region on the ground, then trace the tangents T'_1A and T'_2A. Here we use the inverse operation mentioned earlier. We return points T'_1 and T'_2 on the cone's circle in T_1 and T_2 and obtain the borders between light and shade on the cone's circle.*

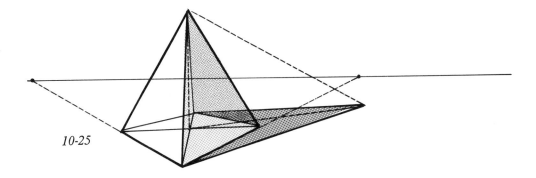

10-25

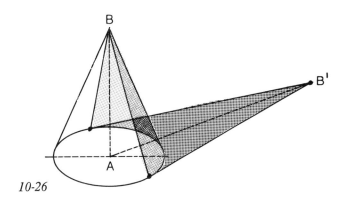

10-26

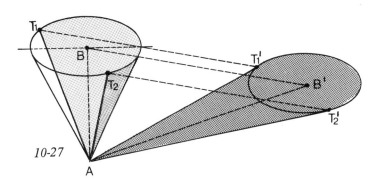

10-27

*You must be aware that such operations as finding the correct angles of the light beams, constructing the cylindrical shadow regions, drawing their section on the ground, and finding the tangents emerging from A can be done with great mathematical accuracy, but a good perspective drawing, rendering, or painting never needs such a scientific approach.

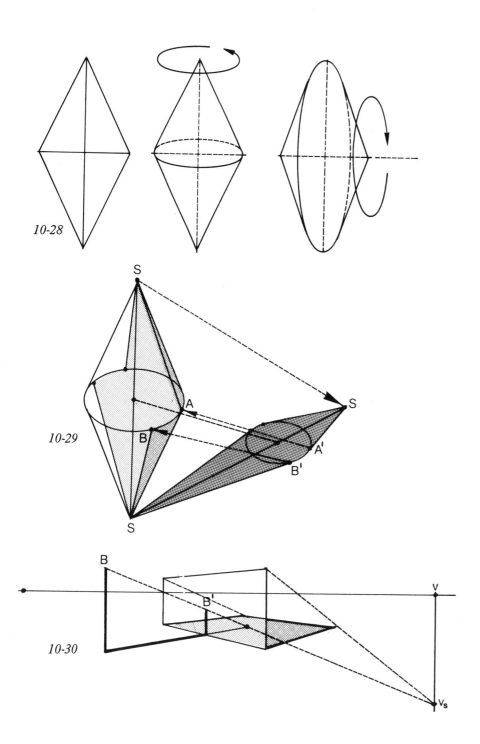

10-28

10-29

10-30

A solid resulting from the rotation of a diamond around one of its diagonals (Fig. 10-28) looks like two cones stemming in opposite directions from the same circular basis. It is useful to construct its shade and shadow in perspective in order to understand better the inverse operation (Fig. 10-29). After finding S'' and the shadow of the basic circle, we trace the tangents $S''A'$ and SB' (for simplicity we show only one side of the construction). The shaded side of the solid is obtained by using the inverse operation. We get A from A', and B from B'. You can see how the borderline between light and shade on the solid precisely determines the outline of the shadow: $S''A'$ determines a line like $S'A$, $A'B'$ a curve like AB, and $B'S$ on a line like BS. For more complex solids and for any case where other solids interfere with a shadow region, look for the *continuity of the outline*. It is there. But let us see what we mean by "continuity."

We will consider our stick lighted by the sun and casting its shadow on the ground (Fig. 10-30). If we place a vertical screen in the shadow region's path, the shadow will *continue* on the screen.

139

Translate the screen back and forth; the shadow will retain its full size, following the line BV_S (Fig. 10-31). If we bring the screen close (Fig. 10-32), the shadow will *continue* on the ground from point M to M'. In Figures 10-33 through 10-49 we study different instances. Line AB is always the stick, the screen(s) are PP', and so on; the continuity of the shadow is drawn with a heavy line. The inverse operation points are marked M and M'. You should study them carefully, because only a brief caption is supplied for each illustration and each instance occurs frequently in shadow constructions.

After studying these drawings, we conclude that constructing shades and shadows means using a few simple methods:

1. Intersection of one-point projection lines toward V and V_S.
2. Intersection of these lines (which actually define the solid shape of the shadow area or umbra) with the solids encountered.

Rotation of screen

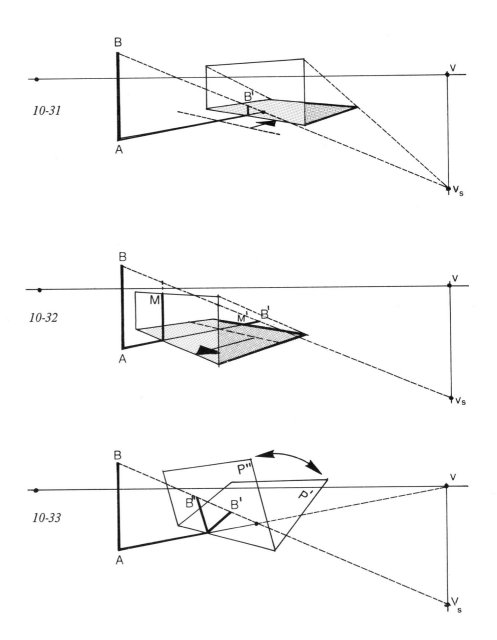

140

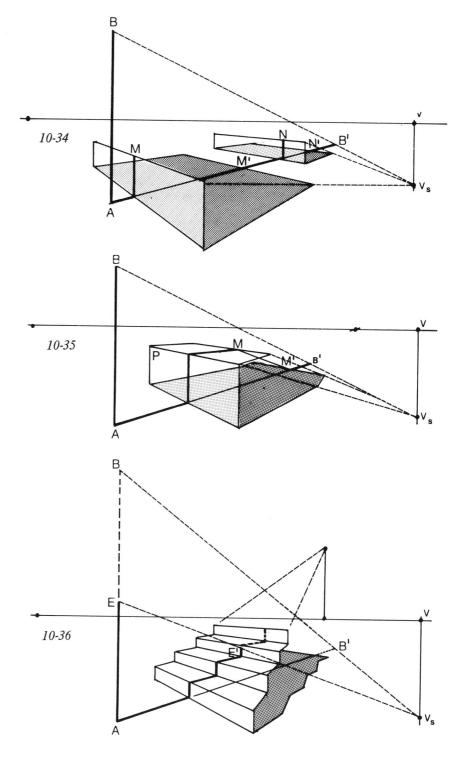

Two screens

10-34

Folded screen (step)

10-35

Steps

10-36

AB and cylinder. Vertical plane ABD cuts a rectangle in the cylinder.

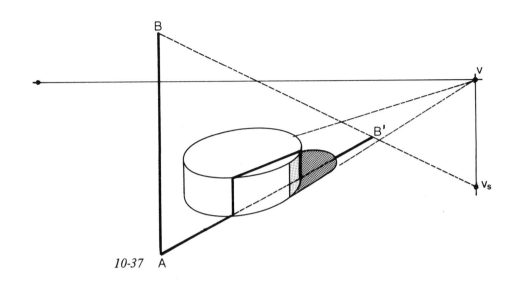

10-37

Slanted stick. Plane ABB′ cuts an ellipse in the cylinder.

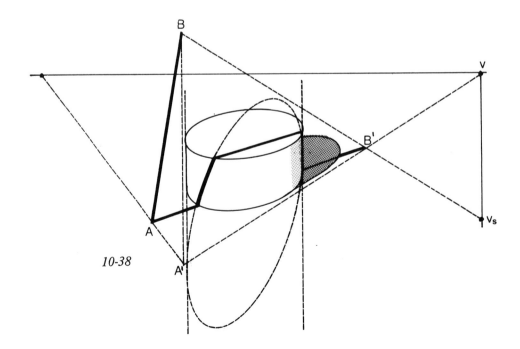

10-38

AB horizontal

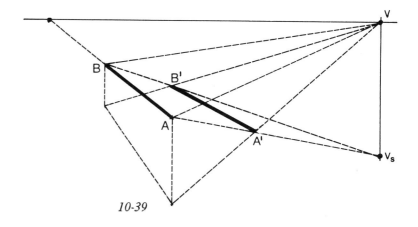

10-39

A'B' intercepted by screen

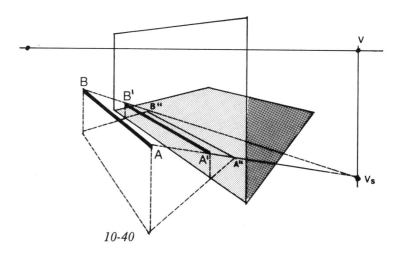

10-40

Incomplete interception of ABB' by the screen (find M from M' through inverse operation)

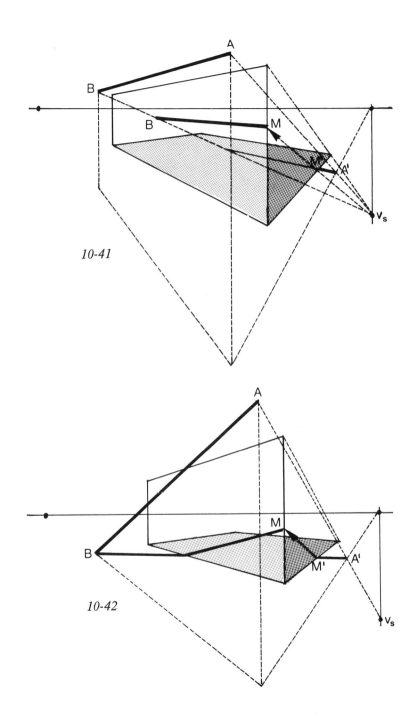

10-41

Incomplete interception of any *A'B' by the screen*

10-42

Wall and normal stick

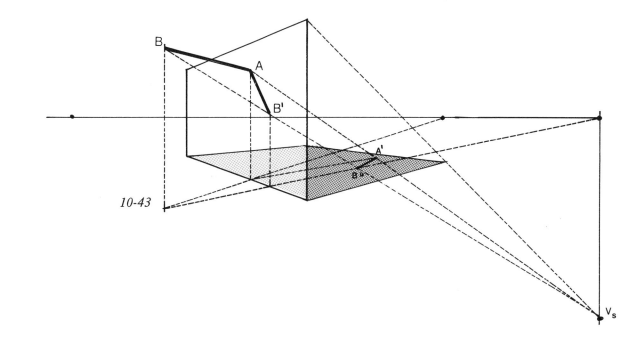

10-43

Wall and corniche

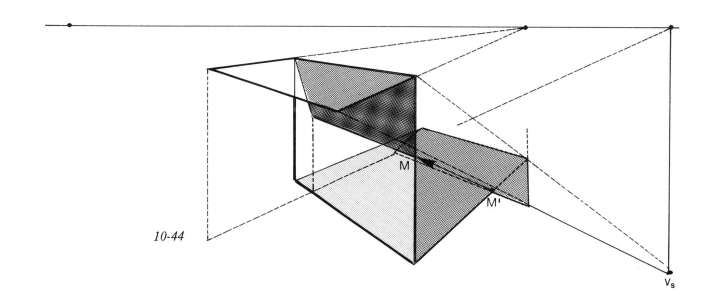

10-44

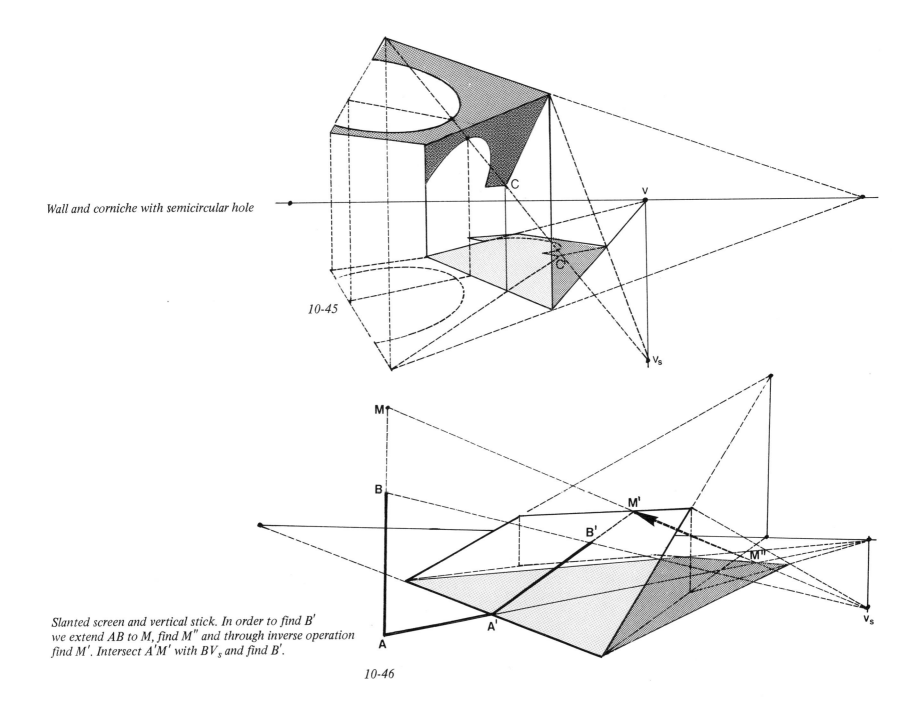

Wall and corniche with semicircular hole

10-45

Slanted screen and vertical stick. In order to find B'
we extend AB to M, find M" and through inverse operation
find M'. Intersect A'M' with BV_s and find B'.

10-46

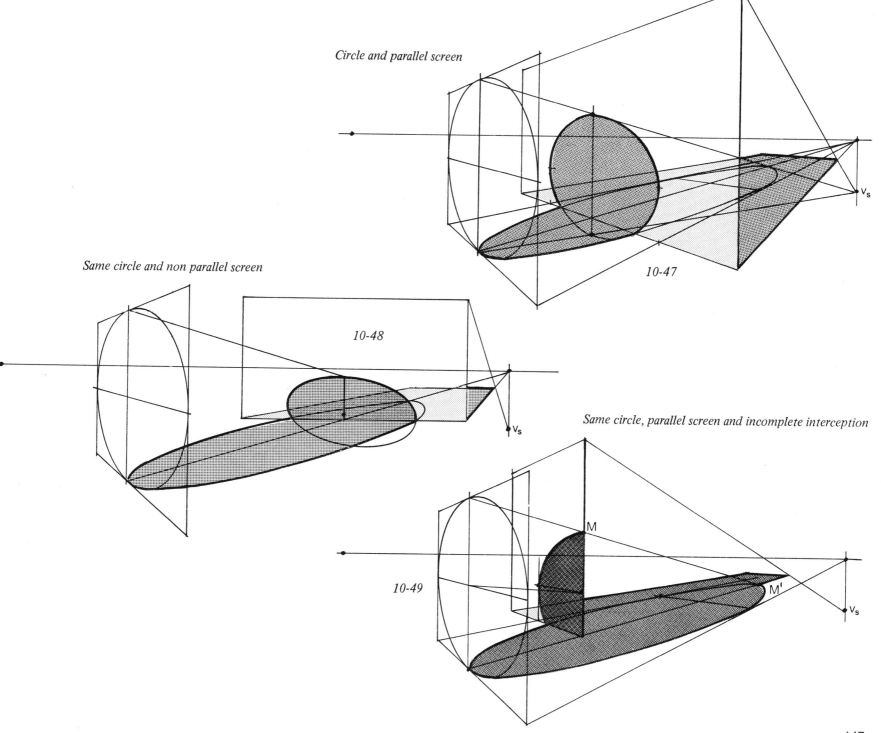

Circle and parallel screen

10-47

Same circle and non parallel screen

10-48

Vs

Same circle, parallel screen and incomplete interception

10-49

M

M'

Vs

147

In order to help your visualization, let us take the example of a sphere (Fig. 10-50). Sunlight will illuminate half of the sphere and leave in shade the other half, with a precisely circular border between. This circle is obviously perpendicular to the direction of the sun's beams. The shadow region is a cylinder. So instead of a sphere, we can use just a two-dimensional circle and obtain the same umbra and the same shadow. This great simplification is rarely possible, but the idea we get is that it is easier to construct a shadow by understanding first the outline of the border between light and shade. In most of our previous illustrations we used only one way of casting shadows, from a sun situated at the left and sending beams toward the right. We suggest that you make your own exercises, moving the sun to the right and casting shadows toward the left. You also have seen that our examples are only a few of the innumerable instances and situations possible. All our examples have been elementary; you can deepen your understanding of shadow construction with the help of more advanced perspective textbooks. Shadow construction should actually be studied first in orthogonal projection and only then in perspective. Many shadows can be constructed only with the help of descriptive geometry, and a full understanding of them goes far beyond their use in perspective. Artists dealing with portraits, for example, must understand the relationship between light and the intricate play of elementary solids hidden in the forms of the human face. But now we must see how color enters the picture.

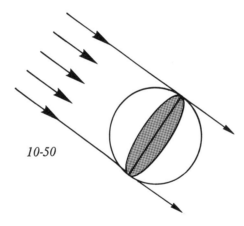

10-50

11. COLOR

You might wonder why we do not use actual color illustrations in this chapter. The major reasons are the following:

1. We are not discussing specific colors or color combinations but what happens with colors in perspective. All our statements are applicable to any color or color combination, even if the examples mention a particular color.
2. We do not wish to give you any particular color combinations.
3. This chapter is our last opportunity to exercise your ability to visualize. We urge you to make the necessary mental efforts and imagine every situation we describe, so that your mental screen will become colorful as well.

In a black and white photograph, the different tones of gray are not only the result of light, shade, and shadow; they are also the "translation" of colors into black and white. Very often architects, architectural renderers, designers, and artists are asked to produce a black and white perspective drawing. In accordance with the requirements for reproducing the drawing, we might have to obtain a clear black and white rendering with no grays or with a detailed spectrum of grays as in a photograph. In either case, we must understand how to treat color in black and white so that it will not compete or be confused with shade and shadow.

As a first step, you should study several black and white photographs and try to reconstitute the original colors mentally. This is rather easy with a portrait but less so with a townscape picture. In a portrait the fleshtone can have many original hues, the lips are more reddish than the fleshtone, and the hair color can be approximated from the contrast with the face and the age of the subject. We can also say that the eyes are either dark or light, but we cannot specify whether light eyes are blue or green. Even from these observations we can say that blue or green eyes (or, simply, *some blue or green tones*) will translate similarly into black and white. But in a townscape we must start with clues: a view on a sunny day will indicate blue for the sky, white for clouds, and green for grass and trees.

As we said in Chapter 10, it is not wise to use 100% (solid) black for shadows, which would not permit the rendering of details within the shadows. In Fig. 11-1 we offer one way of interpreting different tones of color in black and white and how shadow influences them.

The whole list of percents looks like a recipe, but it isn't. If you try to render it accurately you may even find that it doesn't work at all. You would then be compelled to dispense with the percentages and adjust the

tones according to your own intuition. Our example has another purpose: to show that, even when using crude, mechanically selected tones, we have enough variations to define solids in terms of color. Even a black cube will not be represented as a black spot but by two or three surfaces of rather dark tones. The solid (or face of a solid) adjacent to another solid (or face) must have another tone. Otherwise there is no definition. *The judgment that must be made for each pair of adjacent solids is whether the next surface is to be lighter or darker than the one already completed.*

The next step is the full color perspective rendering. Here we enter a realm where the possibilities are unlimited; for centuries artists have used the richest color harmonies imaginable. Even if we know that the sky is blue, the great number of tones and hues of blue utilized by artists proves that "the sky is not the limit," that an artist can use *any* conceivable color for the sky that will enhance and express a certain emotional goal of his artwork. We all have seen green people, red trees, yellow rivers, and so on in works of art. But before becoming so free in expression, we must make a careful study of the realistic relationship between color and perspective.

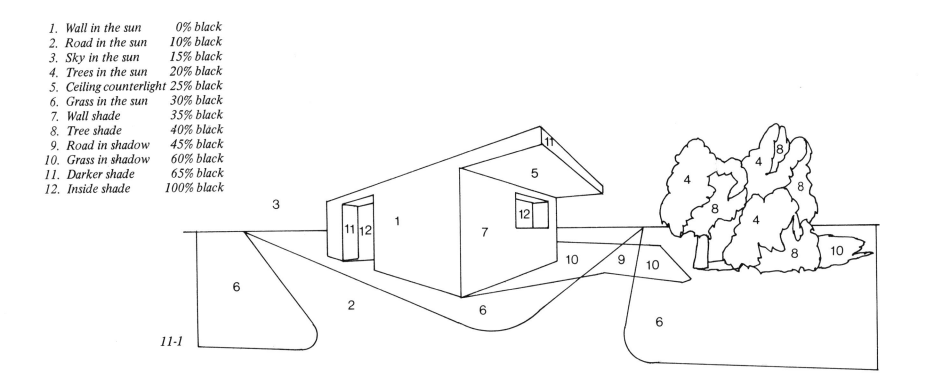

1. Wall in the sun — 0% black
2. Road in the sun — 10% black
3. Sky in the sun — 15% black
4. Trees in the sun — 20% black
5. Ceiling counterlight — 25% black
6. Grass in the sun — 30% black
7. Wall shade — 35% black
8. Tree shade — 40% black
9. Road in shadow — 45% black
10. Grass in shadow — 60% black
11. Darker shade — 65% black
12. Inside shade — 100% black

11-1

As usual, we start with the elementary, the simplest colored wall (Fig. 11-2). For a simple red panel receiving light in the constant direction indicated by the arrows, there are roughly five critical situations:

1. a frontal position, in which the red shows clearly (Fig. 11-2a);

2. a slanted position that sends reflections backward at the same angle as the source, which enhances the color red (Fig. 11-2b);

3. an angle that sends the red straight toward the eyes of the beholder (Fig. 11-2c) and thus shows the most brilliant tone;

4. an angle parallel to the light direction (Fig. 11-2d), so that the red becomes mute;

5. an angle entirely opposite to the light source (Fig. 11-2e) so that the red becomes a shade.

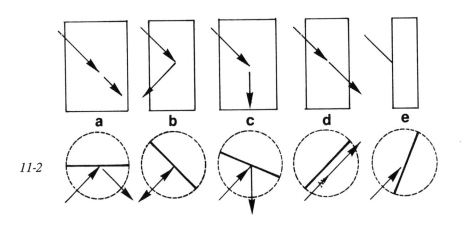

11-2

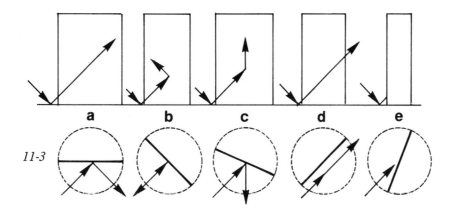

11-3

a b c d e

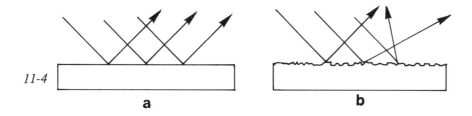

11-4

a b

Obviously, this description is valid for any color (not only red), and it reminds us very much of the descriptions for light and shade. The difference is that the presentation of this first situation is completely abstracted from reality. Such a panel, in space void of atmosphere and far from any material object able to reflect light, will become black for situation (e).

But in our earthly environment such a panel cannot possibly exist. At least two reflecting media will influence the processes of color change: the atmosphere and the ground. So let us consider the situations again. In Fig. 11-3a light from the source hits both panel and ground. The ground reflects most strongly on the lower part of the panel, adding intensity of light *plus* the color of the ground. The result is a change of hue at the lower part of the panel. Interference from the atmosphere is negligible. In Fig. 11-3b and c the result is similar to that in Fig. 11-3a. In Fig. 11-3d there is no direct light or ground reflection; atmospheric reflections begin to show. Finally, in Fig. 11-3e there is again no direct light or ground reflection, but there is strong influence of color from scattered reflected atmospheric blue. The result is a *change of hue in shade.*

Again we have overlooked something: the surface's structure. With very rare exceptions, walls, panels, ground, and any other objects found in our environment are *not* perfectly smooth. The enlarged section of most material surfaces is not as shown in Fig. 11-4a but as in Fig. 11-4b. The difference between smooth and rugged surfaces results in a difference in intensity from light to dark tones, more striking and concentrated for smooth surfaces, more diffuse for rugged ones. (A mirror or chromium steel wall will reflect the actual source of light in almost full intensity, a black velvet wall only a faint grayish tone.)

We have rotated the panel around a vertical axis. We can also repeat the observations while rotating it around a horizontal axis. You can do this yourself, and you will realize that in situation (e)—that is, in shade—the prevalent reflected light will be that from the ground. At this point, instead of rotating a two-dimensional panel we can study the whole process on a vertical cylinder (Fig. 11-5) and a horizontal one (Fig. 11-6). We can now combine the color principles of the two cylinders and understand how a sphere changes colors (Fig. 11-7).

Suppose that the source of light is the sun, the sphere is white, the sky is cloudless blue, and the ground is green grass. In this case, the tones of the lighted side of the sphere will vary from intense white (W) to a yellowish-gray darker tone (the sun is not as pure white as it was some billions of years ago), the atmospheric hue will be bluish, and the ground one greenish. Note that the spectrum colors from yellow to red, which suggest fire, are called *warm colors*, while colors beyond yellow to the other limit of the spectrum (including green, blue, violet, and indigo), being associated with ice, are *cold colors*. It follows in our spherical example that if the light is warm, the hue of the reflected light is cold. Painters have long used this observation and maintained this principle of warm–cold contrast between the light and the reflected light of a solid, often reversing the situation (cold light, warm reflected light). In many instances the reflected light side of the shade receives such strong reflected light from the atmosphere or from other surfaces that the resulting color is no longer the solid's hue but that of the reflective surface. This complex and various interplay creates "light within shade and shadow" in nature and, necessarily, in artwork. Knowing what amount and what kind of light comes from where enables us to combine the proper realistic tones and hues of a colored surface.

Let us now ask the last and most important question. Suppose we have two panels of identical color that look, in perspective, as if their

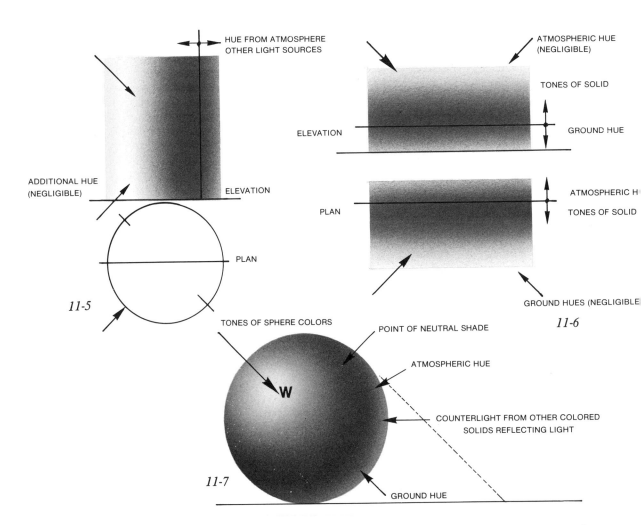

dimensions are also the same (Fig. 11-8). If the distance of the panels from the observer is impossible to detect, how can color give a clue about their relative distance? In other words, how can color enhance the perspective sensation of depth? The answer is twofold:

1. Suppose scattered reflected light from a surface S sends a number of photons onto a measuring screen (Fig. 11-9). If we enlarge the distance between S and the screen, only some of the photons reach it. The tone of color therefore loses intensity.
2. The blanket of atmosphere, with gaseous

molecules, dust, and microscopic drops of water, influences the color as the thickness of the blanket increases. This sort of transparent or translucent wall between eye and remote objects produces various types of intermediate reflections of the light source beams. Clear atmosphere reflects bluish, dust yellowish or reddish, water drops (fog, etc.) grayish green. The result combines with the dimly reflected colors of remote surfaces to create unlimited variations of hues and sometimes completely different tones of color. In other words, close surfaces have intense contrasts, remote ones more blended, more pastel-like colors.

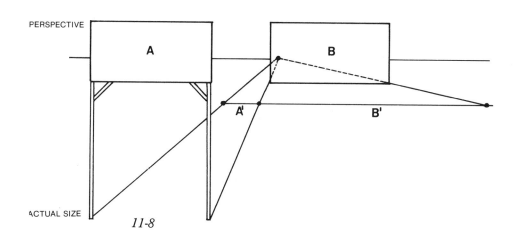

PERSPECTIVE

A

B

A'

B'

ACTUAL SIZE

11-8

Only after mastering the principles studied so far can we take liberties in order to add more drama to a perspective rendering. We saw in Chapter 8 that the mood of a perspective drawing results from certain choices of distance, vanishing points, and so on. But color does increase, sometimes considerably, the impact of our message.

Solids can be rendered bolder and more powerful by increasing the contrast between light and shade and by making the reflected light hue more brilliant. A whole composition looks peaceful when color contrast is rather weak. Depth can be enhanced by coloring the closest objects in bold, powerfully contrasting tones and grading rapidly toward dim, quiet colors as the horizon is approached. These techniques have become so sophisticated during the history of art that painters have learned to express feelings and ideas by eliminating the formal and figurative support of color. This process of abstraction has been reflected in many styles, but their analysis does not fall within the scope of this book.

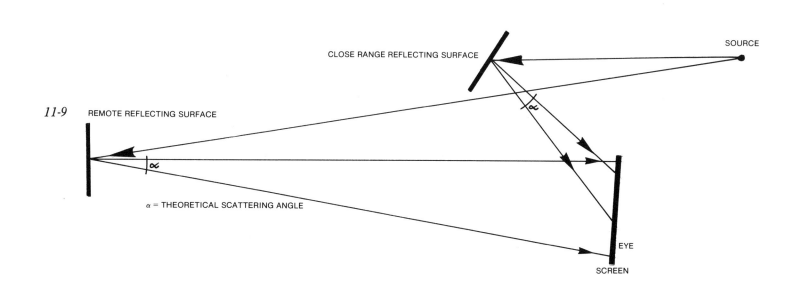

11-9

SOURCE

CLOSE RANGE REFLECTING SURFACE

REMOTE REFLECTING SURFACE

α = THEORETICAL SCATTERING ANGLE

EYE

SCREEN

ANSWERS TO CHAPTER 2

When you consult the answers to the exercises you have done in Chapter 2, you may encounter any of three circumstances:

1.   Your drawing is very much like the drawing given in the answers. This means that you have successfully solved the problem.

2.   Your drawing differs quite a lot from the one shown. In this case you have to understand whether your vision is different or you have made a mistake. There are no two imaginations able to visualize identically, and it is not impossible that your vision is even more interesting than the one in the answers. However, if you have made a mistake, try to understand why *it happened, whether it happened on your mental screen or when you translated your image onto paper.*

3.   Your drawing is altogether wrong. In this case, reverse the whole process: Memorize our drawing and try to see it on your mental screen and work on it in order to compare your wrong results with the correct solution. This is not an ideal way of improving, but it is better than skipping an exercise. You should return several times at different intervals to the wrong exercises until the problem can be very clearly seen and traced on paper. There is no reason at all to be discouraged, because some of the problems are really difficult to visualize and solve and most of them are reviewed completely in the actual course in perspective drawing beginning with Chapter 3.

1.

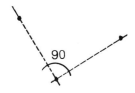

2. There is no difficulty in imagining a V of 45°. However, when you trace it on paper in order to obtain a closer approximation, it is advisable first to trace two perpendiculars and then to cut the 90° angle in two.

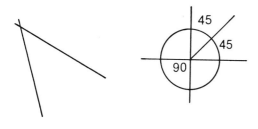

3. There are three possibilities: all four points on one line (a), three points on one line (b), or no three points on a line (c). There are three, five, and six connecting lines, respectively.

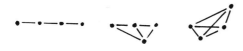

4. The problem is to interpret a flat, frontal drawing in depth, to accustom your mind to elaborate a two-dimensional image into a three-dimensional one. This very simple drawing gives us a multitude of interpretations in perspective. It looks like the abstraction of a road vanishing at the horizon, like the double wake of a boat on the sea after the boat has disappeared beyond the horizon, like two *parallel* pipes, or whatever else you can imagine.

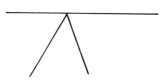

5. There are two ways to interpret the variations. The first is that the distance between the two arms varies because it represents actual larger or smaller widths of the image in perspective. For instance, if this drawing represents a road, then (a) might represent a narrow path, (b) a street, (c) a two-way avenue, (d) a highway. In a perspective drawing, the size is precisely defined by the size of buildings, cars, and human figures. The second interpretation is that it is the height of your eye that changes. In (a) you are looking at the road from the roof of a multistory building, in (b) from the second or third floor of a house, in (c) you are walking on the road, and in (d) you are lying on it. Do not forget that the two interpretations might be combined.

6. Two or three lines intersecting in the same point on the horizon line (a) are parallel. All parallels in the plane or in space vanish in one and only one point. This will be demonstrated in Chapter 3. In the case of the W (b), we have two vanishing points, so the two roads are not parallel.

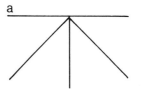

7. Among the inexhaustible number of possibilities, (a) is very common and represents a typical crossroad; (b) represents another pair of nonparallel roads, which intersect somewhere behind our visual field. What the three figures have in common is the fact that they represent two roads vanishing at two different points on the horizon line; hence the roads are not *parallel*. Incredible as it seems, the two roads in Fig. 2-7c intersect somewhere behind the eyes of the observer. This is one of the many strange distortions you will encounter in perspective drawing.

8. Two or more straight lines intersecting in the same point cannot intersect again. As the intersection point is on the horizon line, no matter how the two V's dangle, all lines are parallel.

9. The statement is not complete. If you look at the drawings you will see that two parallel lines can be in different planes, not necessarily only on the earth. According to where we place the dotted lines, they can be the upper edge of a wall (a), the steps of a staircase (b), the upper surfaces of solids (c), and an infinity of other shapes.

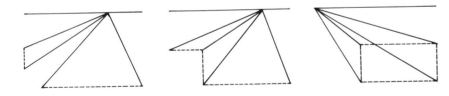

10. Drawing (a) doesn't give us precise information about the relationship between the pole and the earth. Drawings (b) and (c) show us that the pole can be thought of either as mounted on the edge of the road or as on top of a wall. Only a more complete perspective drawing will tell us where the pole is situated.

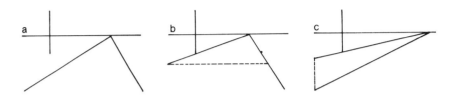

11. The last two edges must be parallel to the lower two, the segments of the upside-down V. Being parallel, they must vanish at the same vanishing point on the horizon line, so in our particular case (c) we will have to build a normal V above the horizon line. Once you have obtained the two V's from the first square, the following squares require no measuring because you already have the necessary elements to build them within their limits.

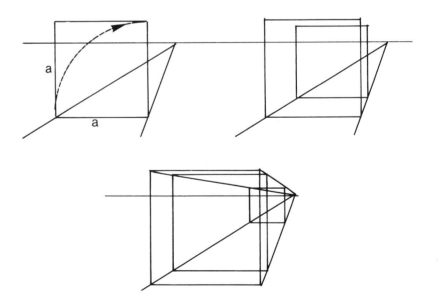

12.

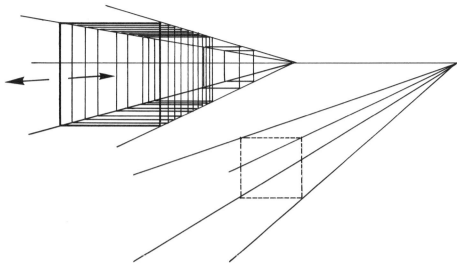

13.

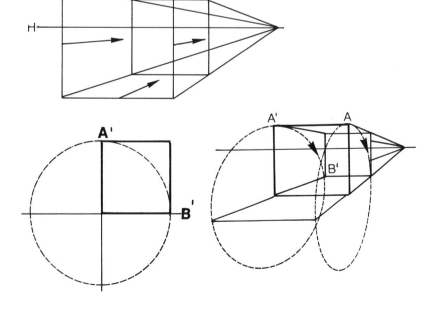

14. We know that the intersection of two planes is a straight line. In our case, the vertical square belongs to a borderless vertical plane, and the intersection of this plane with the earth is the infinite extension of the lower edge of the square, which is parallel to the horizon line.

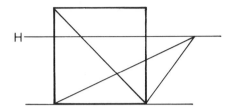

15. In all likelihood, this problem was not easy to solve. Here, the rotation method will give you the first understanding of how to find vanishing lines above and below the horizon lines, which is very useful when you have to draw inclined planes, staircases, hills, roads climbing slopes, and many other lines which do not belong to the earth plane or to a vertical frontal plane. When the square is in the frontal plane, the two vertical edges of the square, being parallel, meet above, at infinity. If we rotate them back 90° (a), they will intersect on the horizon line, forming our old upside-down V. If the rotation stops at only 80° (b), the intersection will occur above the horizon line at a point directly above the 90° intersection point. No matter where we stop the rotation, the intersection point will be vertically above the intersection point on the horizon line. Therefore, for all rotations of a plane, the intersection of a specific group of parallel lines is situated on a vertical line defined by the point of intersection with the horizon line. As this also holds for planes rotated beneath the earth, we see that *all* the vanishing points of the group of parallels are located on a vertical line. Consequently the vanishing line of each specific plane resulting from a rotation will be determined by the specific intersection point and will be parallel to the horizon line. Later we will deal with planes that are not determined by the rotation of a plane that intersects the earth in a line parallel to the horizon line. However, this manipulation of the planes is so important that we ask you to make as many variations as possible and become very familiar with the rotations before proceeding to the following exercises.

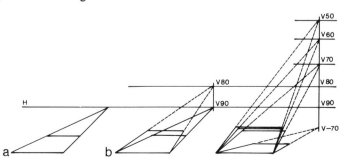

16. The next square (we chose to draw one at the right) has the large frontal edge *a* equal to the same edge of our initial square. This determines the point *p* from which we have to build a parallel to the edge *ee'*, and we know that this parallel vanishes at the same point on the horizon line at which the other two vanishing edges intersect. It will be enough then to extend the smaller frontal edge of our square in order to complete the new one.

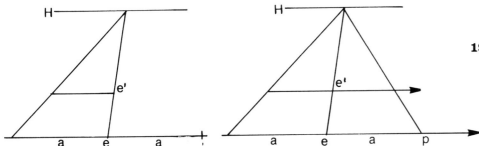

17. All frontal squares will be comprised between the two frontal and undistorted edges of the initial square. We can repeat the length of the frontal edge indefinitely to the right and left and join these points to the vanishing point.

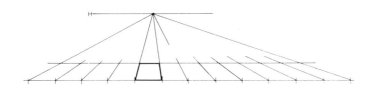

18. Looking at the frontal diagram (a), you can see that the two diagonals are also parallels, so in perspective (b) they must intersect in another point on the horizon line. All diagonals of the same direction will intersect in this point.

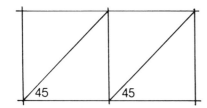

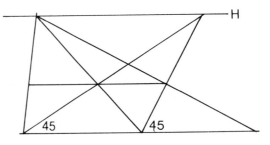

19. For an explanation see the previous answer.

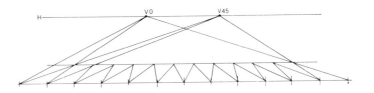

20. Both the diagonals of a square form a 45° angle with the frontal edge of the square (a). Thus their vanishing lines are symmetric about the perpendicular line (vertical) of the square (b). The conclusion is that the two vanishing points of the diagonals must be at equal distances from the vanishing point of the square's edges.

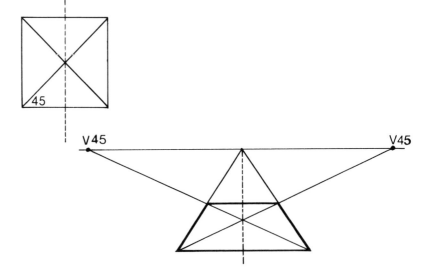

21. The two diagonals give you the center of the square. Trace a horizontal line through this center and a vanishing line parallel to the other two edges, and you have solved the problem.

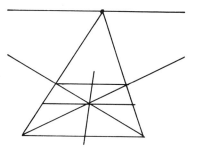

23. You know how to divide a square in four. In the chessboard case, you obtain the first four squares in the way you did before, then take one of the four squares and divide it again into four, and repeat the operation once more with the resulting square. The smallest square will be one-eighth of the large square, so you have a chessboard unit. Don't forget: first the diagonals, then the horizontals, then the vanishing parallels. The upper part of the drawing is not complete. Please complete it!

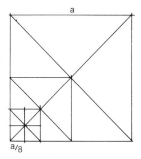

22. The diagonal emerging from *A* will intersect *OB* in *C*, and the diagonal emerging from *B* will intersect *OA* in *D*. From the initial two squares *AEXY* and *XYFB*, regarded as quarters of the proposed larger square (we need two additional ones), we obtain the half-diagonals *AX* and *BX* of the large square. The two smaller squares obtained, *DEWX* and *WXCF*, are actually equal to the first frontal squares.

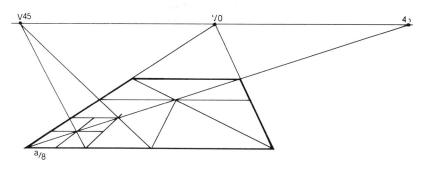

24. The diamond's edge is $a\sqrt{2}$. The perspective distortion can sometimes be considerable.

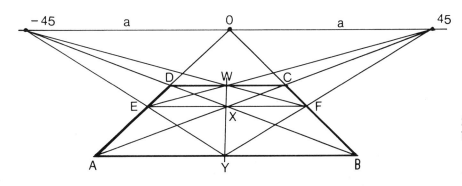

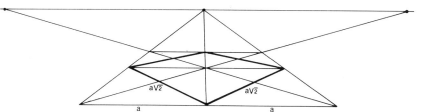

25. The vertical wall is not a square, because its width is $a\sqrt{2}$ and its height (the height of the cube) is only a.

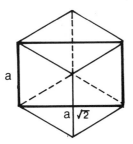

26. You can divide the frontal (horizontal) edge into three without distortion. As you can see in (a), as long as we are talking about squares, all their diagonals in one direction are parallels and thus must go to the same vanishing point. So in (b), you establish the vanishing point O of AB and then from the points C and D trace the diagonals CO and DO. These two diagonals give you the points E and F, which divide the edge BG in three. By tracing parallels to the H line through E and F and then tracing vanishing lines from C and D to P (CP and DP), you have divided the large square into nine smaller ones.

27. In order to divide a square into a number of equal smaller squares, the total number of possible squares must be the square (n^2) of the number of equal divisions (n) of a single edge. For instance, you can divide the edge in two so you will have four smaller squares (2^2), in three so you get nine squares (3^2), in five so you get 25 squares (5^2), and so on. You cannot decide to divide the large square into *any* number of equal smaller squares without taking this very simple law into account. But to divide the square into n smaller squares, you can use the methods described in the previous exercise, first dividing the frontal edge into $\sqrt{n}$ segments and then tracing the necessary diagonals.

28. If you have decided to build the new square on diagonal CB, for instance, then the new square will have two parallel edges (one of them is the diagonal CB), and the two other edges EC and FB will be parallel to AD, the opposite diagonal. So first find the vanishing points V_1 and V_2 of the two initial diagonals, and then trace CV_1 and BV_1, perspective parallels to diagonal AB. You can see that AB is a half-diagonal of the new square, so if you continue AB to the left until it intersects CV_1 in E, you have obtained EC, which is an edge of the new square. If you trace EV_2 parallel to CB, the point F will give you the complete square. You should realize that in this particular case the vanishing points of the diagonals of the first square become vanishing points for the new square's edges and the vanishing point of the two edges of the first square becomes the vanishing point of the new square's diagonal, while the other diagonal remains parallel to the H line. The previous sentence may sound terribly odd, but once you understand it, the whole truth is very simple and obvious.

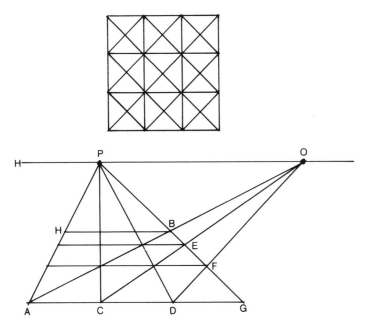

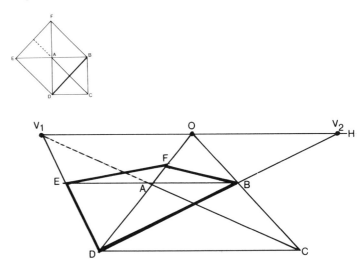

29. Look carefully at the illustration and see how all the diagonals in one direction are unbroken and how, using only V_1, V_2, and O, you can go on building as many squares as necessary.

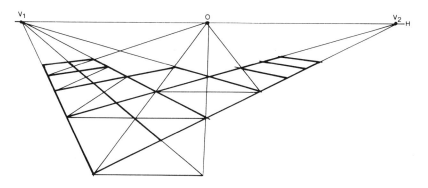

30. Suppose you want to divide square *ABCD* into nine equal squares. You can do this if you have the initial frontal square *ECFD*. Then you divide *DF* into three, obtaining $DM = MN = NF$. If you join *M* and *N* to *O*, the intersection of *MO* and *NO* with *DC* will give you M' and N'', which are the divisions of *DC* into three equal segments DM', $M''N''$, and $N'C$. (They look unequal because of perspective distortion.) *MO* and *NO* divide *BC* as well into BM'', $M''N''$, and $N''C$, so by tracing V_1M', V_1N', and then V_2M'' and V_2N'', you have divided the square into nine.

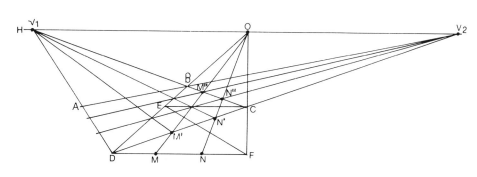

31. The initial square *ABCD* helps you add the adjacent square *BEDF*. Its diagonals give you the middle of this new square so that $DM = DF/2$. In this case *CM* is equal to $CD + DM$ or $CD \times 1.5$.

It is interesting to remark that the vanishing points of the diagonals of this rectangle, *AM* and *CN*, will be different from those of the square's diagonals. Obtaining them will give you facility in building more than one additional rectangle of the same proportion.

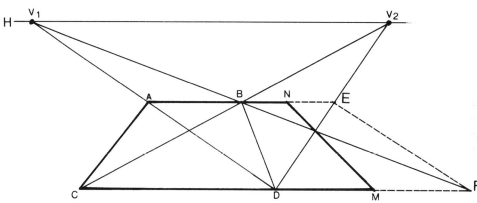

32. It is enough to calculate the value of *na* and add it to the horizontal edge of the initial square.

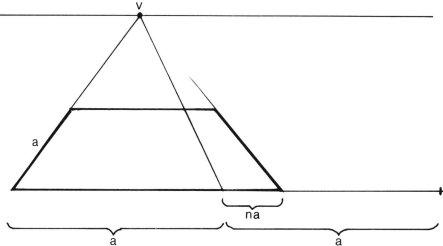

33. Build your first square *ABCD*, then proceed as in Exercise 31, but this time with the second square behind the first.

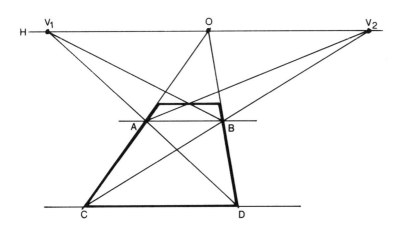

34. If your segment is *AB*, you can assume that this segment is the diagonal of a rectangle with two edges parallel to the *H* line. If you draw through *A* the horizontal *AC* of *random length*, *BC* will become the vanishing edge of the virtual rectangle. By extending *BC* to the *H* line you obtain *V*, the vanishing point of all lines parallel to *BC*. By dividing *AC* into three equal segments *AM*, *MN*, and *NC* and joining points *M* and *N* with *V*, we obtain intersection points *M'* and *N'*, which divide *AB* into three equal segments.

Note: This method is valid, of course, for any number of divisions.

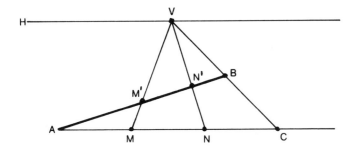

35. Proceed as in Exercise 34, by tracing horizontal *AC* and dividing it into segments in the desired proportion.

36. If your initial segment is *AB*, then *CD*, *CD'*, and *CD"* represent the three possibilities. If vanishing lines *AC* and *BD* intersect on the *H* line, then *AB* and *CD* are equal segments in reality. If *AC* and *BD"* intersect under the *H* line, *CD"* is shorter than *AB*; if they intersect above the *H* line or *under AB*, then *CD'* is larger than *AB*.

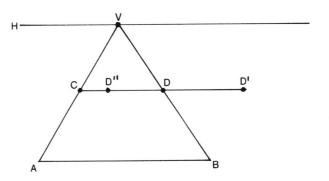

37. Trace a vanishing line through *AC* and from intersection *V* (the vanishing point) trace *VB*. Intersect *VB* with the horizontal through *C*, and this will yield *CD*, the segment equal to *AB*.

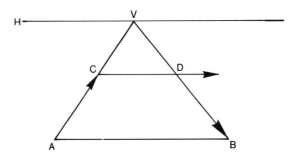

38. No matter where *C* is situated in relation to *AB*, a parallel to *AB* through *C* will vanish in the same vanishing point V_1. So we get the direction of the new segment. Its length requires additional effort. We know that if *AB* equals *CD* (the new segment), then *AC* and *BD* will be not only equal but also parallel. So if *AC* and *BD* are parallel, they will both vanish at another vanishing point V_2. As we can build the first line *AC* and obtain V_2 on the *H* line, we trace V_2B and extend it. Where it intersects *CV* we get *D*, determining the length *CD*.

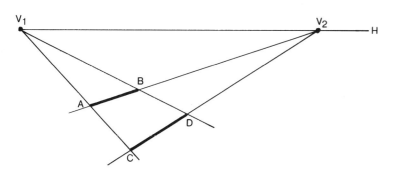

39. Trace the diagonals of the virtual rectangle formed by segments *AB* and *CD* and join their intersection point to the vanishing point *V*. The required segment will be *EF*.

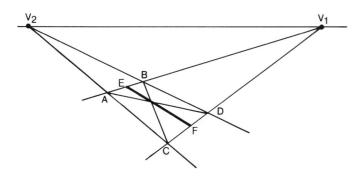

40. The problem is simple when you realize that a triangle twice as large as triangle *ABC* will have the lower edge equal to two lengths of *CB* (which means two edges of the square), the vanishing vertical edge equal to two lengths of *AB* (which means two edges of the square in depth), and the third side the double of the diagonal *AC*.

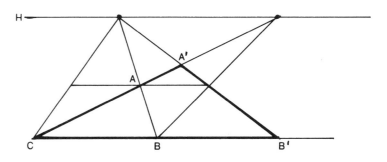

41. The problem is the same as in Exercise 40, but instead of using the entire square at the right, we determine its middle *M* and join *M* to vanishing point V_1. This determines the direction of the third side of the triangle.

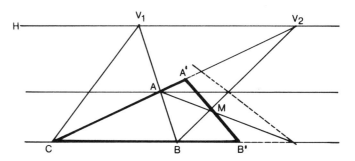

163

42. From position 1, the square moves continuously through positions 2, 3, and 4. Of course, the drawing shows only these four cases, but the motion is continuous and you should come to master this moving image. You have certainly observed thousands of cars, trains, and other moving objects, but did you analyze the perspective changes of the shapes of these objects or understand the perspective laws determining your perceptions? As long as the square moves on frontal rails (parallel to the H line), its horizontal edges always preserve the same undistorted size. The other two edges, which in the first position vanish in point V, remain parallel all during the motion but will always slant toward V. The process is the same if you consider the square stationary and *you* move on a frontal line in the opposite direction. You can see that as the square approaches position 4, the vanishing edges become longer and longer, eventually even becoming longer than the frontal edge. This is an absurd distortion, because it can happen on paper but never in nature. We will analyze this situation in Chapter 9.

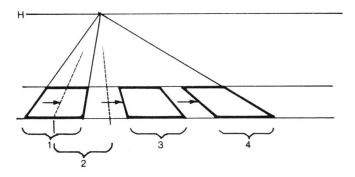

43. We said in the previous answer that the distortions of the square are the same, but this is not a complete analysis. As you move, the vanishing point (called the *eye-point* for lines perpendicular to the H line) also moves from position 1 to 2, 3, 4, and so on. Edge *a* remains the same, while the whole square distorts toward the moving vanishing point like a piece of rubber under pressure.

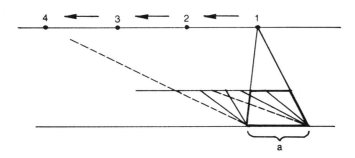

44. The question is how to determine the new square's distorted shape when a_1 becomes $a_2, a_3, \ldots, a_n$ or any other level. As all *a*'s remain parallel and the two other edges remain parallel, the diagonals of any such squares are parallel and vanish at V_2, which is determined by diagonal $A_1 B_1$. The intersections of $V_2 A_1$, $V_2 A_2$, and $V_2 A_3$ with $V_1 B$ determine the level of the upper edge of each square in points B_1, B_2, and B_3, respectively.

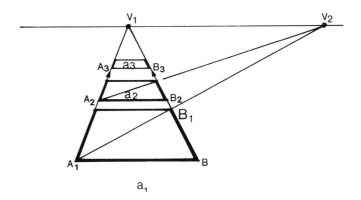

45. Corners *C* and *B*, situated on the diagonal, will move along the vanishing line that is the extension of diagonal *CB* and vanishes in V_2. Points *A* and *D* will also move in the direction parallel to the diagonal, so they also vanish at V_2. So while edge *CD* remains parallel to the *H* line, *AC* and *BD*, moving to $A'C'$ and $B'D'$ and then to any $A''C''$ and $B''D''$, respectively, will all vanish toward V_1.

In one of the previous exercises we saw how to build squares with the help of diagonals. Here we used a method that gives us an infinity of diagonally moving squares.

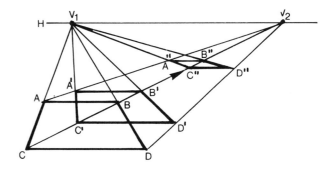

46. If point A of square $ABCD$ moves to the position P (which is chosen arbitrarily), the segment AP determines the direction of motion for all four points A, B, C, and D. In moving they preserve their parallelism, so they vanish at the same point V_2 determined by the intersection of the extension of AP and the H line. Keep in mind that from point P, one edge of the new square remains parallel to the H line and the other remains parallel to AC, so it vanishes at V_1. The other two edges are constructed according to the same observation, point by point.

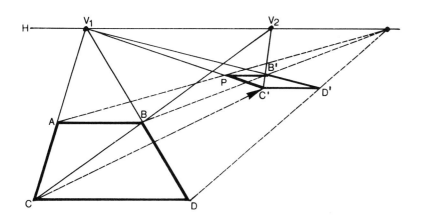

48. Whether you move this square on the horizontal diagonal, on the vertical diagonal, or in the direction of one of the edges, the principle of parallels running toward the same vanishing point is the only guide and means of construction, as in the previous exercise.

49. In order to build the inscribed circle in plane geometry, you trace the square's diagonals to find the center (a). The circle will be tangent to the four edges at their midpoints and will intersect the diagonals in four points, A', B', C', and D'. So you know that eight points of the circle can be determined. Moreover, since the points A', B', C', and D' are on the diagonals, the circle will also be tangent to another square $EFGH$ (b) formed by these four points and their vanishing lines toward V_1 and V_2 (the vanishing points of the diagonals). How do you determine the points A', B', C', and D' in perspective? In plane geometry, the extensions of the lines $A'D'$ and $B'C'$ intersect DC in M and N, respectively. Returning to the perspective square, locate the points M and N on DC and trace parallels to AD and BC (to the eye point), which will intersect the diagonals in the perspective location of points A', B', C', and D'. Now you can easily build the new, diamond-positioned square and trace the circle with the eight tangent points as guidance. Of course, when you work freehand, the circle in perspective will be approximately correct; but you know that any circle in perspective is an ellipse, and you must train your hand accordingly.

Try many different circle constructions, because in every instance the ellipse has a different shape and only training will give you facility in visualizing it before drawing it.

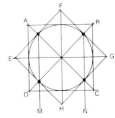

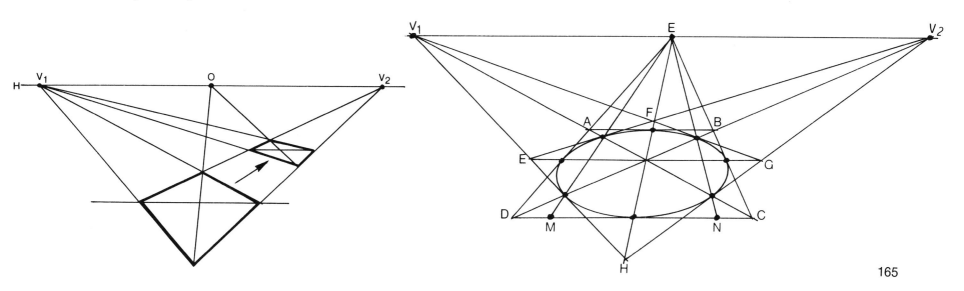

50. This is very much the same problem as in Exercise 49, only reversed. Start first by doing the drawing in plane geometry:

   (a) Draw the square and its diagonals and median lines.
   (b) Draw the circle with radius equal to half a diagonal.
   (c) Draw the circumscribing square *ABCD*.

Transfer square *ABCD* into perspective; then draw the circle as in Exercise 49.

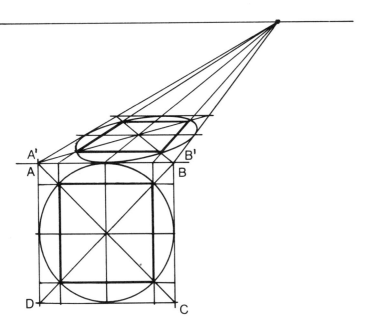

51. Draw the first square *EFGH* in perspective so that *HE* and *FG* are parallel to the *H* line and then mark points *M* and *N* on *GF*. After finding V_1 and V_2 (the vanishing points of the diagonals *EG* and *FH*), draw the parallels through *M*, *N*, *M'*, and *N'*, thus obtaining the second square. You now have the eight vertices of the octagon.

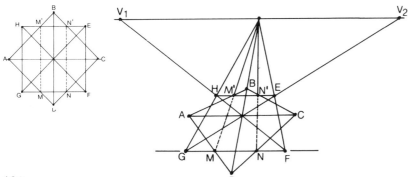

52. Build the square and the circle according to the methods you already know. Mark points *M* and *N* on *CD* and find *M'* and *N'*. The intersections of *MM'* and *NN'* with the circle give you the four remaining vertices of the hexagon (in addition to *A* and *B*).

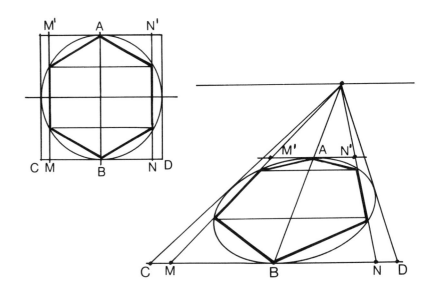

53. If the hexagon *ABCDEF* is already given, *AF* and *CD* determine the E_y vanishing point (eye-point) and *FC* and V_1 vanishing point. You actually do not need the vanishing point of *BC* and *FE*. Study carefully the way hexagons *CHIJKD* and *BLMNHC* have been built, repeat the drawing on your paper and add your own hexagons in areas I, II, III, and IV.

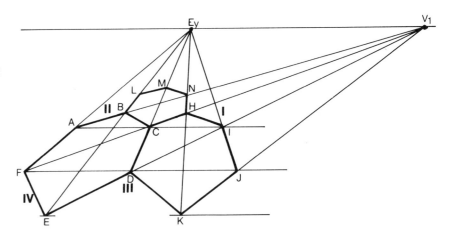

54. In the plan, obtain *PT* parallel to *CB* and then *TN* parallel to *AC* and *BD* (a). Then draw the perspective image of the rectangle and mark points *M* and *N* (b). The vanishing point *V* of the diagonal, together with *T*, will give you the line *VT*, which when extended into the interior of the rectangle will intersect the perpendicular raised on *M* in *P*, the point we are looking for.

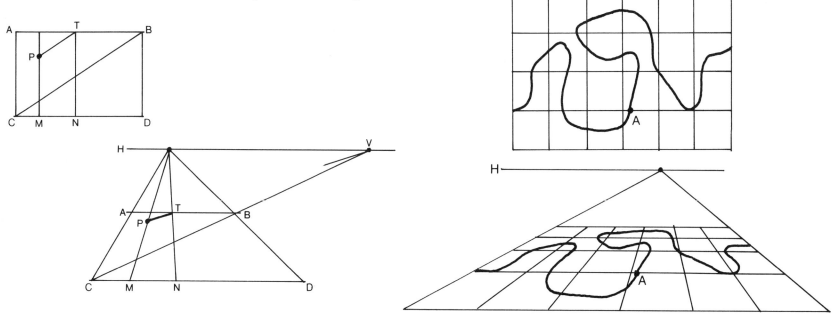

55. Find point *N* by drawing *TN* parallel to *AD* and *BC* (a). Trace rectangle *ABCD* in perspective and mark *M* and *N* (b). Line *NE* will intersect *AB* in *T*, so you obtain *MT*, the section line.

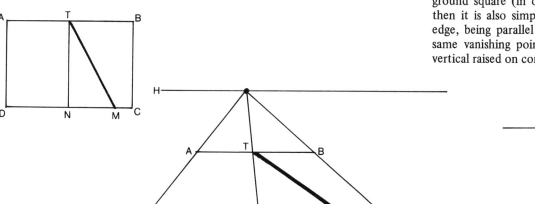

56. Inscribe the map in an area formed by a grid of equal squares. As you can build such a grid of squares in perspective, you can approximate point by point the intersections of the river with the different squares.

57. Building a vertical square on the frontal edges is not a new problem. We dealt with it in Exercises 11, 12, and 13. And if it is simple to raise on one of the corners a vertical that is equal to the frontal (horizontal) edge of the ground square (in order to obtain the vertical edge of the vertical square), then it is also simple to trace the upper horizontal edge, knowing that this edge, being parallel to the vanishing edges of the horizontal square, has the same vanishing point. The length of this upper edge is determined by the vertical raised on corner *A*.

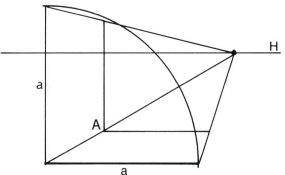

167

58. Just continue the reasoning in Exercise 57.

59. On a frontal square on the ground with edge of length a, the rotation of a lid will be represented by a semi-circle with center at A and radius AB. When the lid is in position AB', $B'C'$ will be the vanishing edge of the lid (parallel to AC and BD, of course). The length of $B'C'$ is determined with an additional construction, one of the construction "tricks" that are so often helpful in perspective drawing. If you project a perpendicular from B' to the horizontal BB'', you obtain a point M. The vanishing line MV must be parallel to AC and $B'C'$, so $MM'DB$ is a rectangle. If we raise a perpendicular from M', then its intersection with $B'V$ will be C', the point we are looking for. Joining C with C' completes the perspective of the slanted lid. Later you will realize that knowing how to determine spatial vanishing points will simplify the construction.

Note: In the two previous exercises we gave you "recipes" for perspective construction. This is not enough for you to understand. Review the two answers point by point and analyze carefully why each point was determined by the construction described.

61. The new square will have edges equal to the diagonal AB, so we must determine this length $(a\sqrt{2})$ in its actual value. We can do this by building a vertical frontal square, tracing its diagonal, and rotating it to a vertical position AD. Actually, AD is the closer of the two vertical edges of the new square. The remote vertical edge will be a vertical raised from B. As the upper vanishing edge is parallel to the basic diagonal, it also vanishes at V, so the intersection point E determines the required square.

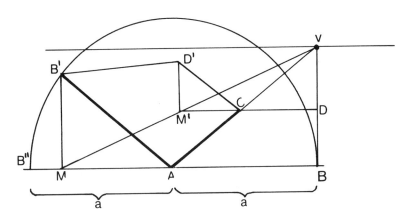

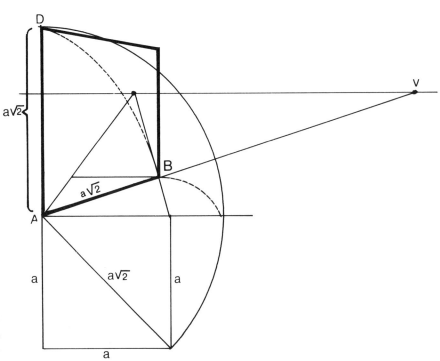

60. First, build a cube on the basic square (a). Then determine frontally the 45° rotation of the lid to position AB (b). Next, trace the level LL' of the upper edge of the lid and continue the same level $L'L''$ on the vertical square $ABCD$ (c). Then, by tracing the diagonal CB and intersecting it with $L'L''$, you obtain the upper point of the slanted lid (d). Finally, by tracing a horizontal line from M through the intersection with the opposite diagonal EF, you obtain the point N, the last point necessary to complete the lid in perspective (e).

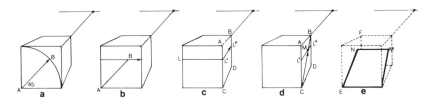

63. Determine the diagonal vanishing points V_1 and V_2 and two verticals equal to the edge of the square (of length a). Join A' with V_2 and B' with V_1, and their intersection will determine the upper edges of the two walls. You can repeat the exercise using the other pair of diagonals.

65. This exercise is based on the same construction used in Exercise 64, with the difference that you will have to define four vanishing points instead of only two. Follow the construction in accordance with the method explained for two walls.

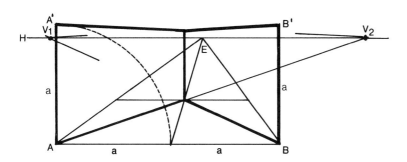

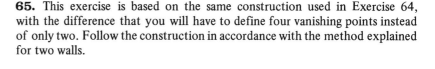

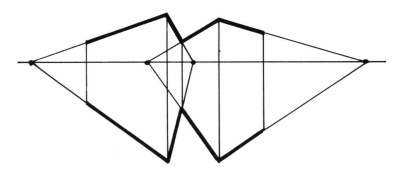

64. The two intersecting lines meet at a point X and vanish on the H line in two vanishing points V_1 and V_2. Take a vertical segment of arbitrary height *wherever you want* on either ground line and join it to the corresponding vanishing point (i.e., if your vertical segment is raised from point P on AV_2, then its top P' will be joined to V_2). At the intersection point X raise a vertical; then Y, the intersection point of $P'V_2$ and this vertical, will determine not only the wall on AV_2 but also the height of the crossing wall.

Note: It is obvious that if we initially raise our height at the point X, we simplify the procedure; but this is not always possible in perspective construction.

66. Given the wall $ABCD$, simply trace its diagonals AD and BC and join their point of intersection P with V. Segment MN divides the wall in half.

Note: It is even simpler to divide this wall in half vertically. A vertical line through P will do it. You will often encounter the situation in which a rectangular surface is divided in half at a quite remote point, as in the drawing. Line AB represents the separation between two *equal* halves of the rectangular wall $CDEF$.

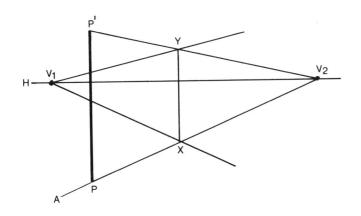

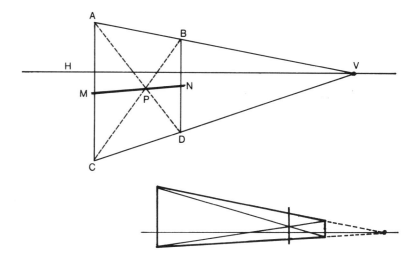

67. Given a square vertical surface in perspective (the distorted dimensions of the square are approximate), trace the diagonals, thus obtaining the middle point *P*. Divide the square into four smaller squares with the help of point *P*. Trace the diagonal *AD* and find the new middle point *M*, which will divide square *APCD* into four smaller squares. Repeat with square *BMNC*. By repeating the operations in the other three squares you will obtain the 8 × 8 (64) squares of the chessboard.

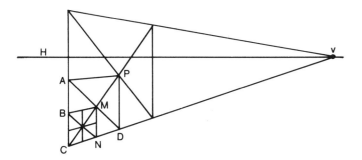

68. Given the vertical square, you know that its vertical edges are frontal in the sense that it has no perspective distortions. If you divide edge *AB* into eight equal parts and then trace the vanishing horizontal from each division to *V*, you obtain eight horizontal divisions. As the diagonal *AC* intersects all these divisions, it determines the points through which you can draw the vertical divisions of the square.

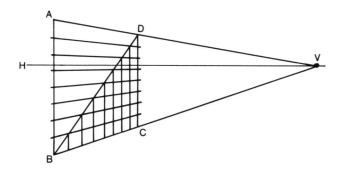

69. Suppose you have to divide rectangle *ABCD* into five equal parts. Take a frontal line from point *D*, parallel to the *H* line and arbitrary in length, and divide it without distortions into five equal segments *Da*, *ab*, *bc*, *cd*, and *dE*. Line *CE* has a vanishing point V_2, which you can use to draw its parallels aV_2, bV_2, cV_2, and dV_2. As the five divisions of *DE* have been chosen equal, any slanting line crossing these parallels will also be divided into equal segments. Thus segments *Da′*, *a′b′*, *b′c′*, *c′d′*, and *d′C* are perspectively distorted equal segments. The verticals from points *a′*, *b′*, *c′*, and *d′* divide the rectangle into five equal parts.

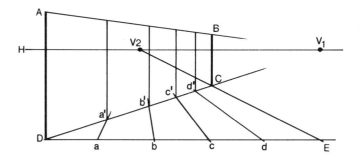

70. You solved this problem in Exercise 68, when you had to divide the vertical into eight segments. Moreover, you should realize that the strips do not have to be equal but can be in any ratios you need. For instance, suppose you want five divisions measured from bottom to top as *a*, 4*a*, 2*a*, *a*, and 3*a* for some unit *a*. Add up these measurements, obtaining 11*a* in this case, and mark the eleven divisions on the vertical as in the figure. The horizontal strips are obtained by the method you already know.

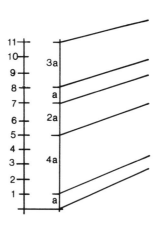

71. You have the square and the vanishing point *V*. Trace the diagonals and, at random, cross the diagonals with a line that also vanishes at *V*. The intersections of this line with the diagonals are the points *M* and *N*. Draw verticals *MO* and *NP*. Segment *OP* is the last side of the new square you need.

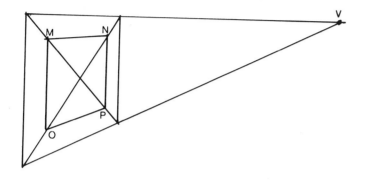

72. If *AD* is the edge of the wall, then *AD*/2 equals *MD* is the length of a side of the inner square. Place a segment *M'N'* of length *MD* in the middle of *AD*, so that *AM'* = *N'D* = *AD*/4. Trace vanishing lines *M'V* and *N'V* and intersect them with diagonal *AC*. You have obtained *PO*, which is the diagonal of the small square, and you can complete the problem by the method you know.

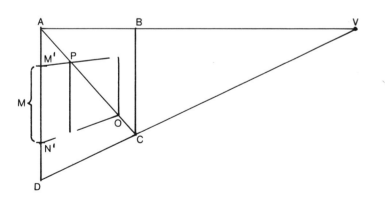

73. Suppose you move (translate) square *ABCD* on the two rails. You know that as long as the rails remain parallel to the *H* line, edge *AB* will not change its size. So, for point *B'*, edge *AB* will become *A'B'*, which is equal and parallel to *AB*. The new position, preserving its parallelism with the initial position, will have top and bottom edges vanishing at the same point *V*. The intersection of *B'V* with rail 2 gives you the point *D'*, which is enough to build the new position of the square with the methods you know. Practice this fundamental exercise with many more positions and get used to visualizing the motion on your mental screen, so that it will appear as a square in continuous motion, always connected to the immobile vanishing point.

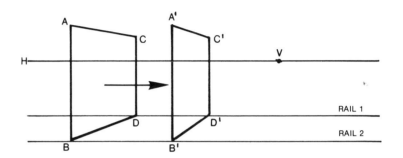

74. Suppose your door *ABCD* rotates around edge *BC*. Both *AB* and *DC* become radii for the circles of rotation described by points *A* and *D*. You can therefore draw these two circles approximately, verifying their correctness with the help of intersections *E* and *F*, which must be situated on the same vertical. Then, if you rotate the point *D* to *D'*, segments *CD'* and *BA'* (*A'* being the intersection of the upper circle with the vertical raised from *D'*) must remain parallel like any other top and bottom edges of a door; so *BA'* and *CD'* vanish at the same, *new* vanishing point *V₂*, determined by the intersection of *CD'* with the *H* line. You can see that point *A'* can be determined without the help of an additional top circle.

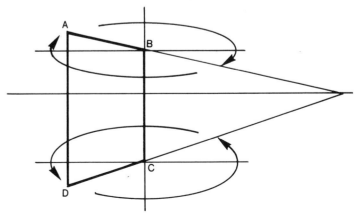

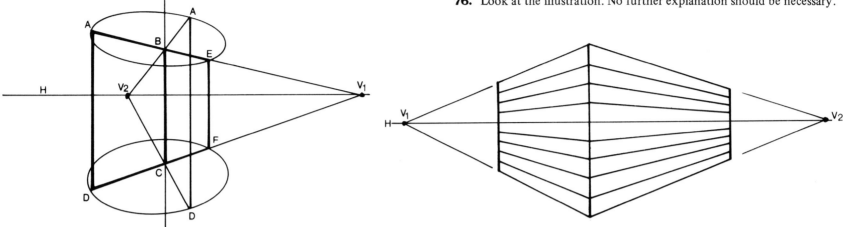

Note: As your circle is approximate, even if the new angle of the door is correct, its length is not precise and only the eye can give you the sensation of whether the drawing is correct or not. We will return to the precise construction of a rotating door in Chapter 7.

75. Square *ABCD*, moving on rails 1 and 2, goes toward vanishing point V_1. Edges *AB* and *CD* vanish at V_2. For positions C', C'', C''', etc., *CD* will become $C'D'$, $C''D''$, $C'''D'''$, etc. Moreover, *AC* will decrease in height from *AC* to $A'C'$, $A''C''$, $A'''C'''$, etc. You should now complete the translated squares yourself.

77. You know how to build the first two walls, given the ground V, *ABC*. You can also decide about the arbitrary height. Repeat the independent construction of the second V, $A'B'C'$, without defining its height. Looking at the illustration, you realize that (if *AB* and *BC* are *not* parallel to $A'B'$ and $B'C'$, respectively) you have a pair of vanishing points for each structure. Line *BC* vanishes at V_2, and your imagination can continue the whole wall based on *BC* as an infinitely long wall vanishing at V_2. All this wall has a constant height. Also, line $A'B'$ vanishes in V_1 and intersects BV_2 in *N*, where the height of the imaginary wall based on BV_2 has the height *NM*. This is the only place where the two imaginary walls intersect, and if both have equal height, it follows that extending the imaginary upper edge of the wall $V_1'M$ will give the correct height for both pairs of walls. To divide the two pairs of walls, follow the same reasoning. You can do it alone.

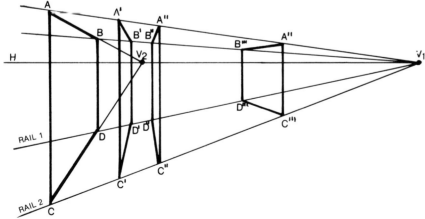

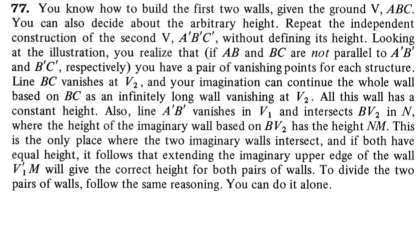

78. This exercise involves nothing new; it just combines methods you already know. Once you have built the cube, find the middle points of the basic and frontal squares with the help of diagonals and divide all faces into four squares.

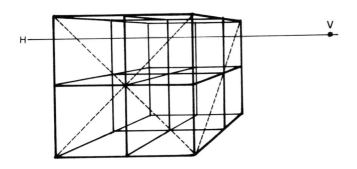

81. Repeat the construction of a perspective vertical chessboard and mark the steps as in (a). For the actual stair construction, you will need another vanishing point V_2 (b). For the time being, your eye will decide which is the proper place of this point on the H line. First build another square parallel to the initial one, trace its diagonal, and extend the vanishing lines of the stair that touch the first square's diagonal. Then, by tracing from each point a vertical and a V_1 vanishing line, you will obtain the corners of each step.

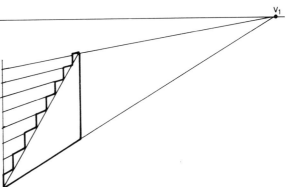

80. The Figure will give you the answer. There is no new theory involved in obtaining it.

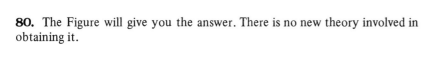

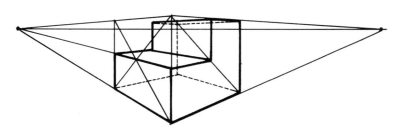

Note: The two diagonals, being parallel, must have a common vanishing point, which cannot possibly be situated on the H line because the diagonals do not belong to the ground plan of the earth but vanish in space. Try to realize where this spatial vanishing point is in relation to V_1, because you will often need it later, in all types of constructions.

82. Given the vertical rectangle $ABCD$ and V_1, decide by eye approximation on a depth vanishing point V_2. Choose at random any thickness you want, creating rectangles $A'B'C'D'$, $A''B''C''D''$, and so on, thus obtaining the other face of the thick wall. Keep in mind that V_2 and V_1 must be vanishing points for groups of parallels that make an angle of $90°$ with each other.

84. On the given wall's front surface, trace the diagonals. Through the middle point thus obtained trace a vertical AB. Then AV_2 and BV_2 will intersect the back face of the wall in C and D. The line CD completes the division of the wall in half.

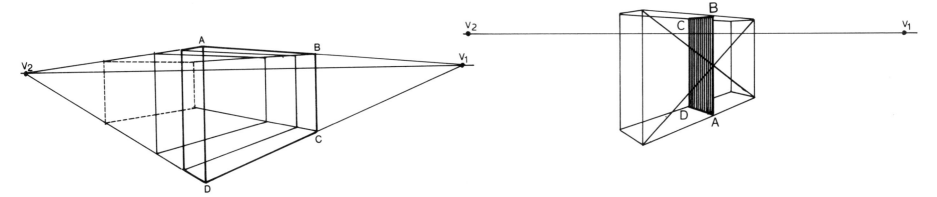

83. After you have decided about the width a of the door, think constantly in terms of parallel lines:

(a) Raise the vertical (and parallel) edges AC and BD of the door.

(b) Decide on the height of the door, mark it on one of the verticals (e.g., at A), and obtain the upper edge of the door, which is parallel to top and bottom of the wall (AV_1).

(c) Trace AV_2, BV_2, CV_2, and DV_2, which give the thickness of the door hole. Where BV_2 and CV_2 intersect EF, construct the other side of the door.

85. After tracing on the ground a square $ABCD$, find its center (by the diagonal method), raise a vertical from it, and choose its height N. Then NA, NB, NC, and ND will be the slanting edges of the pyramid.

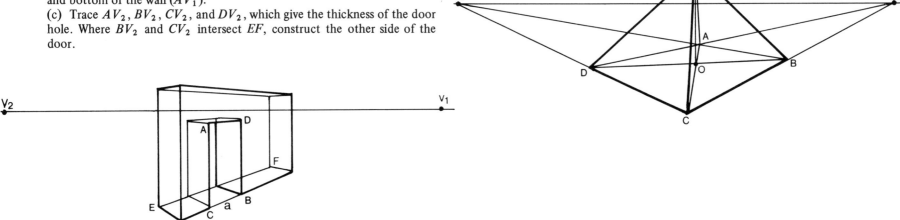

86. Trace the diagonals of the square $ABCD$ to find the center O. Find the vanishing point V_2 of diagonal AC. From A draw the vertical AA' of length a. In perspective, all verticals raised on the wall $AA'V_2$ will be equal because AV_2 and $A'V_2$ are parallel. The vertical at O, intersecting $A'V_2$ in N, will determine the top of the pyramid.

88. The problem differs from Exercise 87 only in the number of edges and the finding of the center of the hexagon. The rest is shown in the illustration.

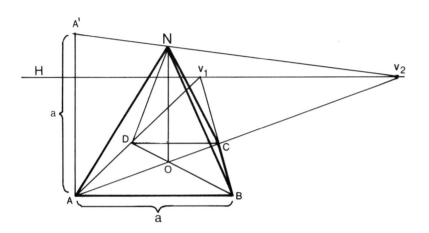

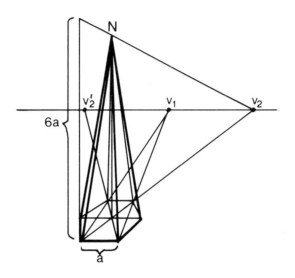

87. As in the previous exercise, raise at A the vertical AA' of length a, equal to the edge of the basic square. If P is the chosen ground point, line AP will vanish in V_2 and $A'V_2$ will be its spatial parallel. Point N, obtained as the intersection of the vertical at P and $A'V_2$, will be the top of the pyramid $ABCDN$.

89. The vanishing edges of the cube go to V_1. Diagonal AB vanishes at V_2. Double the height AC to AD and intersect DV_2 with the vertical from the middle of the square.

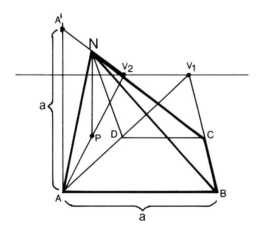

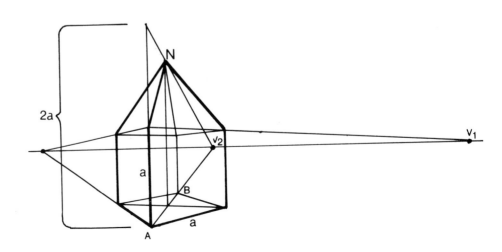

91. Given the square *ABCD*, let *AB* be the edge of the square on which one of the roof's edges leans. If we decide to raise the arbitrary height *H* at *C*, the same height will be obtained for DH^1, by constructing the wall $CDHH^1$, which vanishes at V_2. Now H^1A and *HB* are the slanting edges of the roof.

Note 1: Observe the two right triangles ADH^1 and *BCH*.

Note 2: You can see that AH^1 and *BH* are convergent; that is, they intersect somewhere. Can you say where?

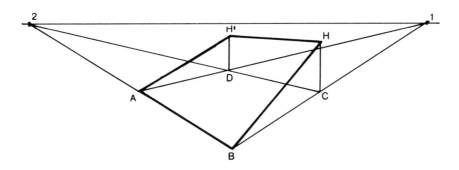

92. Since we want symmetry, we must first double the basic square *ABCD*, and we already know how to do this. From the chosen top *N* we trace *CN* and NC', thus obtaining the double edge closer to us. For the rest, use the method of Exercise 91.

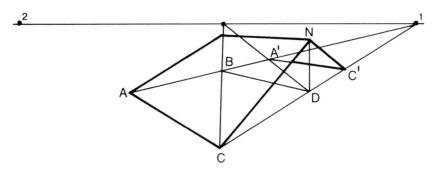

93. This exercise is composed of problems you have already solved.

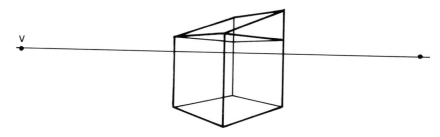

94. Having the basic square *ABCD*, decide on the thickness of the walls, AA' and CC'. Trace vanishing lines $A'V_1$ and $C'V_1$, thus determining the plane of the walls. Verticals through A', C', B', and D' intersected with *MN* and *OP*, respectively, give you the top points of the walls in perspective.

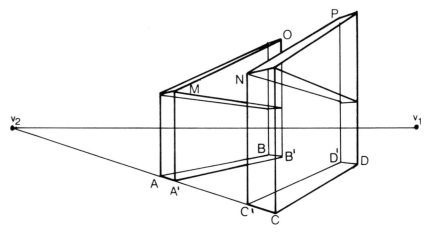

95. There is nothing new in this exercise except that the number of lines becomes rather confusing. You will need to get used to handling so many construction lines.

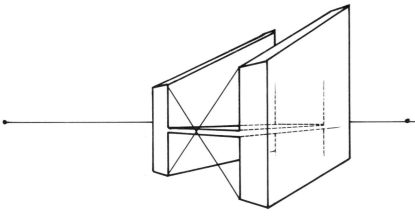

97. Having the rectangular construction, find on the ground the middle line AA' and divide it in four with the diagonals. Segment BC represents the central two quarters of AA'. Raise verticals BB' and CC' of equal (arbitrarily chosen) height and join the four corners of the building with B' and C'.

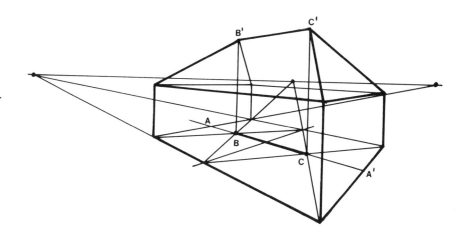

96. After building the first structure, continue building in the rear as many cubes as you want (you know how). Then, by joining A with V_1, you obtain the top height for all the other roofs.

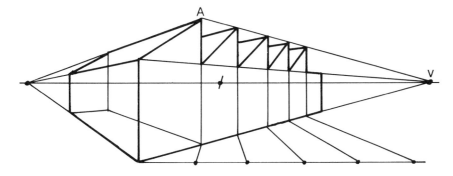

98. First build the square at the top; then mark on it the eight points of the circle intersecting the diagonals and tangents to the middle lines. The vertical edges of the cylinder will be tangent to both circles.

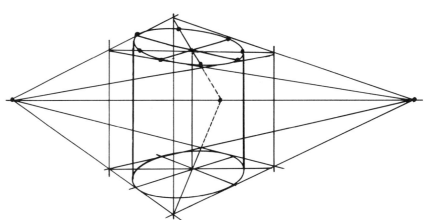

99. From the center of the upper circle, trace tangents to the basic one. If the cone is shorter or taller, the points of tangency will be differently located.

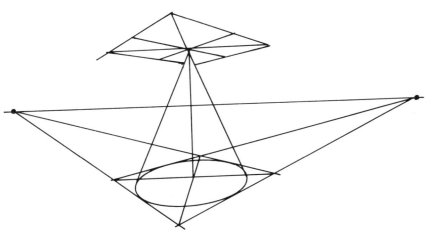

101. First trace the generatrix on the ground and raise on it the triangle *ABC*, obtained by sectioning the cone through its apex and the diameter of its basic circle. Segment *AB* is the diameter and also one of the middle lines of the circumscribing square. The construction of the square is approximate. Its surface belongs to a plane perpendicular to plane *ABC*, and your eye must replace the knowledge that would give you the precise construction. Within the square build the circle and from *C* trace the tangents to it. Observe that the tangents do *not* coincide with generatrices *AC* and *BC*.

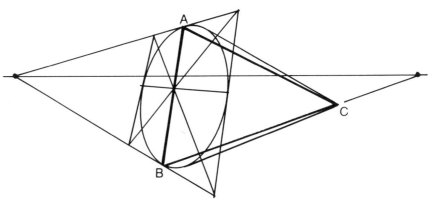

100. First build the prism of square section and on its ends construct the two circular sections of the cylinder. Trace upper and lower tangents to the two circles.

102. First build the cylinder and trace tangents from the center of the ground circle to the upper one.

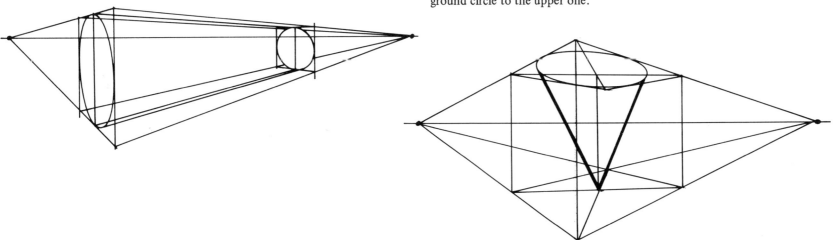

103. The trace of a rolling cylinder on the ground is an indefinitely long and vanishing rectangle of width equal to the cylinder's generatrix. The shape of this rolling cylinder at different sites is determined with the construction of the circumscribing parallelepiped at the site.

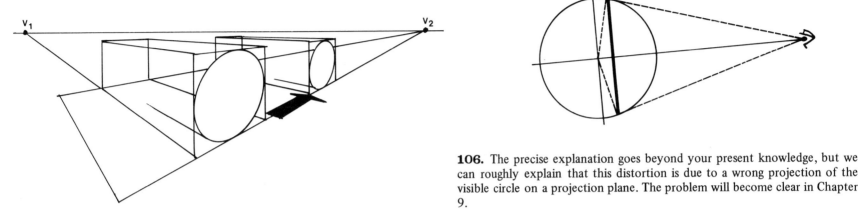

104. A cone rolled on a plane will cover a circular surface of radius equal to the cone's generatrix. In perspective the circle will become an ellipse with major horizontal axis equal to G.

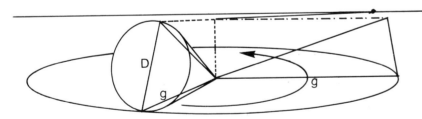

105. The cone formed with the viewer's eye as the apex and the circle of tangence with the sphere is always facing us, so that the line from the eye to the center of that circle is perpendicular to the plane of that circle. Hence the circle is always frontal and undistorted.

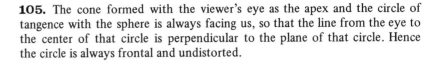

106. The precise explanation goes beyond your present knowledge, but we can roughly explain that this distortion is due to a wrong projection of the visible circle on a projection plane. The problem will become clear in Chapter 9.

107. The distance between the earth and the sun is about 150,000,000 kilometers. For practical reasons the angle of the two tangents to the sun stemming from your eye can be considered zero. Therefore the cone starting from your eye touches the sun on its largest circle.

108. You have edges AB and BC. You also can determine V_1, but not V_2 (which is too far to the right). Use the diagonals trick. Segment AC is one diagonal, and it will be intersected *at its midpoint* by the other diagonal. So find the midpoint M of BC (review Exercise 30) and join it to V_1, thus obtaining O, the intersection point of the two diagonals. Then BO will be half of the second diagonal, which when extended will intersect V_1C in D, the last point of the complete square. Of course, the method is valid for rectangles as well.

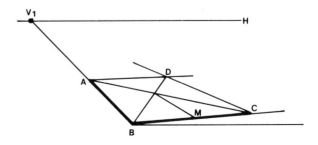

109. You are given wall *ABCD* with vanishing point V_1 and *DE*, the length of wall 2. Enter the realm of imaginary construction. Take a random vanishing point V_R and build the imaginary vanishing wall BDV_R. Then trace V_1E, the imaginary base of another imaginary wall. Their intersection *M* will give you the height of *both* imaginary walls in *N*, which must be the same as *BD*. Extend V_1N to *F* (which is vertically above *E*) and you have the required vanishing edge *BF*, without having V_2.

111. Given vertical *AB* and direction *C*, take an arbitrary V_1, thus creating an imaginary wall ABV_1. Then take another arbitrary V_2 so that V_2C will intersect BV_1. From point *M*, their intersection, raise a vertical *MN*, which determines the common height for both imaginary walls. Extending V_2N to *C'*, we obtain the height of the real wall *ABCC'*. If we divide *AB* in (let us say) two, at point *T*, then TV_1 will intersect *MN* in *T'* and the extension of V_2T' will intersect *CC'* in *T''*. Line *TT''* divides the wall in half horizontally.

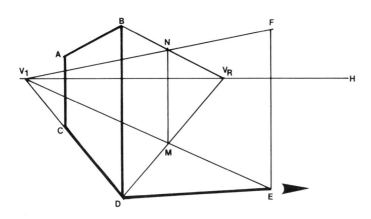

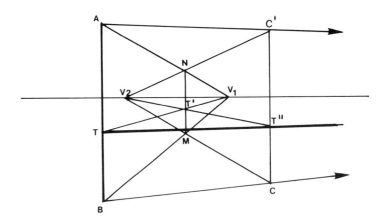

110. You already have walls *ABCD* and *BDEF* and point V_1, but you don't know how to build the other two walls. You actually need only one point, the intersection of the bases of the two other walls, to construct the rest. Then use the trick from Exercise 108. Trace the diagonal *CE*, find the midpoint *M* of *DE*, join it to V_1, find center *O* and extend *DO* to *G*, the point we are looking for. The rest of the construction is left for you.

113. Given the two walls *ABCD* and *A'B'C'D'* vanishing in V_1 and V_2, respectively, divide *AC* into the required number of divisions (four unequal divisions are shown in this example) and trace the divisions on the wall, extending them toward V_1. On the imaginary extension of wall *A'B'C'D'* toward V_2, at the intersection with the imaginary extension of *ABCD* toward V_1, mark the divisions on the vertical *MN* and then turn them onto *A'B'C'D'* from V_2.

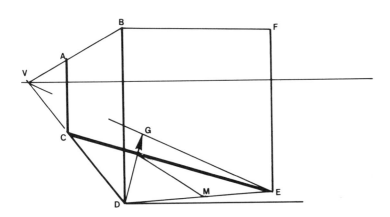

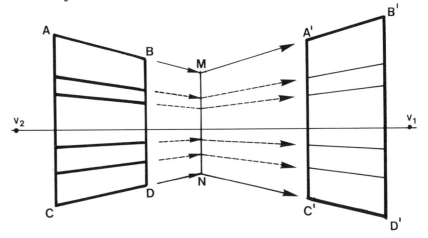

114. Given the points A, B, C, D, and E, raise the chosen vertical AA'. Line AB will vanish at V_1. Line $A'V_1$ determines height BB'. Line BC vanishes at V_2, and $B'V_2$ determines C'. Line BD vanishes in V_3, and the extension V_3B' determines D'. Find V_4 and E'.

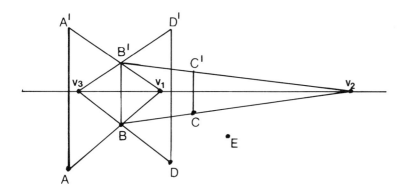

115. Your are given points A, B, C, D, and E and the segment AA'. Line AB will vanish in V_1, and line $A'V_1$ determines point B'. Line BC vanishes in V_2, and the extension of V_2B' determines length CC'. Continue, building DD' and EE'.

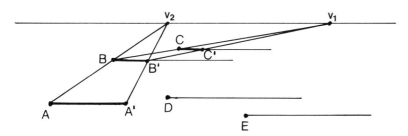

117. Given the surface $ABCD$, sink verticals from each corner and mark on one vertical the depth you choose (Fig. 2-105) The vanishing points will do the rest. The problem is interesting because it has two interpretations. The first is the one given in the exercise. In this case you will be able to see only a part of the underground construction. However, this construction is also valid for finding the basic support $A'B'C'D'$ of an elevated roof $ABCD$. Only related elements in the composition can define the actual position of $ABCD$.

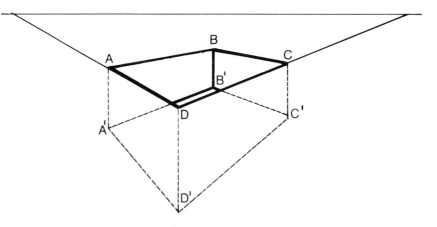

118. By definition, rectangle $ABCD$ corresponds to two squares. On the other hand, we know that the diagonals of each square divide the right angled corners in angles of $45°$. On the diagonals of square $AEFD$, take a random point P, which will be at equal distances from AD and DF. This is enough to construct the rest of the inner rectangle with known methods and with the diagonals of the second square $BCFE$.

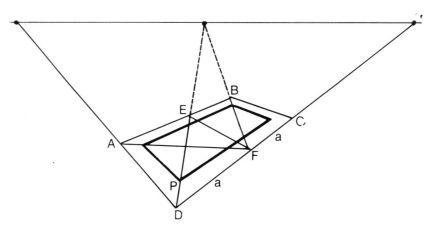

119. Build the first solid. Repeat the diagonals on squares $A'E'F'D'$ and $E'B'C'F'$ and intersect them with the verticals raised on the corners of the inner basic rectangle.

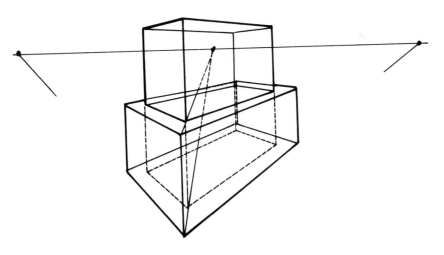

121. Light is a radiation of waves-particles. An atom is composed of a central mass called a nucleus, surrounded by a definite number of satellites called electrons. It is not known whether the electrons are waves or material particles rotating around the nucleus, but under certain conditions electrons change their orbit, moving closer to the nucleus. In this process they loose energy, which is emitted from the atom in a straight trajectory. These small amounts of energy, called photons, have the characteristics both of particles and of waves. We perceive the photons only when they reach the retina, and this is possible in two cases: either when we look at the source emitting them or when a reflecting surface receives the photons from the source atom and bounces them toward our eye. Therefore, from the subjective point of view, light is the brain's decoding of the photonic bombardment of the retina.

122. Photons (or light) emitted by the sun or by stars can be seen by astronauts because the eye faces the source of emission. The earth can also be seen because the light coming from the sun is reflected by the earth's surface and many photons reach the astronaut's eyes. Photons traveling through space void of matter do not encounter reflecting surfaces and therefore cannot bounce toward the astronauts' eyes.

123. The atmosphere is a blanket of gaseous matter surrounding the earth. Matter is composed of molecules, which reflect the photons in an infinite number of directions so that the eye receives them from everywhere around.

124. The moon has no atmosphere, that is, no gaseous molecules to reflect the sun-emitted photons.

125. *Black* is the complete absence of photons.

126. A black surface is a surface capable of absorbing light completely. Since all photons are absorbed, there is no light left to bounce toward your eye.

127. Electrons in an atom emit energies at different levels. The photons therefore carry different amounts of energy. These various energies travel as waves do on the sea, and according to the amount of energy carried, the waves are different in length and frequency. The eye perceives these differences as colors. As the sun emits a specific number of different photons, the combination of all these energies is synthesized by the eye as white.

128. A surface reflecting all sun emitted photons.

129. A surface that absorbs all photons of different energies, except those of a specific wavelength that is perceived by our eye as red.

130. The atmosphere absorbs most of the colors of solar light, letting only the blue wavelength reach our eye. The infinite variation of colors on earth is due to the photons that have escaped the absorption of the atmosphere.

131. Besides the normal gaseous molecules, there are sometimes many dust particles floating in the air. These particles absorb some of the wavelengths and reflect the yellow and the red in accordance with the color of their surface.

132. Because this is the only wavelength available to be reflected.

133. Its texture. We perceive white (or any color) as stronger or weaker depending on the quantity of photons received by the eye. If the reflecting surface is smooth (a), most photons will be reflected in the same direction. If it is rugged (b), some of the photons will be reflected in various directions, not all of them going toward the eye.

134. A one-square-inch screen placed in front of the eye will receive the two photons traveling at a distance *a* from each other and reflected by a surface (a). If the angle of the surface is changed (b), the photons will hit it at the same distance *a* from each other, but they will be reflected at a greater distance from each other. The reduced number of photons per square inch means that the eye receives less light.

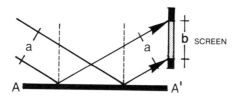

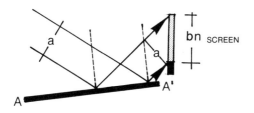

135. Each face of the cube makes a different angle with the source of light, so each of them reflects a different amount of light toward the eye.

136. There are two reasons: (a) Gaseous molecules in the atmosphere reflect some photons from the other side of the cube, which also reflect to our eye. (b) The surrounding objects also reflect the photons they receive according to their color. This is why a so-called shaded surface of the cube will have a slightly different color, depending on the color reflected by the surrounding objects.

137. Because no atmosphere and no surrounding objects reflect any light on the shadowed side.

138. All sources of light radiate it in all directions from the center of the source. A source of light on earth will touch any two targets with two beams. The beams and the distance between the two targets form a triangle with one vertex at the center of the light source. The same thing happens with the light coming from the sun, but the distance to the sun is so enormous in relation to the space between the two targets that the two beams can be considered parallel for practical use in perspective drawing.

139. With good measuring tools you can calculate a fairly accurate distance to the source. Let H_1 and H_2 be the holes and P_1 and P_2 the respective locations of the light beams on the floor. If the triangles H_1EP_1 and H_2EP_2 are similar (a), H_1P_1 and H_2P_2 are parallel, so the source of the light is at an infinite distance, the sun. If the two triangles are not similar (b), simple geometric calculations (based on similarity of triangles and the Pythagorean Theorem) will give you the exact location of the light source.

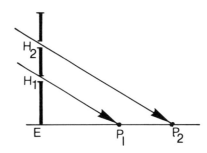

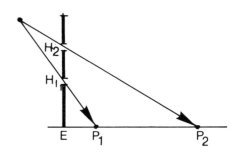

140. The square prevents the photons from reaching the screen. The *shadow area* is the part of the surface of the screen that does not receive photons, and the *shadow region* (or umbra) is the whole volume of shadow between the shadow area and the object creating the shadow. If the light source is the sun, the shadow regions are prismatic. For closer sources of light, they are conical. The prism of shadow being formed by parallel lines and surfaces will leave a shadow identical to the square panel. If you slant the screen (b), the shadow gets longer. If you slant the panel (c), the shadow becomes shorter.

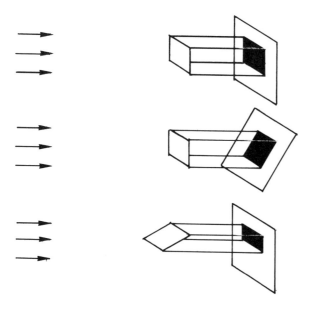

141. The size of the shadow doesn't change, because the sunbeams are like parallel rails on which your hand slides.

142. Panel *ABCD* stops the light coming from the light bulb *O*. Panel *ABCD* and *O* form a pyramid, which continues towards the screen. If *ABCD* is halfway between bulb and screen, then the projection *A'B'* is the double of *AB* and so on, and the area of the shadow is four times the area of the panel. If the panel is moved closer to the screen, the pyramid becomes more elongated, the angle of projection is reduced, and the shadow diminishes in area until, when the panel touches the screen, the shadow's area becomes equal to the panel's. Inversely, if we bring the panel closer to the light bulb, its projected shadow becomes larger and larger until, if *ABCD* touches *O*, the shadow becomes an infinite plane surface.

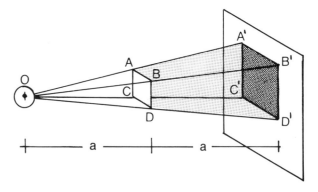

143. Hole *H*, light *L*, and the vertical projection of *H* on the ground *V* form a right triangle. Light source *S* is obviously collinear with *HL*. Consequently a vertical *SP* descending from the source to the ground will form another right triangle *SPL*, which is *similar* to *HVL*. Both triangles belong to the same plane, which intersects the ground in line *PL*. Line *SL* is the light beam and *PL* its *projection* on the ground. You know that a point can be defined as the intersection of two lines. So *L*, the light point (or shadow) we are looking for, can be found at the intersection of the light beam and its projection on the ground, both belonging to the same vertical plane. So for *any* point of shadow cast on the ground, we must define the location *S* of the source, its projection *P*, the material point *H*, and its projection *V*. Lines *SH* and *PV* will give you *L*.

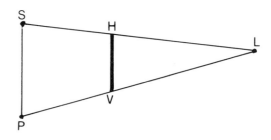

144. Given source S and its projection P and the stick HV, we build the two similar right triangles and find L, the shadow of H, as in the previous exercise (Fig. 2-114). But suppose that the stick is shorter and stops at M. The shadow of M will be found in the same manner, forming the other two right triangles SPL' and MVL', which belong to the same plane as the initial right triangles and thus show the shadow L' on VL. Whatever the height M, its shadow will be situated somewhere on VL, so the totality of points M on the stick will give a totality of L's covering VL. Therefore the shadow of the stick VH is VL.

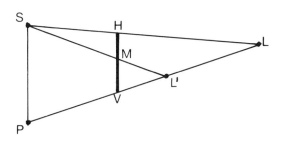

145. The sunbeam SL is stopped by the panel. The intersection of the panel's plane and the plane SPL is the vertical at V_1, which when intersected with SL gives L_1, the top of the shadow of the stick on the panel. So the complete shadow of HV is the broken line VV_1L_1. Observe that the vertical panel can have any angle of rotation around V_1L_1 without changing the position and dimension of the shadow.

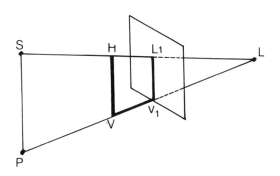

146. Panel $ABCD$ can be regarded theoretically as two vertical sticks joined at the top by line AB. We have reduced the problem to the same one solved in Exercise 144, this time having two sticks instead of one. We know how to find the shadows of AC and BD, which are CA' and DB'. Joining $A'B'$, we have found the complete contour (outline) of the panel's shadow.

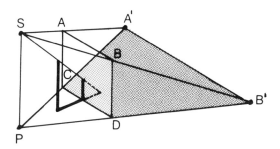

148. The panel being square, AB is parallel to CD. The plane formed by SAB intersects the ground in $A'B'$. Therefore, if AB is parallel to CD (the ground), the plane SAB will intersect the ground in $A'B'$, another parallel to AB. In conclusion, $A'B'$ is parallel to AB, and its imaginary extension will vanish at V, the vanishing point for AB and CD. This property will often simplify the construction of a shadow.

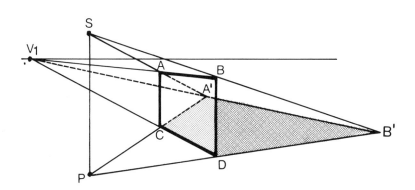

185

149. A cylinder.

150. The frustum of a cone.

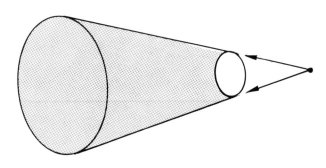

151. A prism of square section.

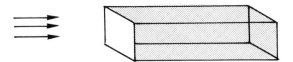

152. The frustum of a pyramid.

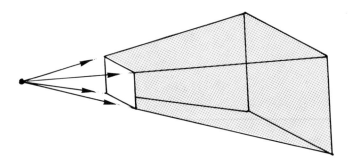

153. A rectangle, if the thickness of the thread is negligible.

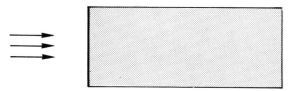

154. A trapezoid, if the thickness of the thread is negligible.

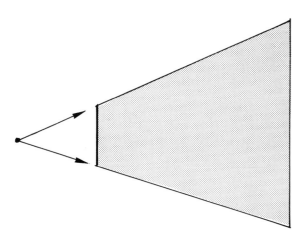

155. A microscopically thin line.

156. The region is actually conical, but for practical purposes it can be considered a line, since the point is so small.

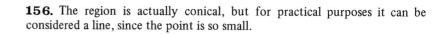

157. Red, orange, yellow, green, blue, indigo, and violet.

158. Red, yellow, and blue, the basic colors that cannot be separated into other color components.

159. Orange (red + yellow), green (blue + yellow), violet (blue + more red), and indigo (red + more blue).

160. Light emitted by the sun is pure photonic energy. No paint has this purity, so the mixture will be grayish.

161. Combinations of blue with orange or of red with green are actually combinations of the three primary colors, resulting in gray. Of course, the percentage of each color in a mixture can be varied to a practically inexhaustible number of tones and hues, and the preponderance of red or blue gives warm or cold tones, respectively.

162. In accordance with the intensity of red and the reflection of the green from the grass, the shadowed side of the cube may have any tone between a brown and a greenish gray.

163. The blanket of gaseous molecules in the air between the mountains and your eye absorbs some wavelengths of the solar spectrum, reflecting the blue in all directions.

164. Dark, strong shadows.

165. All openings receive light but reflect very little. Actually, the holes are not black, but the contrast with the fully illuminated surrounding walls makes them look darker than they actually are.

FURTHER READINGS

General Theory

Pará, E. G., Loving, R. O., and Hill, I. L. *Descriptive Geometry*. New York: Macmillan Publishing Co., 1971.

Architecture

Yarwood, Doreen. *The Architecture of Europe*. New York: Hastings House, 1974.

Art

Atkin, William Wilson. *Architectural Presentation Techniques*. New York: Van Nostrand Reinhold Co., 1976.

Carra, Massimo. *Metaphysical Art*. New York: Praeger Publishers.

Ching, Frank. *Architectural Graphics*. New York: Van Nostrand Reinhold Co., 1975.

——. *Building Construction Illustrated*. New York: Van Nostrand Reinhold Co., 1975.

Coulin, Claudius. *Step-by-Step Perspective Drawing for Architects, Draftsmen, and Designers*. New York: Van Nostrand Reinhold Co., 1971.

Ernst, Bruno. *The Magic Mirror of M. C. Escher*. New York: Ballantine Books, 1976.

Forseth, Kevin. *Graphics for Architecture*. New York: Van Nostrand Reinhold Co., 1979.

Gill, Robert. *VNR Manual of Rendering with Pen and Ink*. New York: Van Nostrand Reinhold Co., 1979.

Laseau, Paul. *Graphic Thinking for Architects and Designers*. New York: Van Nostrand Reinhold Co., 1979.

Lawson, Philip J. *Perspective Charts, Revised Edition*. New York: Van Nostrand Reinhold Co., 1940.

Links, J. G. *Townscape Painting and Drawing*. New York: Harper & Row.

Oles, Paul Stevenson. *Architectural Illustrations*. New York: Van Nostrand Reinhold Co., 1979.

Pischel, Gina. *A World History of Art*. New York: Simon and Schuster, 1975.

Porter, Tom. *How Architects Visualize*. New York: Van Nostrand Reinhold Co., 1979.

Tull, Patricia, and Adler, David, eds. *VNR Metric Handbook of Architectural Graphics*. New York: Van Nostrand Reinhold Co., 1979.

Wang, Thomas C. *Plan and Section Drawing*. New York: Van Nostrand Reinhold Co., 1979.

INDEX

164/2